THE SPELL OF THE MIDNIGHT SUN

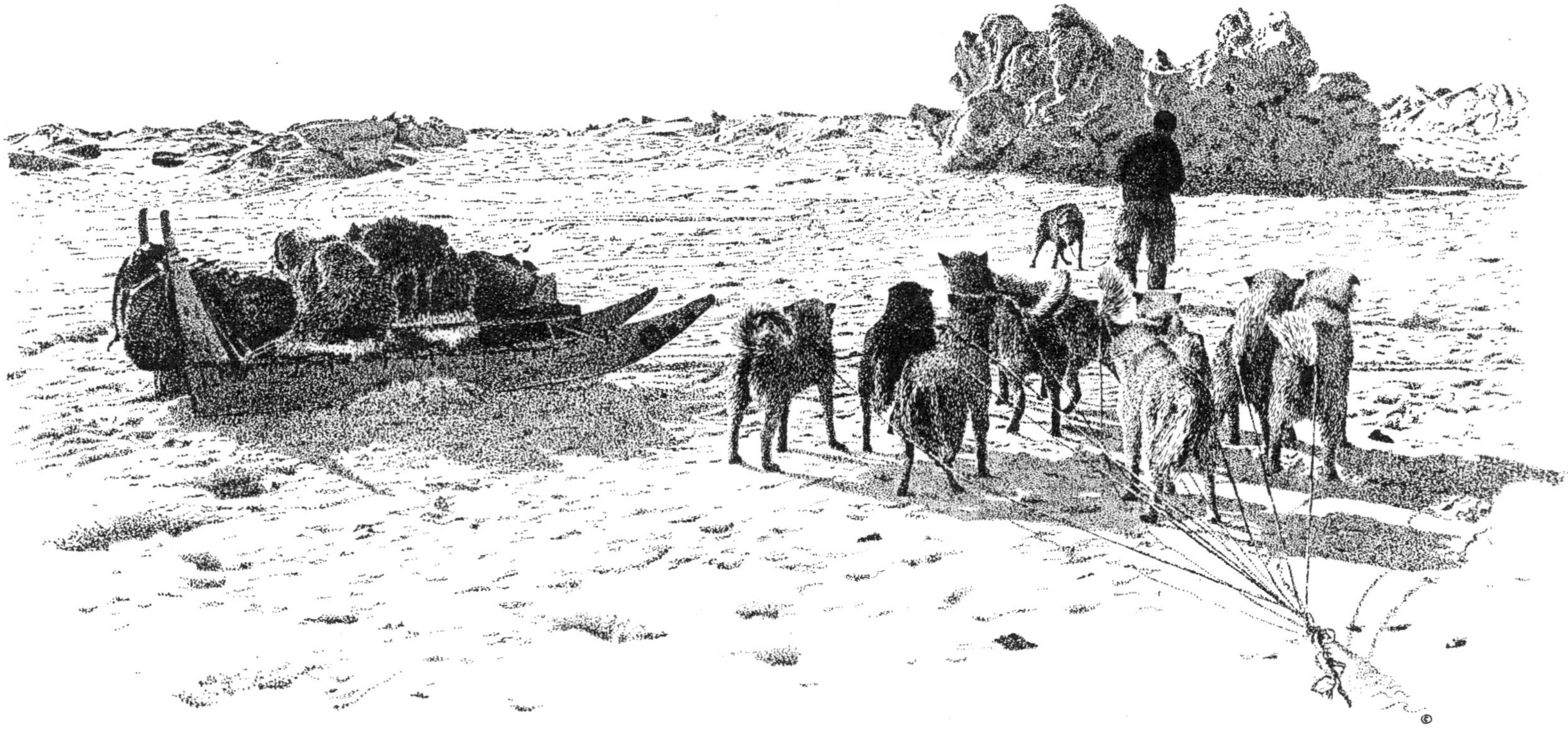

Preparing for the trail.

THE SPELL OF THE MIDNIGHT SUN

Maurice R. Cloughley

Horsdal & Schubart

Horsdal & Schubart Publishers Ltd.
Victoria, BC, Canada

Cover: "Midnight Tea-Break," coloured woodcut by Maurice Cloughley.
All illustrations in the text are by Maurice Cloughley.

This book is set in Lapidary 333 Book Text.

Printed and bound in Canada by Kromar Printing Limited, Winnipeg.

Canadian Cataloguing in Publication Data

Cloughley, Maurice, 1934-
The spell of the midnight sun

ISBN 0-920663-41-9

1. Cloughley, Maurice, 1934- 2.Teachers—Northwest Territories—Biography. 3. Northwest Territories—Biography. 4. Indians of North America—Northwest Territories—Education. 5. Inuit—Northwest Territories—Education. I. Title.
LA2325.C66A3 1995 371.1'0092 C95-910854-8

Table of Contents

This book I dedicate
to my constant and happy companion;
To my guiding star; My compass;
To the clear steady beacon burning bright in the darkness;
To my shipmate;
To my sweetheart.

To Katie,
with all the love that I have.

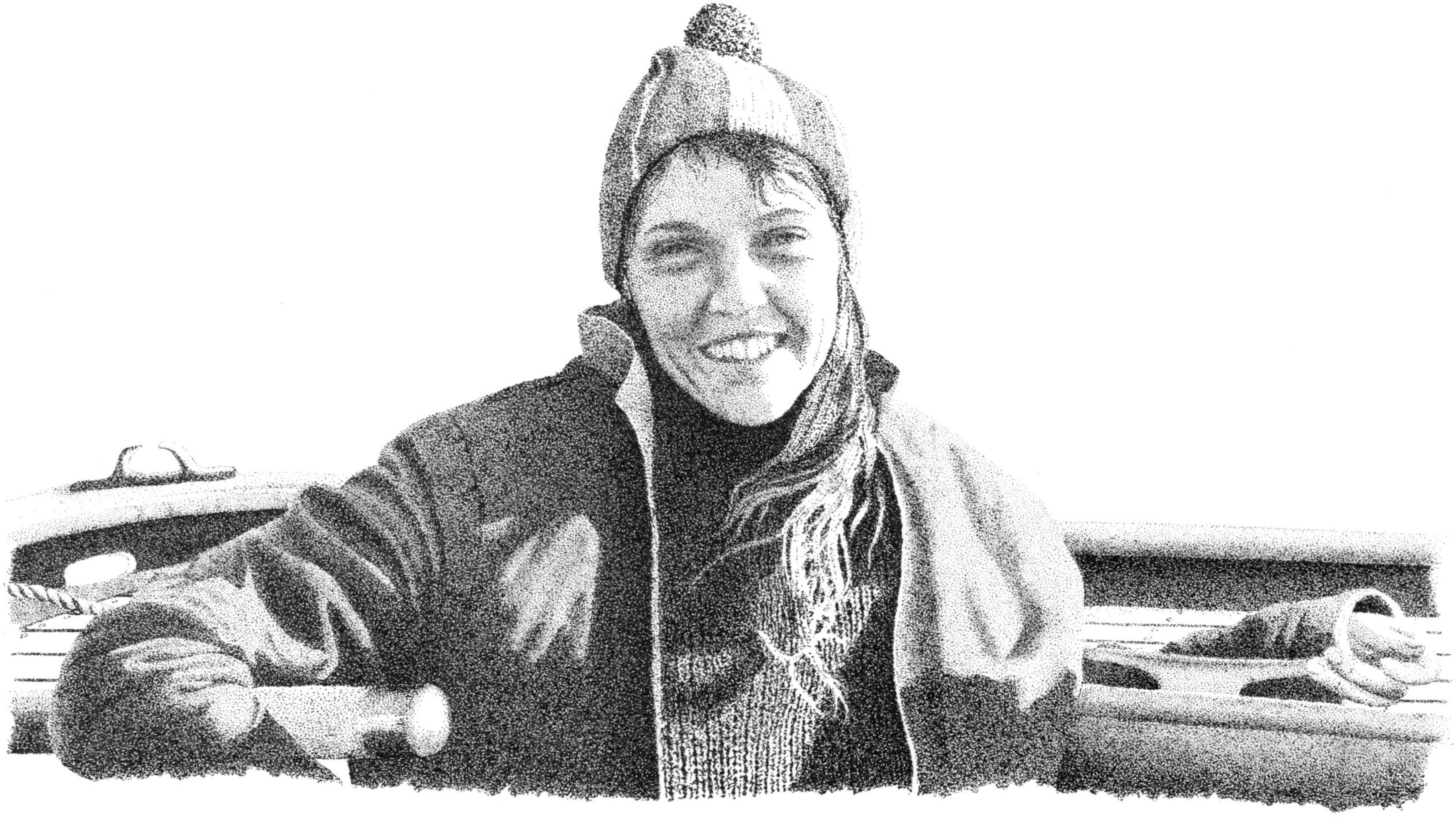

Introduction

I WAS JUST 23 when I arrived in Canada looking for a teaching job. As many young people did back then in the fifties, I was working my way around the world, and teaching at that time was a good job to travel with. Not only were borders, especially Commonwealth borders, wide open to itinerant young workers, but everywhere, it seemed, there was a dire shortage of teachers.

Surprisingly perhaps for such an age, I already had four years' teaching experience behind me, three in my native New Zealand and one in London and Scotland. As it happened, after I'd matriculated from high school I was too young to be accepted directly into teacher training, so the education authorities in New Zealand, perennially hard up in those post-war years for real teachers, sent me off into the South Island high country for a year to fill in time, teaching in a remote, little one-room school with six pupils, the children of local farmers, sheep musterers and rabbit exterminators. The kids came to school each day on horseback, three little beginners, an 11-year-old boy and two girls, nine and ten. I myself was only 16. During that year I enrolled a 15 year old, and he of course called me "*Mister* Cloughley" like the other kids, or better still, "Please Sir." I never thought anything of this at the time. It was the Done Thing, and most New Zealanders in those days were moderately adept at doing the Done Thing when they had to.

They gave me no training whatever to prepare me for all this. I had just finished school, hadn't I? so of course I knew what had to be taught. And that, more or less, was true enough. What I didn't know was *how*. But they handed me a book of blank cheques and said, "At the end of each month write yourself a cheque for eighteen pounds, eleven shillings and ninepence." Anyway, rich or not, I liked that little school and I loved the wild magnificence of those silent mountain ranges rising up from the sheep stations, and in my subsequent years at teachers' college I took the opportunity to specialize in rural education and began to dream and scheme of going eventually into the Maori school system or to get an appointment up in the Polynesian islands, or to some other far undiscovered place even more remote and exotic.

In the meantime, I drifted happily through the undemanding business of attending and graduating from teachers' college. Those years were followed by my first two years' working as a qualified teacher in the farming districts of the far south, and by that time I felt I had at last more or less financed my escape to the more exciting, wider world beyond the seas.

"I'll be back in a couple of years," I told my family as I climbed aboard the bus that would take me finally out of my little home town of Riverton on the south coast of the South Island. "Or maybe three..." but the bus door slammed shut and they may not have heard me. The simple act of climbing onto that bus seemed to me in later years the most important step I ever took, but at the time my only thoughts were for the home I was leaving at last, and my eyes swam a little as the bus left Riverton behind.

One of those years was already behind me, including two summer seasons travelling around Europe, when I flew into Montreal from Prestwick in Scotland. It was June, 1957. One year in Canada, I thought, or maybe two, would help finance my continuing travels down through Latin America, the Amazon, the pampas, before heading back to "settle down."

But it didn't quite work out that way. I suppose nothing in life ever does.

I was wildly excited to find myself at last in this big, dynamic, go-getting continent, the engine, in those days, of the free world's economy. After the tight, crowded cities of Europe, Montreal seemed to me built for giants, with colossal boulevards that took half the morning to cross, great unrestrained skyscrapers that stretched out of sight and huge cars half a block long. There was room to breathe. Perhaps those yarns about Paul Bunyan and the Blue Ox were written by someone fresh out of

Europe? Still, I wasn't much interested in Montreal, nor, for that matter, any other city.

I had ten provinces to choose from, each one a separate nation of its own as far as a teacher was concerned. I didn't speak much French so that took care of Quebec, and I wasn't interested in the gentle little provinces of the east. They were not my North America. We didn't play fishermen and rum runners when we were kids, we played cowboys and Indians, and the West, wild and wide, seemed to me far more romantic and beckoning. I avoided the cost of a hotel by catching the overnight bus to Toronto, and then in the bus station I bought a copy of *The Globe and Mail* and began to pore over the teaching ads. There were pages of them. My eye immediately glued itself to a single small ad among the many hundreds. This one was from the federal Department of Northern Affairs inviting applications for teaching positions in the Northwest Territories, that vast, far-flung and little-known entity to the north of the provinces. I was well aware that a few native people lived up there, but that a school system actually existed in those distant regions was a thrilling discovery. I never bothered to explore Toronto any further, but caught the next bus to Ottawa where I checked in to the YMCA, spruced myself up as much as I could before going to the offices of the department that was responsible for administering those distant regions, and then presented myself in person to the Chief of the Education Division, a suave, grey-haired pipe smoker.

We talked, or rather he did, about the North for some time. There were large maps on the walls showing all of the Canadian North with little coloured pins stuck in here and there where schools had been established, yellow for the mission schools, red for the federal schools, and green for others still being planned. There seemed to be an air of adventure and pioneering among the people in those offices, a sense of excitement at being involved in bringing education across those vast distances to the "primitive" hunters of the Arctic. I wasn't at all sure in my own mind just what those same hunters might do with their education but I didn't let that worry me at the time. My only concern was to persuade the people in those offices that I would be an asset to them in their unfolding adventure.

There was only one problem in all this, a rather major fly in the ointment. *The Globe and Mail* ad had specified *Roman Catholic* teachers. It was after all the end of June and I suppose only a few specific positions remained yet to be filled. At that time, teachers in native communities had to belong to the same religious denomination as the majority of the people in their community, a requirement dictated by the Indian Act and the churches. Perhaps any other arrangement might have infected an aboriginal mind with doubt, disillusionment and loss of faith. The Feds eventually got around to abandoning this vital precautionary measure but that would still take many years and meanwhile I had a problem. Although not by any measure an ardent follower of the church, I had been brought up as a Presbyterian in New Zealand.

But they need Catholics, I thought to myself. Could I not just wing it for a year? Or two? I wanted so desperately to go north.

At the end of my interview with the chief, he set his pipe aside, looked at me and asked the fatal question, "Oh, by the way, what's your religion?"

"Er... Catholic," I said in a small voice, swallowing hard.

He took note of that and told me that he would be pursuing records of my qualifications with the authorities in New Zealand, and would be in touch. I settled down to the life of a casual labourer for a few weeks at $1.10 an hour, keeping myself just barely solvent financially, when at last near the end of July I received the long-awaited message from the chief's office. I was appointed to Fort Norman, an Indian settlement halfway down the Mackenzie River, as classroom teacher of the two-room school there.

This wasn't *quite* as far north as I had hoped to go, but it was much farther north than it might have been and I was deliriously happy.

They took me on strength right away and I found myself in the company of a dozen or so other recruits all getting themselves oriented at headquarters. Apart from myself and an Irishman, they came mostly from the eastern provinces. They were all as young and enthusiastic as I was, but most of the group stayed in the North for only a year or two, or three, and left again.

They seemed, some of them, to be infused with a sense of high mission, an ardent commitment to Do Good, even if it meant having to live in great isolation and going up into an awful climate and enduring a deprived existence amongst strange, incomprehensible people far from the comforts and benefits of civilization. For myself, all these things that seemed rather negative to some of the others were excitingly positive. I really didn't care a fig for the civilized amenities we would leave behind. The chance to go north was a chance to enter a time machine and, at least in my youthful, romantic mind, to voyage backwards a hundred years or more to an earlier, more pristine continent, to the days when North America was still a wilderness and the aboriginal people were still the greater part of the population. I felt myself to be part of a select corps of privileged pioneers, privileged in the sense that, out of all the southern hordes, it was to be given to us few to be amongst indigenous people of a proud, ancient past, people emerging from their nomadic prehistory to the 20th century, and for a time to merge our lives with theirs in their own land.

Our group was given free access to the settlement files and library resources. We learned all about the history of the North, the traders and the missionaries, the search for the Northwest Passage and so on. We passed our physicals. We bound ourselves to secrecy and swore allegiance to the Queen, even the Irishman, who declared he didn't sleep well for a few nights after.

We were introduced to various Northern experts, most notable of whom was the middle-aged English schoolmarm, Margery Hinds. This authoritative, no-nonsense personage had already taught amongst the Lapps of Norway and opened up several new schools in the Northwest Territories, and was now in Ottawa preparatory to launching herself into pioneering yet another new school at Arctic Bay on the northern coast of Baffin Island where 25 young Eskimo children were said to be eagerly awaiting their fate. Most smaller communities of the Eastern Arctic at that time still had no schools, and the new one at Arctic Bay would be by far the most distant and northerly of all.

We held this hardened old warrior-pedagogue in great awe and respect. And for my part in great envy. Even before leaving Ottawa, I was beginning to regret my new religion for it was dawning on me that the most exciting challenges lay in the new schools that were beginning to open up along the Arctic coast, and most of the Eskimos unhappily were Protestant. How I would have loved to trade places with this Englishwoman, this Arctic Amazon, Miss Hinds.

My original dream of going west, young man, was facilitated not by a horse, canoe or stagecoach, but by a first-class ticket at the taxpayers' expense on Canadian National Railways, a journey rolling on and on for long days and nights through the northern woods, the lakesides and the vast prairies to Edmonton. We were met at the station by a federal official who took us to the Corona Hotel where a bed cost us $4.50 for the night. And then at last the flight north. We boarded a rattling old Canadian Pacific DC3 at the municipal airport and were soon leaving, roaring onwards over the wilds of northern Alberta.

"Fasten your seat belts."

"Would you like another coffee, sir?"

"We'll be landing in Fort Smith in ten minutes."

All this was hardly in keeping with the romantic vision I had of the explorer in me. We should have been barging down the Peace River, and portaging the rapids on the Slave River, camping with a group of itinerant Indians, silent, watchful and suspicious, and joining the Hudson's Bay Company steamer, the *Distributor*, for the long passage down the Mackenzie. But this was good enough. I was going north, and this way I was getting there faster. "Yes, I'll have another coffee."

In late August of every second year in those times, the teachers of the North gathered together for a two-week conference in Yellowknife, so that was where we were bound. Yellowknife impressed me vastly. It was a magnificently rough-and-ready, hard-drinking frontier town, a get-rich-quick gold town far beyond the highways, set in the midst of a marvellous, hard-rock wilderness shaped by the primeval cold. It was quite a small place then. The Gold Range Hotel at the time was in the process of construction but we were quartered there anyway, and given beds, or at least mattresses, in the few rooms that already had windows fitted. We trampled back and forth through sawdust and shavings and the usual litter of a half-finished building, but this was the North and nobody minded. I shared a bare plywood room with the principal from Coppermine, a youngish fellow with whom I spent many a bibulous night celebrating all over the town and many a penitential hangover the morning after. This was the thing you did in Yellowknife, and I for one was happy to do in Rome as the Romans. Wisdom always returned before breakfast and remained through most of the day's lectures, but it never survived the lengthening shadows and returning thirst of another afternoon.

I always loved those conferences, but I never really learned anything vitally useful in them except inadvertently, things having nothing to do with the original intent of the exercise. Still, we were told all about native culture by sociologists from Alaska and all about reading programs by a lady from Alberta, and home economics by another one from Ottawa. An inadequate attempt was made to unveil the (to me) very great mystery of how to confront a classroom of children who have absolutely no common language with their teacher, and to understand them, and to be understood by them, and, more than that, to develop in them an eager fluency in English. (I often tried, in the North, to cast my mind back to my own elementary school and to imagine how difficult our education would have been as children if our classrooms had been run by alien, pig-tailed Chinese who understood nothing of our own history, culture or language, nor cared, who were equally incomprehensible to our parents and who insisted on talking to us in nothing but their own sing-song Mandarin Chinese and making us learn to write in Chinese characters with a bamboo brush. I always saw myself in the North as exactly such an outsider.) The advice we were given was awful. 1. Outlaw all talking that is not in English. 2. Set aside a formal Basic English period each day for instructing the children as a group in spoken English using a boring little book called *English Through Pictures*. These ideas were actually quite a bit worse than useless.

One of the recurring themes in that conference was the idea, much in vogue in Ottawa, that the native people had to be integrated into the mainstream of Canadian life. There were many interpretations of this, but nobody really challenged it as a desirable goal. Change was not seen as a two-way street. The enormous changes ahead were to be theirs alone, and we were to be the agents of that change, being very much involved in its speed and direction. And our involvement went far beyond the classroom. While the rest of Canada managed to get by with just plain teachers, the Northwest Territories had "Welfare Teachers." This was a special designation placing us in a category similar to all other civil servants in that, while we put in the usual two hundred days of teaching each year, we had to work at all other times too, with only the same three-week annual vacation that other government employees got.

We were expected to do "welfare work"! Anything falling into the general category of Doing Good was considered welfare work. This in fact was serious enough business in certain remote little settlements like Fort Franklin where the teacher had to act as dispenser of medicine, radio operator, social worker, Indian Agent, diesel-power-plant operator, game warden, dog officer and general factotum, but in the larger places it was a little more difficult to define the role, and it generally had more to do with the ongoing educational and recreational needs of children and adults. Most teachers at that time chose to remain at their posts right through every second summer "doing welfare work" so that they could accumulate six weeks of vacation time Outside for the following year. A great deal of time and earnest talk were expended at the conference on our roles as Welfare Teachers, and I wondered what on earth could possibly be expected of me once I got to Fort Norman. I liked teaching but I didn't quite see myself as changing the world.

We were told about the rations we would receive and how to complete our expense claims and our monthly reports. We were put through a first-aid course on how to set bones, deliver babies, stitch wounds and pull teeth, for many of us were going to places where no medical facilities existed. (I managed to pass the artificial resuscitation part of this course by actually doing it on an actual victim at Long Lake on my first day in the North.)

Eventually, August, the earnest lectures and the wild partying were all over, and Max Ward's bush planes were chartered to ship us off, north, south, east and west to all those distant little settlements. We said our sentimental, relieved goodbyes and flew off to the northwest in a single-engine Otter over the vast array of uncountable lakes on the great Canadian Shield.

And so my Northern years began. I loved the Northland with a wild, absorbing passion, and year after year I delayed my always-intended return to my own home. After two years at Fort Norman, I transferred to Fort Franklin on the shores of Great Bear Lake, and it was during the long winters there that I first conceived the idea of emulating my various boyhood heroes, Joshua Slocum, Captain Voss, Erling Tambs, W.A. Robinson and others by getting myself a small sailboat and making a transocean voyage, a most unusual thing in those days, foolhardy even, especially for a total novice. Returning home to New Zealand by plane or ship as a passenger suddenly seemed tame and anticlimactic, just as did the awful notion of "settling down" once there. I was in need of new adventure.

I subscribed in those bachelor years to yachting magazines and read every cruising book I could lay my hands on, so that, although I had no practical experience whatever of sailing, and had never even been on a sailboat, I did gradually teach myself all the elements of seamanship and navigation that could be learned from the pages of books. Perhaps I could single-hand my own boat from England to New Zealand? My daydreams did not end there either. Steeped as I was in the stirring history of the North and the long search for the Northwest Passage, I fantasized that I might take a sailboat up into the Arctic someday, and attempt the Passage myself. In those times such a thing had never been done. I was aware too that no vessel of any description at that time had ever completely circumnavigated the Americas. What a thing to achieve! What a dream!

What a *dreamer!*

So these tantalizing prospects finally persuaded me to send in my resignation to the superintendent, and from Fort Franklin I went to England and learned to sail. It was quite wonderful. How good it was to be young with a head brimming over with seemingly achievable dreams! But along the way, two things happened: one was that I found my pocket wasn't deep enough to afford both the 25-footer I wanted, and the expense of the long voyage to the other side of the world. The other, infinitely more important, infinitely happier thing was that I met Katie. She was involved in the sailing club that I had joined in Devon. She came from Greenwich in London, so, after crewing on an assortment of sailing yachts, crossing the Channel back and forth several times, after a Biscay gale in a schooner-rigged sieve and shipwreck on the Spanish coast, it was to Greenwich that I resorted for a year, teaching nice little working-class nine year olds, and attending navigation classes on board the *Cutty Sark* in the winter, recapitulating all that I had studied in Fort Franklin.

London was Katie's world, and she had scarcely travelled out of it farther than the south coast. Still, for all that, we shared similar dreams of travel, high adventure and of cruising someday to faraway places. But as I saw it, those dreams could be fulfilled only by my returning to the Canadian North, which itself, luckily, was an exciting prospect for Katie as well.

Katie and I were married in London in the early summer of 1963. We honeymooned on Lake Victoria and the source of the Nile in Tanzania, travelled to the Mountains of the Moon, gadded about amongst the tall, elegant tribespeople of the southern Sudan — the Dinka, the Nuer, the Shilluk and the Nuba — in what was still then a wondrous and happy Garden of Eden. We rode horses over the Sahara sands and climbed the great pyramids of Giza, marvelled at the Acropolis, Pompeii, Pisa, Paris, and caught a liner at last to Canada.

We lived for three happy years at Split Lake, a Cree Indian reserve in the spruce-and-river wilderness of northern Manitoba, and, in 1966, we transferred to Arctic Bay on northern Baffin Island for a year. Then followed two years at Grise Fiord on Ellesmere Island, and it was during the intervening summer of 1968 that we flew to England and found the sailboat of our dreams, a 34-foot wooden ketch which we named *Nanook of the North*. In 1969 we left the Arctic, flew back again to England, and sailed away.

And so the pattern of our lives was set. There were limits to how much of that extreme isolation we could handle at a time before going mad, and five years or so in those tiny distant settlements were usually quite enough. So we lived in the North for a few years at a time, saving our money, and then sailed away for a few years at a time and spent it all. We completed a world circumnavigation after we left Ellesmere Island, very much more than fulfilling our original dreams, and it took us five years and 47,000 ocean miles before we left *Nanook* behind on a mooring in Nova Scotia and returned again to the Arctic, this time to Clyde River on Baffin Island for two years, and later to Resolute Bay. Then followed a four-year voyage which included four Atlantic crossings, a passage to Peru and Easter Island, and a year in New Zealand before sailing north in 1983 through Micronesia to Skagway, Alaska. We based our boat there for two winters, and on Vancouver Island for several more while we lived again in the North, this time in Tungsten in the west, on the Yukon border, and then finally to Rae Lakes. Our third extended voyage began in 1989 when we sailed north to revisit

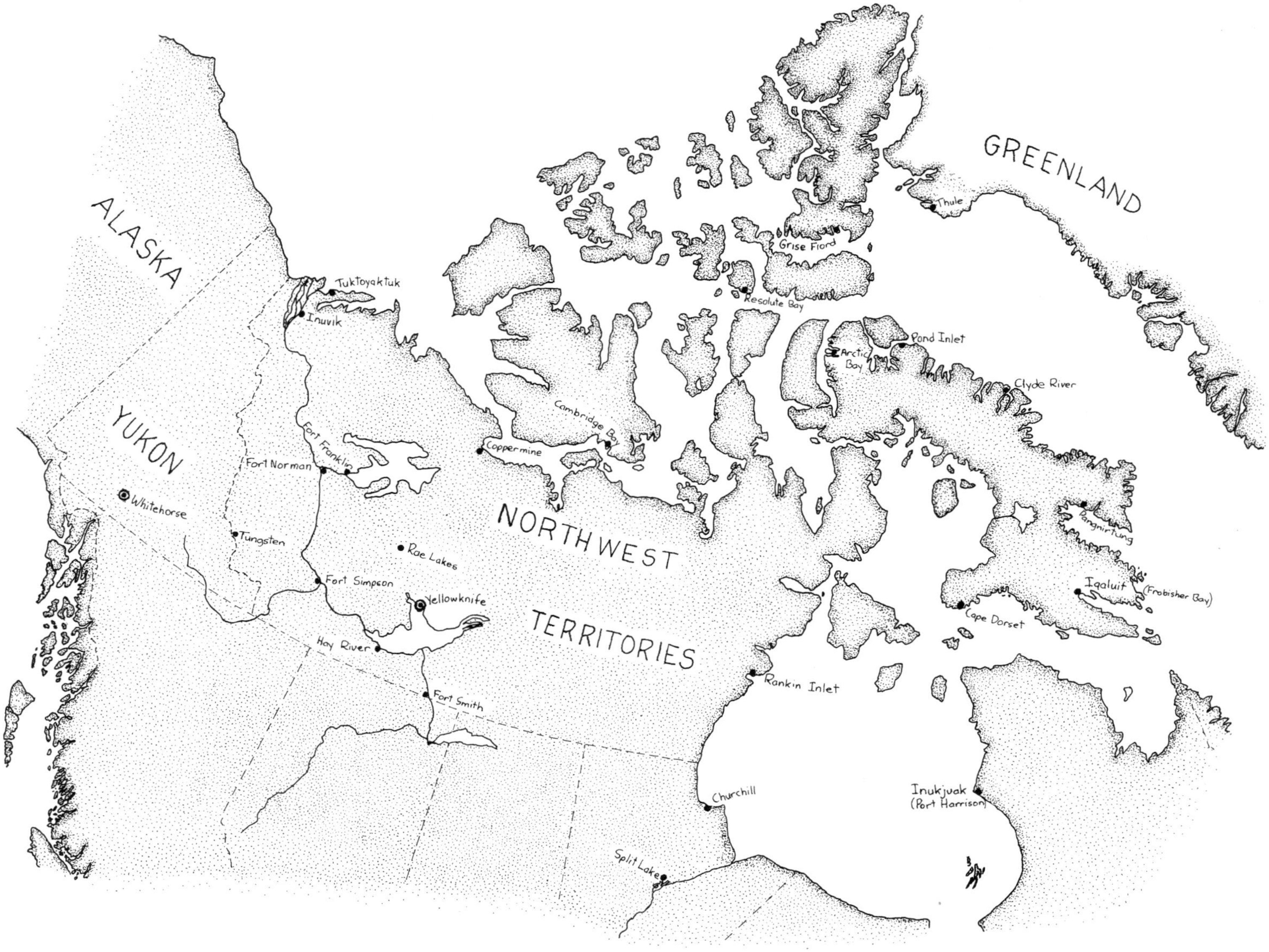
ALASKA
YUKON
GREENLAND
NORTHWEST
TERRITORIES
Tuktoyaktuk
Inuvik
Fort Franklin
Fort Norman
Whitehorse
Tungsten
Rae Lakes
Fort Simpson
Yellowknife
Hay River
Fort Smith
Coppermine
Cambridge Bay
Resolute Bay
Grise Fiord
Thule
Arctic Bay
Pond Inlet
Clyde River
Pangnirtung
Iqaluit
(Frobisher Bay)
Cape Dorset
Rankin Inlet
Churchill
Split Lake
Inukjuak
(Port Harrison)

our much-loved Alaska, covering the entire coast right up to the Eskimo community of Teller near Bering Strait. We crossed from there to the Siberian port of Provideniya in what was still then the Soviet Union, and from there turned south to follow the entire west coast of the Americas to Cape Horn, and beyond that, apparently forgetting to turn the boat in any other direction, until we reached a south latitude of 63°. Forty days from the Falklands and we were in Cape Town. Sixty days from there and we were back in Nova Scotia.

So in this way, our lives kept alternating: the North; the sea; the North again, back and forth. And while, far to the south beyond the equator, rolling along over the white-capped seas to the sweet, seductive, incessant music of the southeast trade, or the shriek of the belligerent westerlies, I dreamed again of seeing the Great Bear wheeling counter-clockwise around Polaris, and of gazing overhead again at the wondrous aurora high above the snowy wastes, so too, in the depths of those bitter, Arctic winters-without-end, did I gaze up at the northern sky and long to see again, through the rigging and past the ever-moving sails, the greater, clearer, brighter sweep of the Milky Way of southern skies, and my own native Southern Cross wheeling in its turn, clockwise, around its own celestial pole.

We loved both sides of this alternating life, but although many people professed to envy us, it was not a life that would have suited everybody, for it often carried with it varying degrees of privation, discomfort and danger, long separation from loved ones, lengthy periods of tedium, and often the near or total absence of many of the "necessary" luxuries of modern life. We were "minimalists" long before the term was invented. We have hardly ever had a television. We have never owned a car, or wanted to, nor do we have drivers' licences (I have driven about 30 miles in my life), and we have never owned a house. Occasionally we yearned for a modest little cottage of our own somewhere, but the closer we came to actually doing something about this the more we were frightened off by the realization that owning your own home means that you have to keep coming back to the same old place all the time.

* * *

We have a friend on Vancouver Island named Michael Greenfield. Michael had once cruised in his own boat from British Columbia to the islands of the South Pacific and back again, and although he had the desire to find his freedom and sail away once more, he was much too involved with his family and business to actually do it. After our voyage to Bering Strait, we returned to Vancouver Island, and spent a brief winter there preparing for the voyage south to Chile. Katie sometimes went to the same hairdresser as Michael, and, in the course of general chit-chat, Katie had told the woman all about our lives. So the hairdresser knew all about us, and on one occasion when Michael went there to have his hair cut she began talking to him about the Cloughleys. "Those poor people!" she said. "Imagine! They don't have jobs. They have to live by trying to sell pictures of the Arctic. They have hardly any really nice clothes. Katie has only one decent pair of shoes, and I don't think he can even afford to get a proper haircut. They don't know anything about what's showing on television because they haven't even got one. They don't have a car, not even one between the two of them. They have to walk everywhere. They don't own a house, and I don't suppose they could even rent one. They have no family to fall back on, and they just have to live on a leaky old wooden boat. Those people have nothing!"

Michael stared straight at her for a moment, and then said, slowly and deliberately, "Those people have everything!"

Well, maybe there were little grains of truth in each of these two opposite conclusions. But it all depends on your own perspective.

A Winter at Fort Norman

Halfway down the Mackenzie River, where its wide, muddy waters are joined by the clear, cold stream of the Bear River draining out of Great Bear Lake, lies the attractive little Indian village of Fort Norman. No one seems to know how the place got its name, but Norman himself was probably some functionary of the old fur-trading North West Company. A hundred and eighty people lived there in 1957, not counting a small assortment of White outsiders like myself, posted to the place on various pretexts. Fort Norman had a two-room school and it was here that I took up my first-ever teaching position in Canada.

The native people, legally at least (and these things mattered in 1957 as well as long after) were quite a mixture, ranging from Treaty Indian, through Non-Treaty, to Métis, and dwindling on through varying shades of almost (but not *Quite*) White. It was a delightful little place, and towards each other, the people including the Quite Whites were all mostly friendly and well-intentioned if not always well-informed or even well-acquainted. The settlement was sited above a bank sloping steeply up from the North's Old Man River, the mighty Mackenzie. Above this bank there were two terraces, one well above the other, and by long established (but unintended) precedent, these ancient formations served to define quite distinctly one's status: who you were, where you came from, where you belonged. All the native people of whatever category lived in their tired old log cabins or tents on the lower terrace nearer the river, and all the Whites lived in or adjacent to their workplace on the upper level. This quite unplanned arrangement seemed to suit everyone. There wasn't a lot of room for many more on the lower terrace and the Indians liked being close to the river, while the Quite Whites seemed to be happy having their own larger enclave at some distance and elevation from The Rest.

A more-or-less road meandered along the upper level connecting all the elements of this higher enclave. (Like all roads, this one had started out as just a dirt track, but there were now two tractors at Fort Norman, so that made it a road.) Two Mounties manned the stockade at the western end of this road, and not far from their detachment was the Roman Catholic church which normally had two Oblate priests in residence. Then came a Department of Transport radio station followed by the Indian Agency. The Hudson's Bay Company post was across the road overlooking the native village and the river. Next came the federal day school where Frank Frey, the principal, lived. The game warden's office was across the road, and at the end was the nursing station.

It was to this elevated stratum that I clearly belonged. The Whites decided things and ran things, even including each other, and while in our various capacities we all dealt with the local people on a daily basis, there was always the unspoken but clear understanding that socially we confined ourselves to our own kind. Oh dear! This was hardly why I came North and secretly I was more than a little disappointed to find myself bound by these expectations, but I wasn't about to change the world.

A small house, a design known across the North as a 512 for its square footage, was being shipped in for me to Fort Norman, but as this wasn't built yet, I had to board with the Freys for a few weeks. They lived upstairs in the school building itself, which was a common design in the North in the early fifties: two classrooms side by side separated by a folding partition that facilitated the conversion of the school into a community hall but did nothing to dampen the noise of either class in the adjacent classroom. A hallway separated these two rooms from furnace room, toilets, storage space, office and corridors, and directly above these rooms was the three-bedroom apartment of the principal.

Eventually, the old *George Askew*, last stern-wheeler on the Mackenzie River system, nosed a load of barges gently against the river bank. Piles of building materials were offloaded onto the beach, and within a short time my 512 got built at the edge of

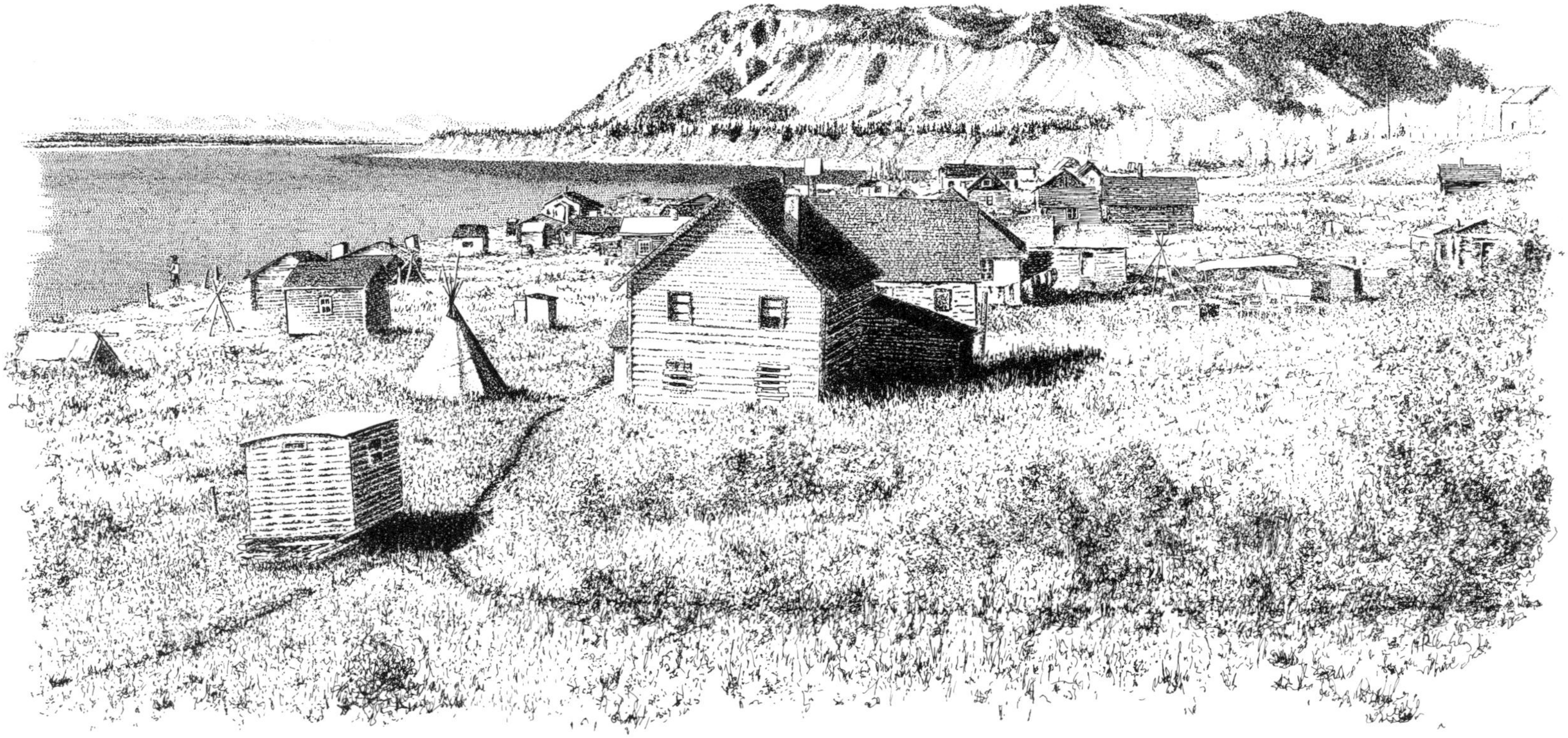

Fort Norman, 1957.

the school playground, and I moved into my first-ever home of my own. It felt great and I was very happy with it. I got a Métis man to provide me with a 45-gallon steel gasoline drum with the top hacked out and replaced with a plywood cover. This drum I painted inside and out, and that was my water tank. It was filled periodically in the summer season by pump and canvas fire hose from the river, but on the advice of my neighbours who warned me gloomily of problems ahead, I laid in a stock of ice blocks against the house in case of need and especially for use in spring when the river water would be filthy.

School started right away in September and I busied myself for a few weeks in my work as the leaves turned colour and fell, and, falling with them, the enchanting snow and the temperatures. All this was humdrum to everyone else but it was novel and exotic to me and I was enthralled. The ground froze. The lakes froze. We flooded a rectangular skating rink in the school playground, and that froze.

I bought an outdoor thermometer at the Bay and nailed it at my cabin entrance so I could monitor the temperatures as they stepped steadily day by day down the old Fahrenheit scale until I

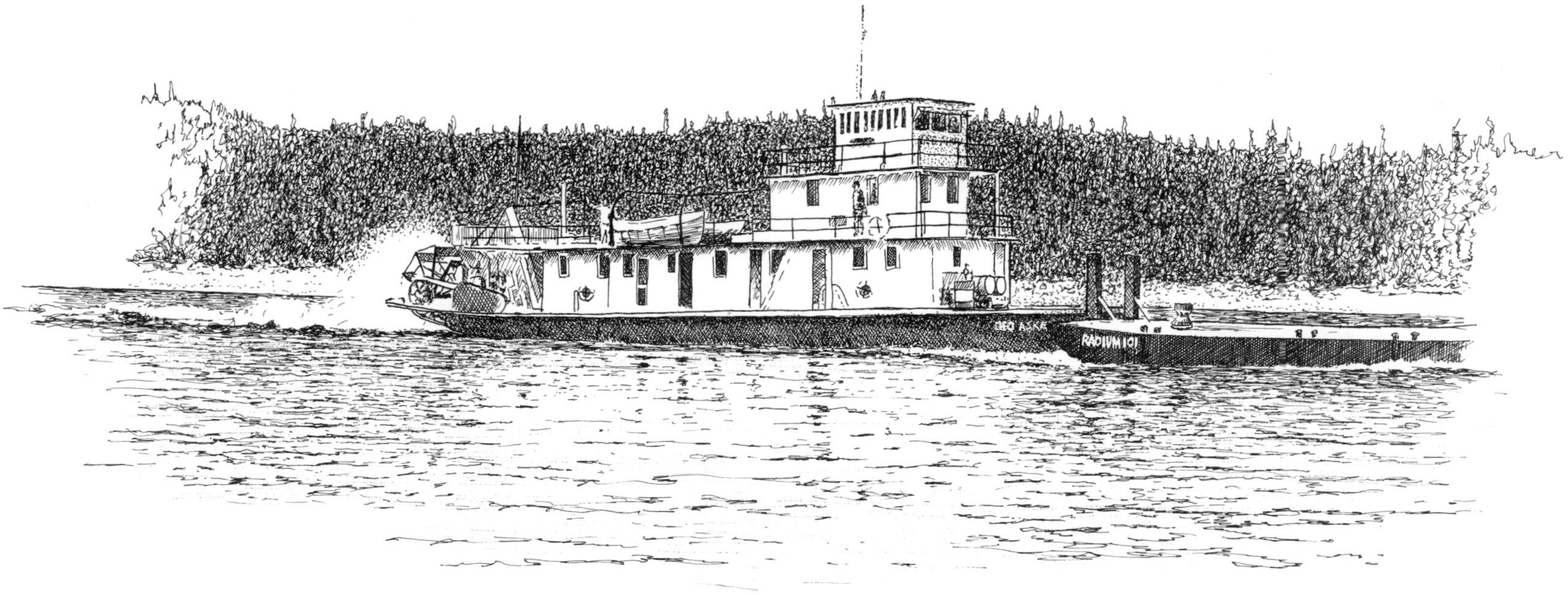

The stern-wheeler GEORGE ASKEW.

could add the unaccustomed term "below zero" in my letters home to New Zealand. I was thrilled and wonderstruck at the amazing cold. The river began at first to carry thin, colourless, skim ice along on its surface. This soon congealed into small, rounded, ice pans and then larger and larger pans until they floated everywhere over the wide, vapour-smoking surface of the great, silent river, leaving us cut off for six weeks from the bush planes that normally ran a scheduled service into our settlement every two weeks from Norman Wells. Finally and suddenly the running ice stopped running as it jammed up tight from one bank to the other, a jumbled mass in most places, but flat and smooth enough in some areas to allow us a winter airstrip.

Twenty-five degrees below gradually became 40 below and occasionally, towards dark December, dropped all the way to 60 below and more, the air feeling like acid on the skin, while tall columns of white smoke rose steadily from every home straight up into the dense, quiet, absolutely still air, curling up amongst those unfamiliar Northern Hemisphere constellations and that other exotic wonder, the Northern Lights. I was enchanted with the beauty of it all and often stood outside at night, spellbound, for as long as I could endure the cold, gazing up at the stupendous displays of swirling light, the multi-coloured curtains dancing in the northern sky, and listening to the soft crackle of my own breath freezing in the still air. And occasionally I caught a glimpse too of that other wonder of the time, the newly born Sputnik circling the world like an omen of great changes. And then this time it was not I alone who stood gazing up in wonder and disbelief at what was up there, but everyone else as well.

My little house was heated only by the oil-burning cookstove, unlike all the other White houses which had similar cookstoves, but depended for heat on forced-air furnaces. I thought nothing of this. Homes in New Zealand were generally heated, if at all, by the cookstove, and when my frequent White visitors came in and kept their parkas on, and complained to me of the cold, I replied, "Well, of course it's a bit cold in here. It's cold outside, isn't it? Move closer to the stove." The trouble was that while it was absolutely frigid in wintertime at floor level, it was likely to be baking hot at the ceiling. The snow kicked from my mukluks would skitter across the linoleum tiles when I came inside from 50 below, and would just lie there for long hours as snow, until it evaporated in the desiccated air. Meanwhile, butter melted in the top cupboards. Ideally, to be comfortable, one needed to be horizontal, halfway up or so, and occasionally during the cold snaps I took to abandoning my double bed in the first bedroom in favour of the upper bunk in the tiny second bedroom.

Except for the butter and lard, most of my tinned rations too had to be relocated upwards. The government had shipped an "A ration" down the river to sustain a single teacher at Fort Norman through the year, and after the mountain of cardboard boxes had been hauled up to the 512, they deducted $35 a month from my salary to offset the cost. To prevent it all from freezing I piled it up on top of the wardrobes. The lower kitchen cupboards were ice-cold all winter.

I once reached for my electric iron to attend to ironing my laundry during a cold snap. It resided on one of those bottom shelves, and I was surprised to find how cold the thing was to the touch. Without really thinking what I was doing I licked it to see just how cold it really felt. I instantly knew. My tongue was stuck fast, frozen onto the flat surface. It hurt like hell when I tried to drag it off, so I desisted and stood there in a panic holding the damned iron flat against my face and trying to think what to do. Eventually of course it occurred to me: plug the bloody thing in! Slowly my tongue eased away and I was left to gaze at the white patch on the iron and marvel at the wonders of science.

The pokey little toilet room in that 512 was just as cold as the cupboards. All the other White establishments in the settlement were provided with flush toilets (the chronic water shortage usually limited each toilet to just one flush per day), and underground cesspits outside, and these systems worked well enough much of the time. But my 512 had a toilet that was just a folding lid over a galvanized pail. No need here to worry about how often I could afford to flush. Such basic buckets as these, common things in the North, are lined each day with a fresh "honey bag" of black plastic, but in those earlier times there were no plastic bags. The pail itself received all contributions, and the pail itself had to be taken out and emptied. In my case, right through the winter, these contributions immediately froze solid in that little side room and every weekend I was faced with

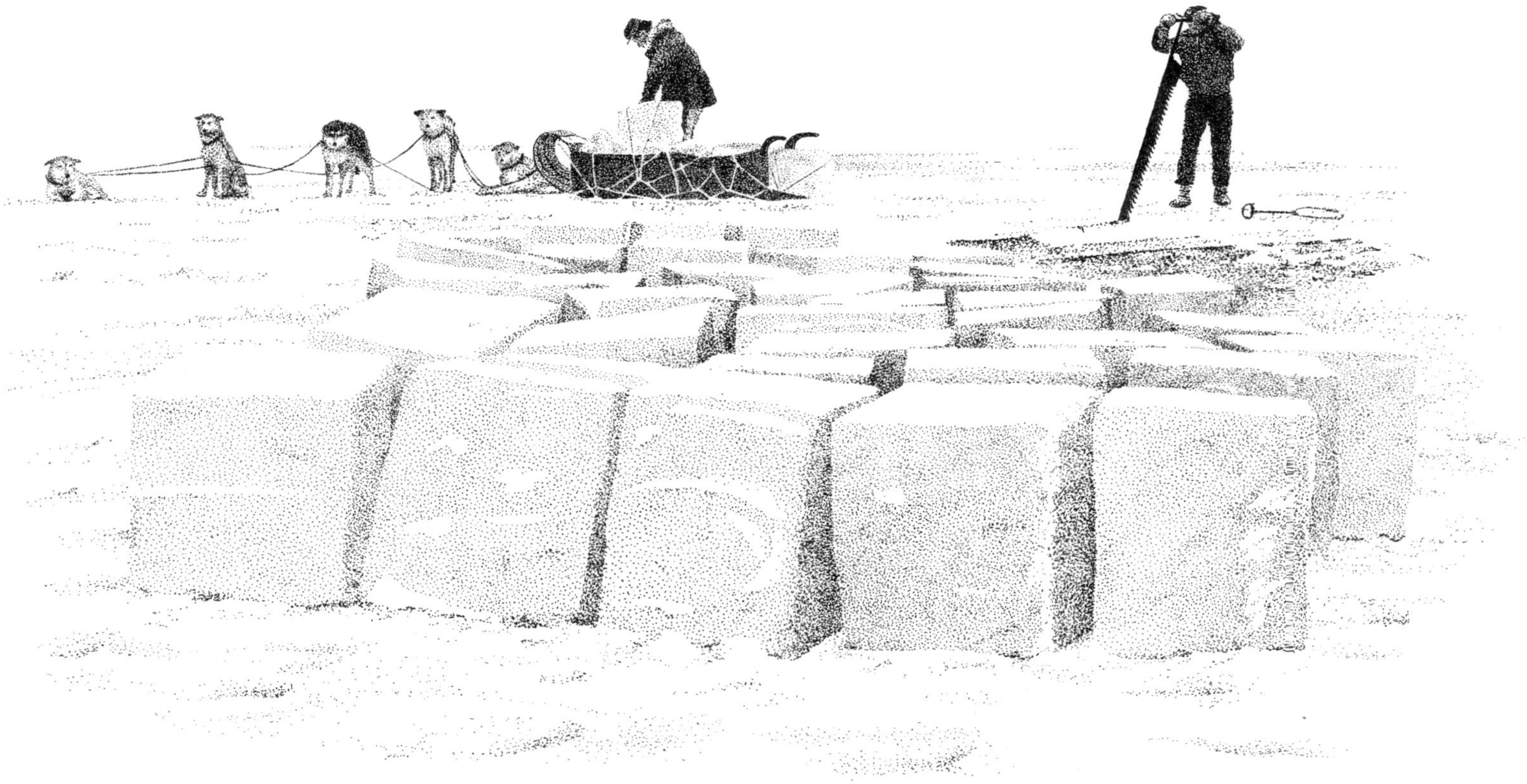

Cutting ice blocks after freeze-up.

the problem of emptying the rock-solid pail. I'd bring the object in to share the living room with me on Saturday mornings. I'd take it out to a hole back in the bush around 11 A.M., turn it upside down and shake it. Nothing! I'd bring it back in, elevate it on a chair and leave it for another two hours. Still nothing. I'd put it up onto a box on top of the chair and if a couple of hours at that height didn't loosen the block I'd say, "What the hell..." and give it a place of high honour on top of a chair on top of the kitchen table close to the stove, keeping an eye out meanwhile in case I got visitors. (On one occasion, I did get visited at about this stage so the pail was rushed back to its proper place before they came in. They stayed a long time and the whole process had to be started all over again the next day.) But even up at that height the thawing was sometimes far too gradual for my impatience, and in exasperation, before the afternoon was through, I would plant the ghastly thing right on the cookstove itself.

I loved Fort Norman. The people, including the Whites, were a wonderful mixture, and although I felt rather too insulated by social constraints from the far more interesting life on the lower terrace, life on the upper one was never dull. I was the youngest of all the White adults, and with the open, tolerant and uncritical (or vacuous) mind that distinguishes youth, I liked them all. Yet as the winter developed, all these various people to my amazement got on each other's nerves. The Hudson's Bay manager hated the priests, and the Indian Agent reckoned the Hudson's Bay manager was cheating the trappers. The cops were mad at the principal for refusing to take over non-Treaty welfare, the principal was incensed with the game warden because he never did any work and his many children were unsupervised, running around with the Indians and heading for ruin (I thought they were delightful kids), the nurse thought the D.O.T. radio operator was a conniving crook, not to mention the Indian Agent, and the Indian Agent was fit to be tied over indications that the game warden was after his wife, or had already proceeded beyond mere pursuit. The wife of the principal thought that the single cop ought to set a better example to the young people and leave the nursing station at a respectable hour instead of two o'clock in the morning, while the D.O.T. man infuriated all the still-compatible rest by shutting down the power plant whenever they, the still-compatible rest, gathered together for a private showing of one of the Community Club movies. And so it went on. The petty bickering and the cliques and the cat-calling were something marvellous to see. I just couldn't understand why so many nice people couldn't manage to get along better. I alone had the ear of everyone, as well as a strong disinclination to gossip, so like it or not I was subjected unwittingly to everyone's side of every issue, all in varying degrees a little silly and parochial, but all of it fading happily with the approach of spring.

Welcome diversion from these matters might easily have been had on the more exotic lower terrace. To me, the Indian people, their tortuous language, their stark and dreadful economy, their alien customs and ways of thinking, and their incredibly hard lives in the wilderness were a source of enormous fascination, and I longed to know them better, although they seemed at times to be almost unknowable.

Of course, giving added weight to these silent desires, there were the inevitable sirens, precursors of shipwreck as the sin-obsessed priests would gladly have reminded me. One of the Menalaya girls for example was hardly 19 when I first seriously noticed her at a watering hole on the frozen river bank. She was one of the Mountain Indians. She had that lovely, clear-skinned, moon-faced freshness of one long accustomed to living most of the year in the bush. She seemed sullen and sulky, and she knew no English, or at least admitted to none. I shot long glances at her many times, but I never saw her smile, at me or anyone else, and the deep, sultry thoughts which she kept behind those almost-almond, liquid-black eyes were just as hopelessly hidden from me as was the perfect, amber-golden form which I knew must dwell hidden within all those ugly layers of bulky Hudson's Bay underwear, innerwear and outerwear. Her smoky scent of aromatic moosehide musk, redolent of distant camps, was all she ever let me steal from her, and for the rest, she seemed as unapproachable, unknowable, unattainable and remote as if she had lived on the moon, no matter how many pretexts I invented for dropping by, oh so casually, at her parents' home whenever duty called me to the village.

But of course we were bound by the curious sort of well-intentioned social apartheid that was inherent in the colonial mentality of the time, an ethic far more rigid than it ever was or

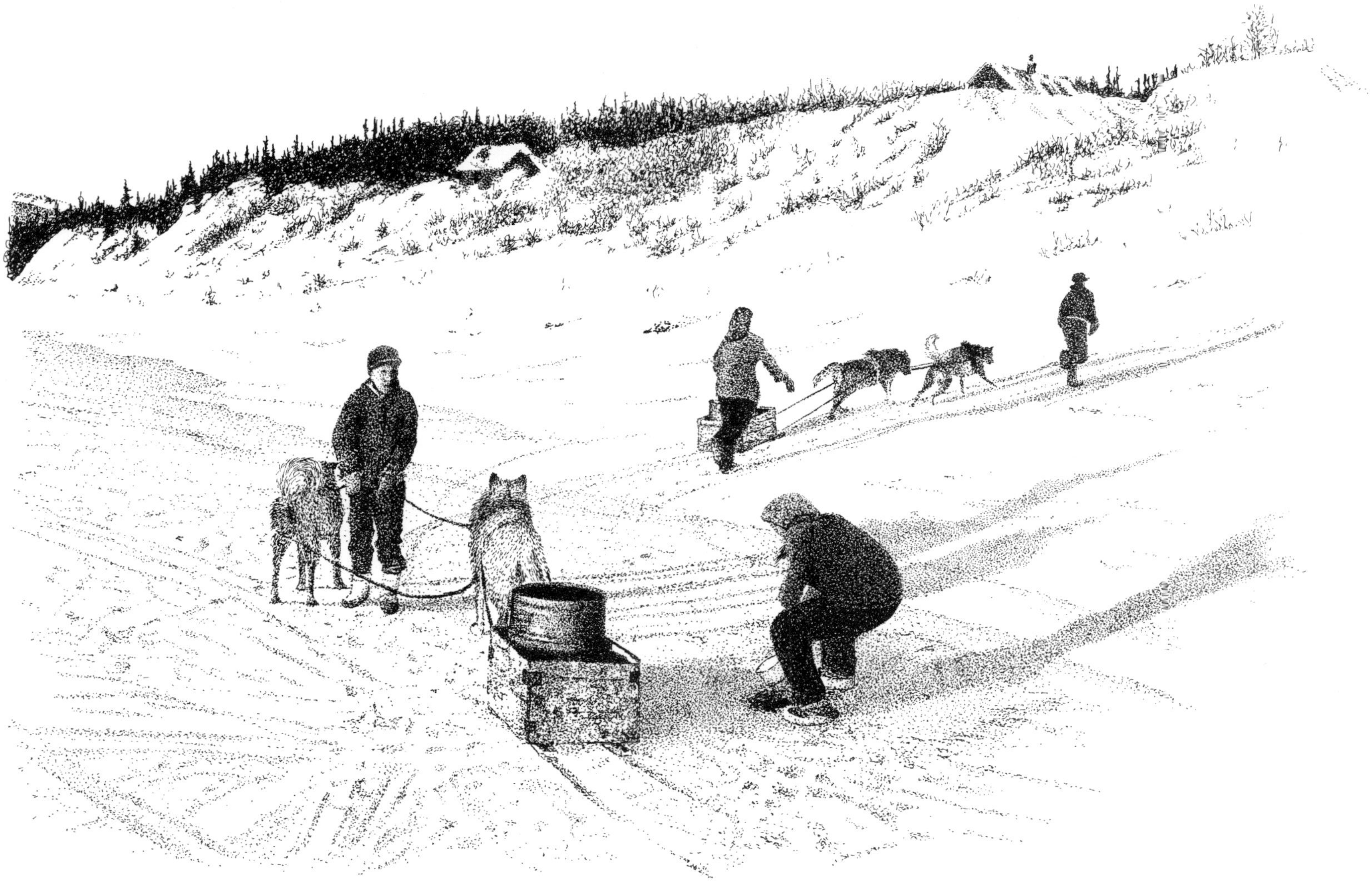

Children getting water from the Mackenzie.

could have been in my native New Zealand, so everyone on the upper level knew (and saw to it gently that I knew) that too much socializing down the bank was, in 1957, almost a definition of being "bushed." And if that hadn't penetrated my innocence, there were in any case other ongoing and more immediate demands on my time and attention.

My teaching kept me busy all day every day, and I loved it. I always returned to the classroom for long hours beyond the time when I had released my charges back out into their wider world, and this became a consistent practice through all my years in the North, for a multi-grade classroom demands thorough, meticulous planning every day if it is going to run smoothly.

I was forever being invited out for supper to one or another of the White homes. I kept a record for several months and discovered that I averaged only one evening meal at home every week. This went on all the time and occasionally, absent minded as I was, I would accept two invitations for the same evening. But various people dined at various hours, and if I realized my mistake in time I was usually able to take in both meals, one after the other, not that I needed or wanted them both, but I was always much too embarrassed at my idiotic forgetfulness to back out of either one. Luckily, people were accustomed to my fairly prompt departure from the dining table, because they knew I would still have preparation work to do in the evenings. The only time when I could not quite manage this doubling-up trick was on Christmas Day when I realized that I was being expected for nearly the whole day at both the RCMP and the HBC, having many weeks before given them both my verbal acceptance. I was long, thin and young, with a fine appetite, and gradually I came to be known amongst the other Whites as "Yon Cassius."

I enjoyed my work with the Indian kids. I realize now that I was hopelessly stodgy, middle-class and conventional in my approach at the outset, but that gradually changed as I came to know the people and their culture better and learned to approach things from their point of view, to relax, to be inventive and innovative and to throw some fun into the program. Anyway, for almost the first time since graduating in New Zealand I discovered that I could actually enjoy teaching, that if the program was fun the kids were fun (these kids anyway) and that it was all very rewarding as well as challenging.

But the standards were not very impressive. To many of the native families, school attendance was a matter of no great importance and in many cases it was more or less left to the child himself to decide if he wanted to show up. The parents were good natured about it, but still made no real effort to ensure regular attendance. The half-dozen White children and those of the Métis were always there when the bell rang at nine o'clock and as a result their academic performance was fine, but the rest were a mixed bag.

Reasoning that school was supposed to be what it almost never is, an exciting place, a wonderland of discovery, an irresistible magnet, I began to turn as much as possible from traditional chalk and talk, to put some excitement into the program and to get the kids doing, laughing, singing, creating, rather than just sitting. All this certainly helped improve and broaden my own teaching skills, but attendance still remained a problem.

Forget the three Rs and throw a party! Did all the kids show up? No, they did not. Gradually I began to realize that even if school could be transformed into a dizzying kaleidoscope of exciting, delightful, stimulating adventures, that might still not be enough to ensure that all the students actually and regularly appeared. The only thing that would do so was what the White and Métis children had, parents who valued what the school offered and what it stood for.

Sometimes the Mounties would do a sweep of the village for us and herd sleepy, grumpy, little groups up the hill, and this seemed to have an effect for a while, because not only did the cops threaten to cut the parents off their family allowance if they didn't get their kids to school (a thing theoretically possible but never in fact carried out), but more importantly there were often large enamel pots brimful of illicit home brew stewing away under the beds in those little cabins. The cops had a nose for those pots and some of the parents realized that having extraneous kids hanging around at home on weekdays was an invitation to the cops to come snooping around. So, one way or another, the kids were just as likely to be driven as drawn to their studies.

The Métis children were nicely and naturally sort of bilingual regardless of school, at least understanding both languages even if they didn't regularly use both, but it was quite natural that they were about the only ones who were. I'd been given the junior class by Frank that first year, the little ones from five to ten years or so, and most of them used their native Slavey quite exclusively until they were shunted, or inveigled, up the hill to their studies, and even then they insisted on speaking their mother tongue with each other, quite in defiance of all reason when clearly they were being given the far better alternative of speaking English. (So, anyway, was the perspective of those days.) Adults told me of being spanked, in the earlier old mission schools (if they'd been so privileged as to attend them) for speaking their own language to each other in class. Slavey should be prohibited while the kids are in school. Many teachers believed this, and practised it. It had been advocated in Yellowknife (not the spanking, of course, but the demand) along with other guaranteed remedies to the language problem like the infamous little pocketbook *English Through Pictures*. This hideously boring but ubiquitous text was to be found in huge quantities in every school in the North. The "pictures" of the title, appearing repetitively on every page, were little stick figures, and the two-volume text was a step-by-step course in learning to hate learning English.

At first I experimented with both those official remedies, never thinking at first to blame anything but myself when I didn't like the results. But the ban on the native Slavey language seemed unworkable and unfair, not to say insulting, and since it clearly threatened to widen the gulf between the Indian kids and their alien teacher, I gave up trying, though greatly against Frank's wishes. But my indifferent results with text-book-based English teaching I blamed for a long time on myself rather than anything else, and for this first year I persevered rather unhappily.

I wasn't at all sure what I could or should do in the way of "welfare work," but we were expected to fill out a Welfare Report each month and send it in to our headquarters at Fort Smith, so something had to be done if that blank form was to contain anything. Many teachers of those times came North fired with a fervent zeal to Do Good, especially in their first year, and their Welfare Reports must have made fascinating reading. The end result, all too often, was that they did more harm than good, offending and alienating with their paternalistic charity, their patronizing helpfulness, when all that was required of them, really, was to kick over their pedestal, to relax, to learn a little of the language, to laugh and rub shoulders with others, to act like normal, fallible humans, and above all to acquire and to show that they had acquired, a degree of respect for the native people and their way of life.

My contribution to "welfare work" was pretty low key. I played an active but not a prominent part in community work, I made sure that the adults, and most especially the parents, knew me as a real person rather than as a function, and I responded to immediate community needs as any normal citizen would, rather than as would one bound on saving the world.

I did run a twice-weekly adult evening class: English literacy and simple mathematics. Frank called me aside and warned me about this. "You're going to get a lot of young women," he pointed out. "You'll need to treat them with some reserve, and be sure that they leave school promptly at the end of classes. Chances are they will be enrolling more for what you may have to offer them after classes, rather than during." Frank was very Catholic. I was a perfectly normal healthy young bachelor, and I couldn't bring myself to value my chastity quite as highly as he did, or to feel that I needed to take precautionary measures to protect myself and to ensure that these scheming young wenches would not have their wicked wicked way. However, my classes ran smoothly all that year, and the one to follow, and somewhat to my regret, Frank's puritan fears proved to be almost entirely without foundation.

All this time I was endeavouring to keep up the pretence of being a Catholic myself. This wasn't easy. I swallowed hard every other Sunday or so and wandered along to the church to sit at the back, and attempt to act as if I had been used to it all ever since infancy. But I could make no sense whatever of the mumbo-jumbo Latin mass, and of course I was much too embarrassed to ask anyone for a crash course in understanding what was going on. When people stood up, I stood up. When everyone around me sat down, I did too. When they knelt, which they did rather frequently, I knelt too, though it came a little hard, for my knees are perhaps the most Presbyterian part of my whole being. But at times some stood while others sat, or knelt. And then I was left in confusion, remaining at my seat and gazing abstractedly at the floor. The priests could never quite know what to make of me. I never went forward to receive communion. I never confessed to anything and I never contributed a brass bean to the church. Yet I co-operated with them at school to a fault, and as much as was within my powers, I tried hard to give them and everyone else the impression that I was, if not a perfect Catholic, then at least someone with a nominal interest in the church, with some faint, vestigial loyalty to its teaching. This all went very much against the grain, yet I forced myself to keep it up for I had put myself in this position and I felt I owed it to both the people and the department to preserve the pretence of my commitment. On the surface, I was a semi-active lukewarm follower. Just below that surface I was laughing ruefully to myself at my ridiculous situation. But beneath that again, in my heart, I detested it all. Still, not just for this first year but for the four more that were to follow it, I kept this up, never once even hinting to my very closest friends that I was anything other than what I pretended to be. Happily such things don't matter any longer, but they mattered then, and it was the only flaw in my paradise.

As fall became winter in Fort Norman and the lakes and rivers all froze solid, the native people began hitching their dogs, and life gradually took on a different rhythm. The Mountain Indians, a group of families who frequented the great ranges far to the west of the river, over towards the Yukon, were the most traditionally Indian of all the people, and of all the children theirs were the most accustomed to the bush life, the most skilled at lighting fires, handling dogs, setting traps and using guns, and the least accomplished in the White Man's school. They were so seldom in it.

After celebrating Christmas and seeing the New Year in at Fort Norman, the men of the mountains loaded up their tents, traps, guns and grubstake, and off they went with their wives and kids, travelling great distances by dog team westward beyond the river to their traditional lands where they remained hunting until the spring. Then, as the winter snows began to melt, the men constructed great canoe frames, strong and elegant, out of green spruce, while the women set to, stitching tightly together the mooseskins taken in the winter. These water-tight skin covers were then stretched and bound over the spruce frames to form enormous, buoyant canoes, each capable of carrying several adults as well as all their kids, dogs, sleighs, tents and equipment. A long steering oar was fitted into a spruce oarlock on the stern. Paddles were shaped, mostly for working across the currents because the long journey ahead was all downstream. They came down the Keele or Gravel River and camped at the confluence with the Mackenzie until the great river itself, Deh Cho, was ready to break. Then within a day or two after the ice of the mighty Mackenzie finally let go with its customary chaos, sometime in the first half of May, the quiet, reclusive, English-resistant Mountain Indians showed up again at Fort Norman, their wondrous canoes, dating back in form to pre-history, tethered to the tangled blocks of river ice on the shore, and our classes began to swell again, the lovely (but outlawed!) Slavey language began to reassert itself, and the classroom smelled again of smoked caribou, fragrant spruce boughs, fish, duck feathers and moosehide.

But it was not only the Mountain Indians who disappeared en masse during the school year. Most of the hunters went off to their assigned traplines at varying times through the winter, sometimes taking their wives and children, sometimes not, sometimes staying away six weeks at a time, sometimes only a few days. At school we had to get used to the almost constant coming and going of so many of the native children, and the carefully-thought-out groupings I organized based on the wide range of abilities in the classroom would last for only a few days at a time and then become nonsense. We did manage to keep attendance artificially propped up at times by persuading parents who were heading off to the bush to board their children out with other folks. These foster parents got $1.50 per day per child, and every Thursday afternoon they came up to the school and waited for the principal to type out a little chit to the Hudson's Bay Company for so many dollars to buy food for these kids. But everyone was always complaining that the money was just spent by the foster parents on themselves and that they never really took proper care of the kids, and no doubt that was sometimes true. Anyway, with the approach of spring even this tactic didn't work anymore because then almost everyone took off with their dogs, tents and little canoes for hunting muskrat over the last of the winter snows to their traditional spring camps along the many lakes and rivers located in different directions from the settlement.

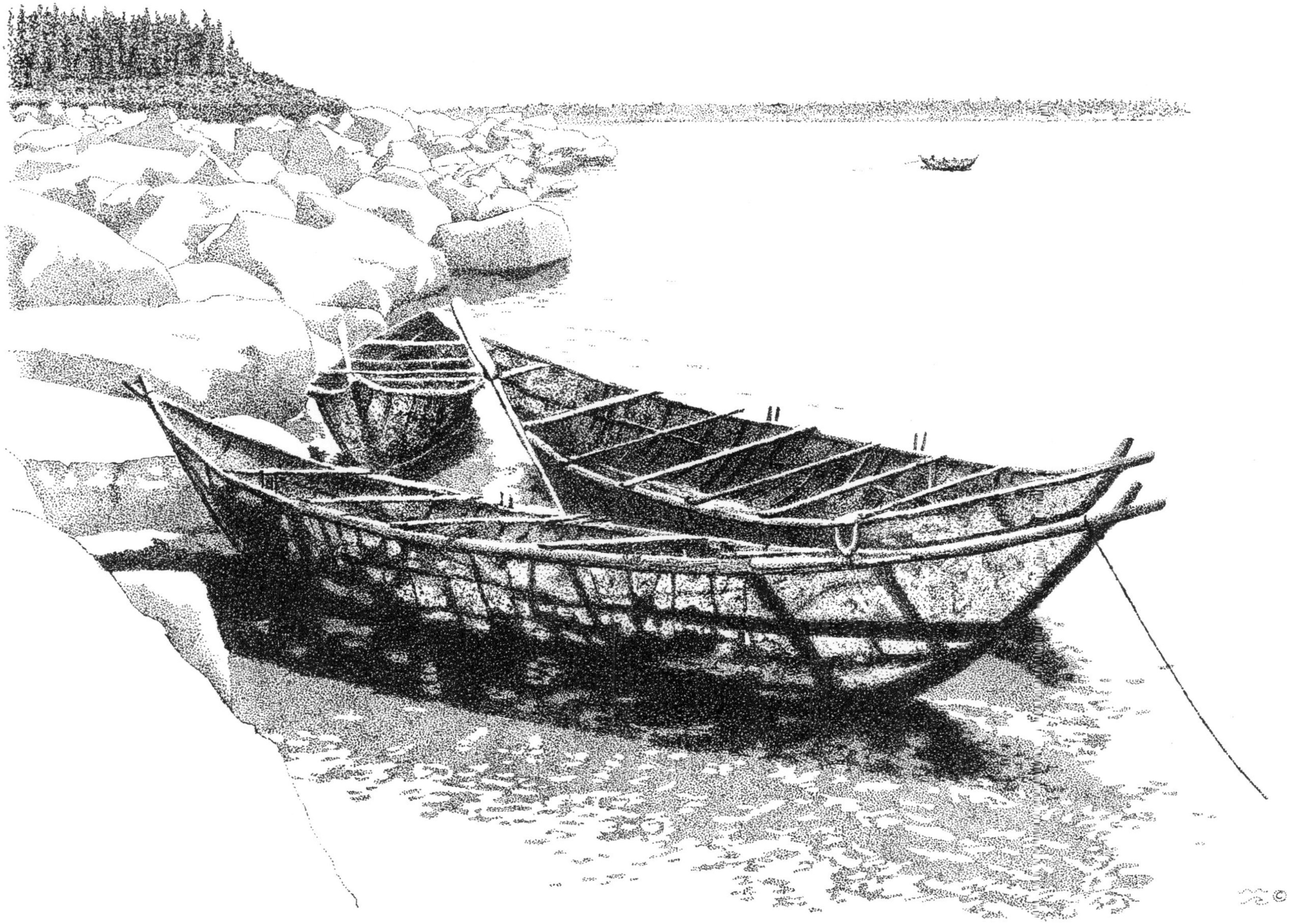

Mooseskin canoes at Fort Norman.

This was the high point of everyone's year, the lovely happy season of the spring break-up, the awakening time between the dark severity of winter and the mosquito plagues of early summer. We changed from moosehide mukluks to rubber gumboots, and the bush planes based down the river at Norman Wells went south to Edmonton to change from winter skis to summer floats. This meant we were again cut off for six weeks from contact with the outside world and enjoyed the happy assurance that our respective bosses had no way of flying in and bothering us. So just as it was the happiest of times for the Indians, so they were happy days too for the Whites remaining in the settlement. We started growing beards. We visited more and gossiped less. We ran a lottery on the exact time the river would break up. We roasted wieners over camp fires and drank beer until sunrise at two in the morning and wandered happily home in our gumboots through slushy snow, flooding streams and deep mud.

And if I felt a little less than ready to face another day of teaching a few short hours later, well there were only six children anyway, our numbers having dwindled steadily from 24 in each class, and my six were just as disinclined to hard work as I was, they too having had too little sleep. So with the three Rs given their rightful due, we made kites in the classroom and cookies in my cabin, and went out to look for bird nests. We gathered ice from the river bank and salt from my rations and came back to crank ice cream out of an old wooden churn. We tramped miles up along the river bank to examine the burning coal seams first recorded by Alexander Mackenzie himself, and burning there still on the banks of the river. The children sank screaming through apparently solid ground knee-deep into warm ashes so we retreated discreetly and returned to school to write stories and draw pictures, and to sip hot chocolate while I read to them *The Adventures of Huckleberry Finn*.

It was a happy time.

Gradually the ice of the frozen river lost its winter lock on the shore, and began to inch upwards as the spring runoff from the Liard and the Nahanni, the Keele, the Slave, the Peace, the Hay and all the other myriad smaller tributaries upstream added their extra weight to our Old Man River. Brief groaning, grinding sounds began to echo up occasionally from the expanse of winter ice. Cracks opened up out in the middle, closed and opened again. Except for the kids playing at the edge, everyone stayed off the ice as it gradually rose higher and higher on the swollen stream, and contented themselves with just gazing at it from the bank, wondering....

Then suddenly late one evening, in the almost broad daylight of almost midnight, she let go! What almighty chaos! We could hear the muffled roar from back in the woods. We rushed to the bank and there it was heaving and thundering, the entire river surface in churning, chaotic tumult, endless square miles of winter ice Arctic bound at last, grinding and hurling and crashing against itself in rapturous release, tossing thousand-ton blocks high up onto the muddy banks just as ocean waves toss foam. The sight was quite overwhelming, and I stood there staring for hours, almost speechless. Here at last was the famous break-up on the Mackenzie.

So I had not (as I had dreamed in boyhood) seen the sun rise over Samarkand? Not after all cycled Africa from Cairo to the Cape? Not climbed the Matterhorn, or even kayaked the Irrawaddy? Well, who cares? I thought. I have witnessed the great spring break-up at Fort Norman.

And with that, the Mountain Indians returned in their great canoes, (for within days the river cleared itself) and these were soon followed by other families coming down the Bear River from Willow Lake and Kelly Lake and the other favoured spots of spring, bringing back their beaver and muskrat furs and their happy families, faces glossy from a diet of ducks and fish, and burned almost black from sun glare and woodsmoke. Fort Norman came alive again.

All through the hours of night the caribou-skin drums pounded rhythmically down in the village, and from as far away as the school we could hear the drummers bellowing in unison their manic, falsetto, celebratory chants as men and women, old folks and kids jostled around in a long circle, Indian file. And again the next night, and again the next. What infection there is in the thundering of primitive drums! The Quite Whites, having on long-established principle distanced themselves delicately from too much social familiarity with the common populations of the lower terrace, now felt that the drum dances ought really to be none of their affair, amusing and exotic though they found it, and for the most part they stayed away, although with smiles on their faces they did listen to the distant rhythm. ("The natives are restless tonight!") I couldn't quite be bothered with their ridiculous restraint, and I and the game warden and two of his kids went down to the little cabin where everyone had gathered, and joined in, pounding our feet around the circle like everyone else, as the old women rocked back on their chairs, their hands clapped together in front of them, laughing in delight at the sight of us.

May quickly became June and we used the little Indian Agency tractor to plough up part of the school playground. This we divided into many small plots and assigned each plot to two of the older students, or to three or four of the younger ones. They loved it. They raked and harrowed until their beds were smooth and soft. They made little furrows and planted crooked lines of beans and potatoes and lettuce and peas and radishes. They watered these patches daily and lavished ridiculous attention on them, and before long various things were poking up through the soil to the delight of everyone, and then grew like weeds in the almost continuous daylight.

This was in marked contrast to the attitude of the adults. The Indian Agent was forever trying to encourage the native people to grow their own vegetables, and to some degree it would have been possible at Fort Norman. But this was a thing unheard of, and all his efforts, free ploughing, free seeds, free persuasion, met with nothing but disappointment, frustration and an indifference bordering on scorn. Gardening was not a seasonal exercise that the adults had any interest in, despite the Indian Agency and the obvious example of the priests who every year grew a bonanza of potatoes and cabbages in their backyard. Whoever heard of a successful moose hunter eating cabbage? Or far worse even than that, having to bend down over the dirt to grow the damn things in the first place? That was priests' work.

But children have the happy knack of stepping out of their own culture at times, examining, exploring and experimenting with life in other ways. This is one of the many endearing things about children, this ability to go far beyond their own culture and to embrace things that their parents would never dream of. The White children of Fort Norman, as a small example, were far better integrated into the social life and language of the village than were the White adults (and would have been a great deal more so if it were not for parental constraints placed upon them). The social and economic life of the whole huge North country is changing profoundly and, although it is possible to regret much of it, on balance those changes seem to me for the better. The interesting thing is that it is all made possible by children, yesterday's children for today, today's for tomorrow. Without children our societies, cultures and customs would remain quite stagnant. A good thing too I hear some people say, and I know sometimes how they feel, but I am not much for the conservatives, the static-state traditionalists. I am more for that one eternal constant of the universe, that more painful thing, change: theirs, ours, everybody's (but ours especially) and it will come, if we are wise enough to let it, and to guide it gently, through children.

I was impatient to see more of the vast Northland, but you couldn't transfer after just one year, so I stayed on for a second at Fort Norman. The Freys had by then departed, and since I was asked to take over Frank's job as principal, I happily handed over the junior class to the tenderer care of a newly appointed lady from the South. But in 1959, I asked to be transferred farther north. The superintendent wanted me to go to Tuktoyaktuk, but my religion was all wrong, and much to my surprise I was sent instead up the Bear River, to take over the challenging position of Welfare Principal at Fort Franklin, succeeding a famous character called Bill Bowerman.

In later years, it took a chartered Twin Otter to move all our personal effects from one settlement to another. In 1959, all I had was a suitcase. This I carried down the river bank at the end of June, and put it aboard the *George Askew*, the old stern-wheeler working the Bear River, and flew off south for the six-week break that I was entitled to after my first two years in the North. I travelled by bus all the way from Edmonton to Guatemala and the Yucatan, to explore the ruins of the Maya before settling for a time on the chilly shores of Great Bear Lake.

Feast and Famine

Those "A rations" we got in the earlier days used to bore me to distraction. Every year the same old stuff, great square tins of beef from Canada Packers, oval tins of ham from Burns, cases of chicken haddie, flour, sugar, jam, two dozen tins of sardines, one dozen tins of Irish stew, evaporated milk, on and on the same every year. In every new settlement I went to it was the same old story. The previous occupant (if there had been one) had left behind on the bottom shelves under the sink all the things you didn't want, those identical stacks of dried chopped onions, tins of stale spices, packets of rancid walnuts and great stacks of egg powder, the stuff that nobody could stand.

The Department of Northern Affairs provided all its employees with an "A ration" for each adult, and a "B ration" for each child to get them through their year in the wilderness. Each summer it was offloaded from the river barge or the ocean-going ship and dumped on the settlement beach, a small mountain of cardboard boxes with "Maurice Cloughley, Welfare Teacher" stencilled on each box. There was nothing remotely either fresh or frozen. It was tinned or it was dried, and much of it was both.

We were always being assured that some dietary expert down South, living amongst all those lettuces, pork chops and oranges, had calculated our rations to be entirely adequate to our physical needs, and so we happily lived with that assurance, but at times the boredom of our daily bread was almost enough to put one off eating. Admittedly in my first bachelor years I benefitted greatly from the superior cuisine of other households and also from the odd fact that different departments or agencies got different rations. The Mounties got real, not instant, potatoes. The Indian Agent got occasional shipments of frozen meat, and the nursing station always had fresh eggs. But those were other branches of government and our own department did not see any need for such frills. So, what's for supper? Open up another tin of beef and onion stew. Throw in a tin of peas. Stir up a dollop of instant mash. Maybe finish up with another tin of black cherries. No more black cherries? Oh well, a tin of fruit salad then. Try sprinkling, say, Red River Cereal on it this time to make it seem like something different.

But who could complain? We lived a comfortable, secure existence in a land of uncertain hunting and dire, if intermittent, poverty. Rumours (soon to become national headlines) began leaking out from the Keewatin in those years, of starvation and death amongst the small, isolated Inuit populations of Ennadai Lake and Padlei, inland communities almost totally dependent on the then-dwindling caribou herds. But even in the Mackenzie Valley, where all the southern support systems sort of existed in rudimentary form, life was remarkably difficult much of the time. Hunting was uncertain at best. The caribou appeared in smaller numbers if they appeared at all. There was always the occasional moose, but like everything else it was shared around many households, so that never lasted long. Fishing was okay but you didn't catch much fish by living a settlement existence. You had to travel far away to the best places, and remain there once your nets were under the ice. Even then, much of the fish had to go to feeding the dogs.

In the settlement itself, many of the dogs more or less starved, especially in the summertime when they were tied up on the river bank and abandoned for weeks on end without attention. That they survived those summers of misery and neglect, hunger and thirst, on the end of a short chain or scrap of wire was, to me, amazing enough, but that they then went on to live through the awesome winters that followed, surviving savage temperatures on the most meagre of diets (when they even had one at all) and when called on, working long, brutal hours on the trail as well, would have been to me quite beyond belief had I not been there to witness it. Poor dogs, I often felt aghast at their condition, their hard lot in life, and sorry for their misery but truly the Indian people of the settlement seemed to have an ongoing struggle to feed just themselves and were often hardly in a position to do much better for their dogs.

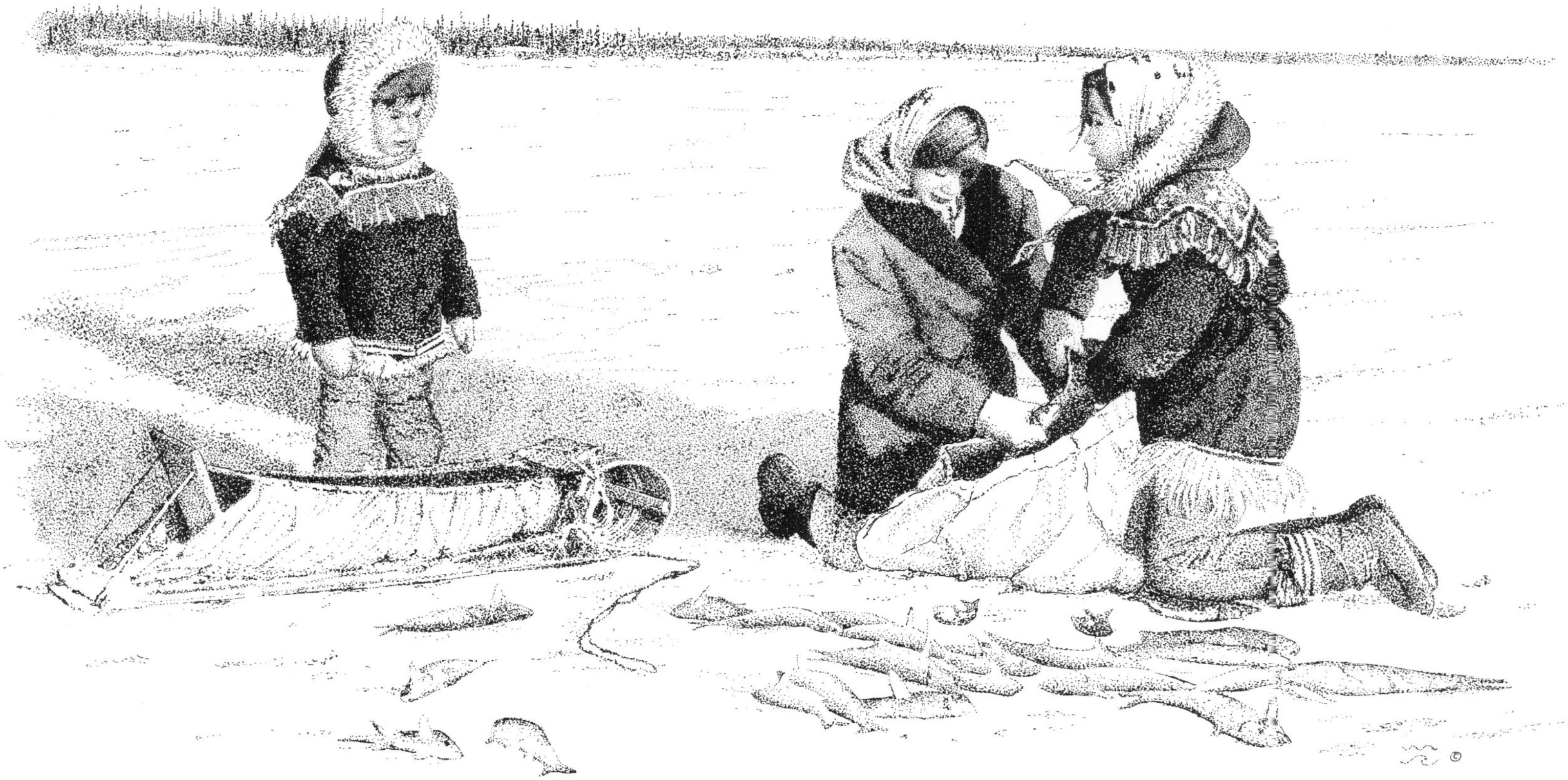

Herring harvest, Great Bear Lake.

So food was always a problem, and the life of the people, still so intimately dependent in those times on the natural world, was closely linked to the elemental business of finding enough of it. The vast land itself was truly rich enough for a multitude but only if they spread themselves thinly on the surface, and then were mobile enough and skilled enough to get it. It was a land for nomads. The migratory birds and the caribou could be expected to appear (or not to appear) in their great numbers regardless of the concentrations of humans, but generally, as soon as people moved in to permanent settlements and remained there, the demands on the local fish stocks, the moose, beaver, bear and everything else within easy reach of the community became greatly depleted by human competition. And generally, too, the people who chose the bush life tended, if they knew what they were doing, to live well off the fat of the land, though certainly not always, as the poor people of Ennadai Lake could have testified.

For many, the easiest recourse of all was simply to go up the hill to the Indian Agent or the Mountie, or administrator, or teacher, whoever handled such things, and ask for welfare assistance.

The problem tended to come to school each day at nine o'clock. In nearly all of those many little Northern settlements where I worked, at least some, sometimes most of the children, came to school breakfastless. It was never an invariable thing but it was usually there to some degree as a daily reality, especially in the earlier days. It was a problem transcending settlements, economic conditions, seasons, cultures; many of the kids for much of the time came to school sleepy-eyed, snotty-nosed, tousle-haired and empty-stomached. They were always so endearing, those Northern children, and I often felt, when they arrived in the mornings, looking confused and grumpy, like putting my arms around them reassuringly, telling them that school wasn't so bad after all, that they would enjoy working with their friends, and promising them a little snack once we had done a few things.

For a long time I was unsure about the reasons for this chronic problem. Even in hard times, there was nearly always something, some morsel to eat at home, not much but something: a lump of bannock, a pot of boiled sealmeat, a smoked fish, a kettle of black tea. And obviously the people loved their kids. But they didn't fuss over them the way White parents did. Their love seemed rather to take the form of just giving them their freedom. It was simply natural and expected that, as much as they were able, the kids would fend for themselves. In some places, I was amused at the contrast between the native children of tender years and the much more dependent White children. The six- and seven-year-old native kids could stick up for themselves. They would put their boots and parkas on at the end of the day and go crashing out the front door in their usual state of happy anarchy. The little White children would wait to catch the teacher's attention and ask politely for help in tying bootlaces or closing up a stuck zipper. They were used to being fussed over, to having their needs anticipated and met for them, including of course breakfast. And their needs were met, whereas for the local native kids it could be anybody's guess.

It was always obvious, even to a casual observer in the classroom, that the children functioned better when they had something inside them. They worked faster and communicated better. They were more alert, happier, louder, busier.

So what was to be done about this business? The nurse at Fort Norman brought along to the school a huge jar filled with small, oval-shaped, cod-liver-oil capsules. This long-standing remedy for everything was recommended as an essential additive to the diet of the local children, and so we passed the little brown plastic things to the kids each day. The soft outer envelope of these capsules was intended to spare the recipient the unpleasantness of having to taste the awful fish oil inside, which most city kids would have gagged on, but these ones crunched hard to rupture the outer casing and chewed appreciatively as the tasty oil swam around their mouths. It could be smelled in the room an hour later. But that was hardly breakfast.

So we also used to order great tall cardboard tubs of whole milk powder. Each day at morning recess several cupfuls of this were measured into a big aluminum pot full of water, whisked into frothy milk and ladled out into little Melmac cups to be gulped down by the incoming flood when the bell rang.

We also had vitamin biscuits to go with the milk, boxes and boxes of the boring things. For many years these were shipped in by the federal authorities as a dietary supplement for school children, and for decades they were to be found in excessive quantities in every native school in the North. I tried eating them many times. They were solid and stolid, square, hard and tasteless. I suppose they were therefore, almost by definition, good for you. They were alleged anyway to be laden with all kinds of vitamins and other nutritious things as well. Perhaps they had been assessed and recommended by the same experts who so glowingly guaranteed to us our "A rations." (While we were in the Cree settlement of Split Lake I could not for a long time figure out why all the loose dogs liked to hang around the school at recess time, but it was simply that we passed those vitamin biscuits out to the students as they went out for recess, and as often as not they threw a large portion of them to the dogs.) At all events, some decades later, an urgent memo came around to all schools advising that a new study had found these famous biscuits to be not merely useless, but potentially hazardous if taken in any quantity, or taken very regularly, and we were told in no uncertain terms to discard all remaining stocks forthwith. And so the pendulum swings.

Gradually the school authorities in Ottawa became increasingly aware of the problem of empty bellies in the classroom, and a specially funded School Lunch Program was set up. It was left largely to the individual school to look after the details. What would be served? When? Who does the cooking? The washing up? Some schools were able to inveigle local parents into helping with the kitchen work, but usually they wanted to be paid and would have nothing to do with helping in a volunteer program even though they were keen on the free meal their kids were getting.

This always puzzled me a bit. The Northern peoples had always lived a close communal existence which consisted largely of sharing amongst all whatever was to be had. To do otherwise was rightly considered selfish and reprehensible. To a generous degree they shared their food with their neighbours. They shared their wood supply, if there was a need and a surplus. They shared their dogs, their welfare cheques, their cabins, their camps, their equipment, their wives (or husbands), their children too if there were some to spare and others wanted them. But all this open-hearted communal sharing didn't extend to working-bee volunteerism. It was the "gummint" that wanted the kids to go to school in the first place, so of course it's the gummint's job to feed them when they're in school, and if we help the gummint to do that work, then the gummint ought to pay us.

Actually (and surprisingly, for the North has long become a sort of welfare state gone berserk) the gummint thought otherwise, and apart from teaching staff, the only volunteers I ever had, and happy eager ones at that, were the children themselves, from about nine and upwards. Porridge and milk on Mondays, macaroni and cheese on Tuesdays, chicken soup Wednesdays, bannock and fish Thursdays, milk and vitamin biscuits with cheese spread on Fridays, or maybe a bean stew or something else.

The kids loved it. They vied with each other for the privileges of the kitchen. They learned to read recipes, measure quantities in teaspoons, pints, ounces, pounds, or (later on) in the metric system. They learned to calculate times and temperatures, learned about housekeeping, hygiene and kitchen safety, and while such things at home were held to be the exclusive rightful drudgery of females, at school the boys were just as eager as the girls to roll their sleeves up, take over and produce steaming tasty snacks for all the rest at morning recess. It was the happiest moment of each morning and I suppose it all helped to bond them a little to their school. But from my own perspective it meant far more than just the pleasure of a belly full of porridge. It was a golden opportunity to teach in an incidental but vivid and effective way basic English, reading, mathematics, geography, science and just about everything else. I could never quite understand the attitude of teachers in those little places who grumbled to me that the school snacks robbed them of ten minutes of their spelling period.

It was freeze-up time in Fort Franklin when we came across a yarn in the old Grade Five reader about making Hudson Bay beans. They were cooked overnight in an underground oven of embers and earth. So hurry outside and dig those holes. Get your fires going in the pit and somebody from each fire rush off and borrow a pot with a lid. Now what does it say here? Soak two cups of beans. What does soak mean? Add onions. Never mind, open up a tin of dried onions. I've got lots. Brown sugar or molasses, a bit of caribou meat, salt, vinegar, a teaspoon of dry mustard. What's mustard? What's a teaspoon? This is a teaspoon. The ones who could read a little bit had to read better. The ones who couldn't didn't know much English anyway and they had to listen intently for my instructions, and in so doing their grasp of English gradually improved. Communicate, communicate! By the end of the day, five mounds of black tundra dirt were tamped down over five pots, and the next morning, what a feast!

In Grise Fiord they tried chopped muktuk (narwhal skin) added to chicken soup. In Rae Lakes they made their own wild blueberry jam in fall to go with bannock in winter. In Clyde River we made an Arctic haggis of seal liver, lungs and heart, with rolled oats, all ground up together, and boiled in a smelly seal stomach. This was a wild success so we repeated the concoction in Resolute Bay where the students also grew alfalfa seeds or mung beans, adding the shoots to bean stew with muskox, and once, to raw chopped Arctic char from Somerset Island.

I always liked to open the eyes of these Northern children to other cultures, other values and other ways of living in distant parts of the world, if only as an antidote to the powerful culture of White North America that increasingly intruded into settlements and dominated their education system. So I would tell them of the Masai and the Maoris, the Incas, the Solomon Island Melanesians, and the atoll-dwelling Polynesians, showing them slides and telling them tales of our adventures in those far places. But they needed more than just stories. How do you actually make a shell necklace? Well, they had to make them. What does a coconut really look like, and how does it taste? So I managed to bring coconuts into the Arctic as I returned from a convention in Montreal, and the whole class tasted the sweet juice, and chewed appreciatively on the strange white flesh. "It tastes like soap!" was one opinion. So then I had to tell them all about making soap from copra. "That's why soap sometimes tastes like coconut," I explained.

In one school the children had never seen an orange, let alone eaten one, so I wangled a small case of the things, charging the enormous air-freight bill to a local community-development fund. Each child got one orange, and each child, after eating the orange, then set to and ate the skin as well. They loved anything exotic.

Food could take on some pretty amazing forms in the North. One of the Arctic Bay hunters told me of dining on young murre chicks taken from the cliffs of Lancaster Sound generations ago.

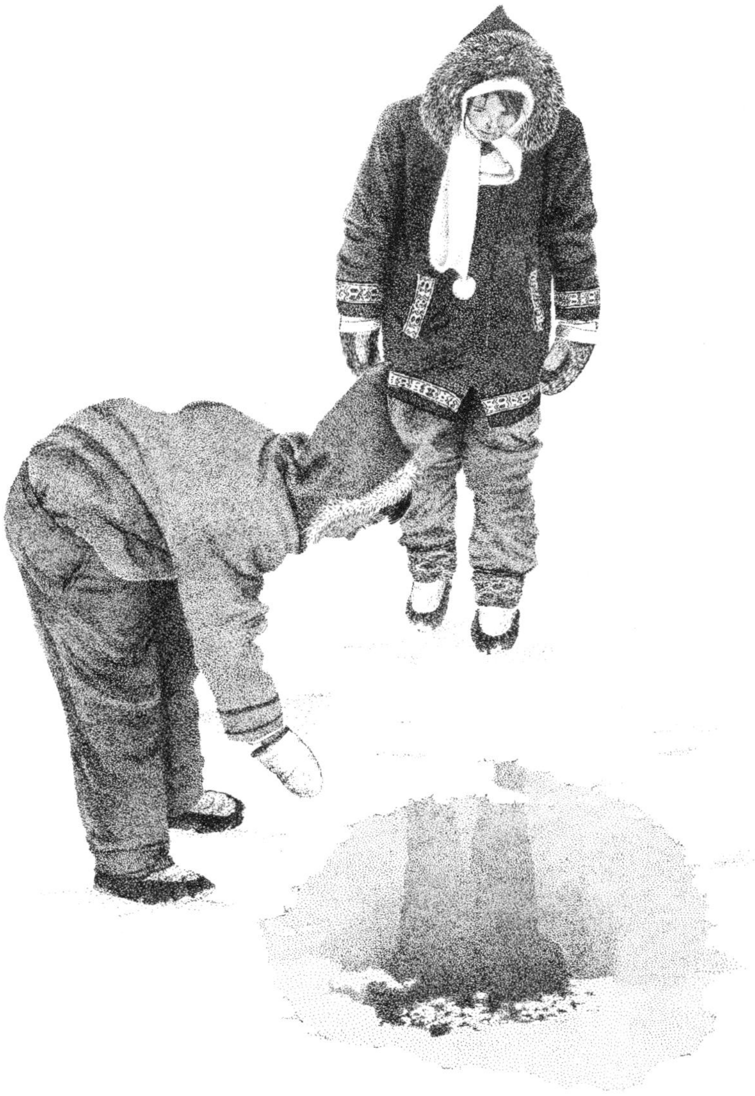

Where the seal got away.

These chicks were taken in large numbers in early summer. They were gutted and stuffed en masse, feathers and all, into sealskins that still had thick blubber lining the inside. These skins were then sewn up and cached under rocks, leaving the bird carcasses to fester and mature nicely in seal fat until the coming of winter. The Cree of northern Manitoba saw to it that Katie and I dined from time to time, as they did, on muskrat, beaver tail, roast haunch of black bear, white swan and sturgeon, exotic things that brought an occasional change from the more mundane moose, whitefish and great northern pike. But then in Manitoba under Indian Affairs we didn't receive an "A ration" with its tins of meatballs, or beef and onion stew — just the basic supplies of the Hudson's Bay Company store — so we needed to gluttonize the wilderness a little.

Not, though, anything like as much as our Northern hosts. We enjoyed eating frozen raw char a few times in our igloos at the camps near Arctic Bay and, when it was available, frozen raw caribou meat. If this tender, dark flesh was just beginning to thaw, it had the consistency of hard ice cream, and the juiciness of a peach. Boiled walrus skin was fine about once, a sort of cross between gristle and solidified custard. But we became squeamish at frozen raw seal, we hated polar bear, and we couldn't bring ourselves to contemplate some of the now-neglected desserts that, according to some of the hunters, the great Northland offered up: rabbit's eyes, the milk in season of a freshly killed seal or caribou, or the supposedly delicious larvae of the warble fly. This summer tormentor of the caribou herds lays its eggs in the skin of the animals. The larvae hatch and develop just under the skin through the winter, and when a caribou is freshly killed the white grubs can be squeezed out and gobbled up like berries.

A young man of Great Bear Lake once took me moose hunting in late fall. Though I was happy enough to help eat them when they were offered, I never had any interest in the killing of wild animals and I suppose in that respect I made a poor Northerner, but Victor took me along for the ride anyway. Our moose, when we got one, was cut into manageable chunks for the tiring hike back through the bush to the river. Victor saved some of the blood in the billy can that he used for boiling tea, and he also kept the stomach and tossed it with the rest of the meat into the bottom of our canoe. We crunched our way back up the river to the settlement, slamming repeatedly into small running ice pans and then, frozen stiff, unloaded our welcome cargo. Victor at the time had no shed of his own and asked if he could stash a part of the meat in the unheated warehouse behind the school. Along with the meat, he also brought the stomach. He took out part, but not all, of the semi-digested mush inside the stomach, and then added his billy of blood to what remained, stirring it all up together. He then stitched up the ends of the stomach and left it on the warehouse floor to mature until the spring. I was always afraid that he would show up to claim it sometime and invite me to share the contents with him, but in the spring, long after it had thawed, it was borne off to his home, and to my relief I was left alone to my boring "A ration."

I suppose the final word on Northern cuisine belongs to Arctic Bay. The school superintendent was based in Frobisher Bay as it was then called. He was a short chap with a gimpy leg and at times a grumpy manner which eventually brought him into enough bother with enough teachers that in due course he was removed to another region. He came into Arctic Bay once or twice in the winter to see how I was shaping up. He stayed at our house, but somewhat to our disappointment he never brought much with him in the way of fresh food, obtainable down in Frobisher, but unheard of in Arctic Bay in those times. But he did bring along in his luggage a bottle of rye whisky.

I always made my own beer in the North, and at that time I was using a large, yellow, plastic garbage bin with a white plastic lid as a brewing keg. It sat on the kitchen floor. I would syphon the fermented brew from the keg into bottles, cap them and store them on the ration shelves. At the time of the superintendent's visit I had a big batch going in full ferment, enough for seven dozen bottles. I was getting low on tins of malt so that had to keep me going for a while.

The superintendent declined my proffered home brew (from a mature earlier batch of course) and we talked on and on until late at night while he worked away at the bottle of rye. He was a chain smoker, and the fingers of his right hand were always stained dark brown from nicotine. He was a frail man in rather poor health, but that didn't stop him from incessantly smoking. When he prepared to leave on his charter flight next day I

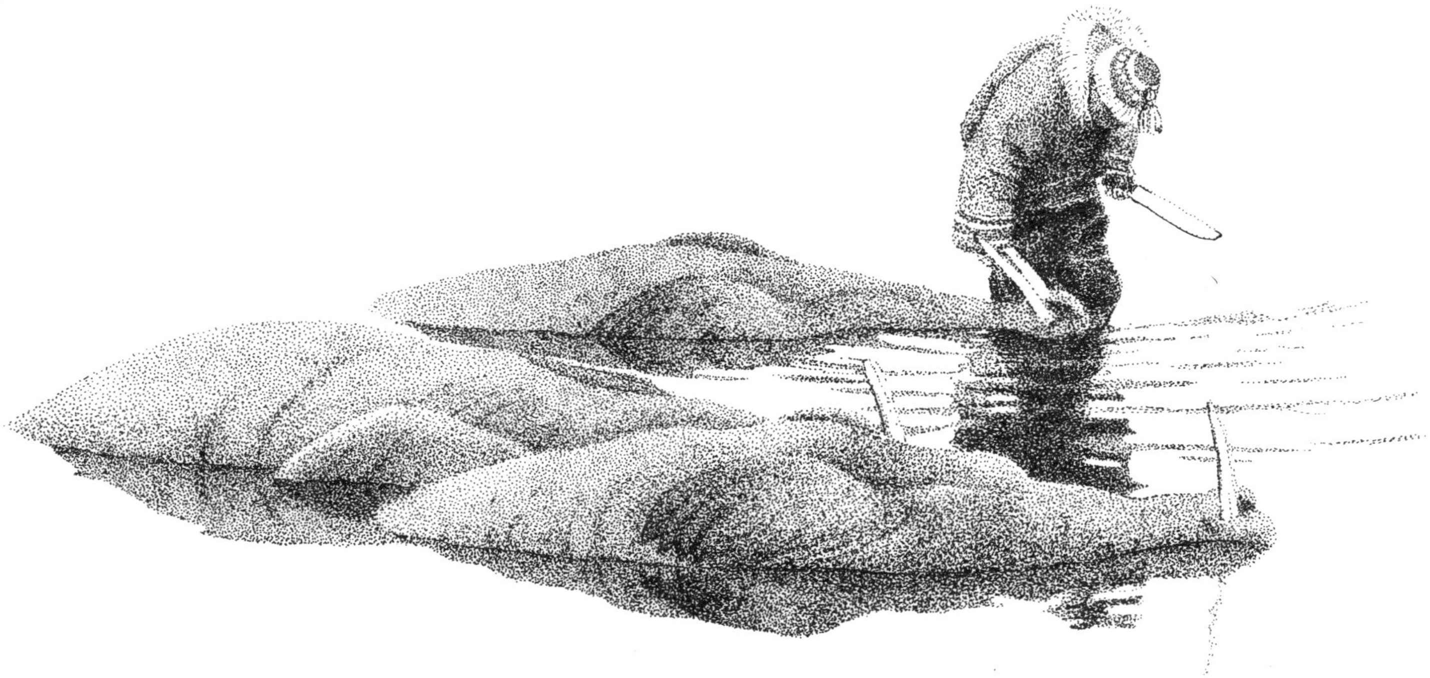

End of a walrus hunt.

suggested he might like to take the bottle of rye with him to finish off in Resolute on his way home. There were still a few ounces left. He hesitated for a second but checked himself in time and insisted on leaving it. Gee thanks.

The plane came in to collect him and, sometime after he had gone and we had returned from the sea ice to our home, I glanced into the large brewing keg to see how my beer was doing. My eyes were greeted with a truly gruesome sight, enough to bring tears to the eyes of angels if they had had to live in Arctic Bay in those times. The superintendent had taken the large ashtray, brimming over with his dirty old butts and ashes, and emptied it into my keg of beer, thinking that to be the garbage bin.

He made one more visit to Arctic Bay at the end of the school year, not so much to visit the school but rather to accompany some officials who were introducing a home-economics program for the women of the community. The Inuit at that time were being provided for the first time ever with modern prefabricated homes, heated, watered, furnished, electrified, and the general objective was to teach people how to use their new homes and care for them properly: how to clean, how to protect children from electricity, how to safeguard against fire, how to care for appliances, how to conserve energy and so on. So they brought a home-economics adult educator with them who would remain in Arctic Bay to run the program.

This little group stayed overnight at our house, which was the only government residence in use at Arctic Bay at the time, and again we were disappointed that they didn't bring with them any of the fresh goodies that could be bought (for a price!) in Frobisher. *Where were the strawberries?* But on the other hand, while we longed to sink our teeth into something fresh from the distant South, they for their part hinted broadly that they would like to sink theirs into something distinctively Northern.

Well, but what? They could have had their fill if they had just wandered around the settlement and visited the people now so happily ensconced in their new, heated, prefabricated homes. A piece of bannock here, a cup of sweet black tea there, grab an *ulu*, sit down to a dark seal carcass and carve away to heart's content. But I wasn't a hunter, and all we had in our house were the dreaded "A rations."

Katie and I consulted. There had been a lot of lemmings that year up on the sunny slopes behind the little settlement and the children had been rather fond of bringing these, dead or alive, to school. So I let the word out that after school I would pay one dollar each for the first eight or so brought in, so long as they were already dead. Meanwhile Katie made a pie crust. We spread the furry little bodies around the crust in a circle, heads to the centre, covered them over completely with a white meringue filling, and popped them in the oven just long enough to brown the top of the meringue.

Our visitors gathered together at our house at the end of the day for a few beers and a spaghetti and meatball supper. Then with a flourish Katie placed dessert in the centre of the table, and announced, "Here is your Northern treat. We often have this on Sundays instead of strawberries and ice cream. Just help yourselves."

They did. There was a sudden, brief, horrified silence from our little home-economics contingent, and somebody shrieked, "Oh no! What's this?"

"Eat it up," Katie said, "you'll just love it. It's lemming meringue pie."

Wild Bill

He burned down the little one-room school at the Dogrib settlement of Fort Rae in 1954, if not intentionally then certainly carelessly, and that's how Bill Bowerman got himself transferred out of there to become Welfare Principal of Fort Franklin, a tiny and exceedingly remote settlement of 180 Indian people on the shores of Great Bear Lake. According to Wild Bill, his services as a teacher/administrator amongst the Indians were in such high demand that the federal Department of Northern Affairs had had to negotiate hard to get him on loan from the federal Department of Indian Affairs, though a little unkind delving might have revealed that the Indian Agent at Rae was only too eager to be rid of him, and that his destroying of the school there was the last straw.

At all events Fort Franklin was exactly what Bill was looking for, a traditional Indian community with no Indian Agent, a place devoid of any government services whatever other than what he himself would provide. And there he held sway for five years. During part of that time I got to know Wild Bill well and eventually succeeded him in 1959 when ill health sent him south into retirement.

Wild Bill Bowerman had the bearing and manner of someone who had once enjoyed an army officer's rank. In those times an officer's background, running a platoon, brigade or company of soldiers in wartime, was seen for some weird reason as being almost the ideal qualification for a subsequent career with Indian Affairs running the Indians, and various officials of that department were still fond of having themselves called Brigadier This or Colonel That long after leaving the military.

But Bill had gone rather to seed since his military days. He was a little shorter than average, but thick and stocky, with a big nose, baggy eyes, a loud voice and a much too generous paunch. He arrived at Fort Franklin by river barge with his wife and young family. Naturally, back in those earlier times, the arrival of the annual supply barge at the settlement dock in front of the school was a major event bringing everyone out of their tents and cabins and down to the lake shore to watch all the action, and especially on this occasion to see what the new teacher looked like.

As Bill strode importantly ashore to the front of the gathering crowd, the chief at that time, old Francis Ayah, stepped forward to welcome the new teacher to the domains of the Sahtu Dene, the Great Bear Lake people, and to introduce himself as chief.

Wild Bill replied in that loud voice of his, "Well, you may be the chief, but I think everyone better get it straight that when I come into the settlement, I'm the one who runs things."

And on that note began the five-year-long Dominion of Bowermania on Great Bear Lake, the Middle Ages of the Sahtu Dene.

Once Wild Bill got himself established in the principal's apartment upstairs above the school, he was not long in turning his attention to what he liked best, running things in his own inimitable style with no one of any consequence running him, or trying to, or even looking over his shoulder. He wangled a canoe and outboard motor for the school, and set the school janitor to rounding up a certain amount of camping equipment, and off he set, the janitor acting as guide, in a series of mini-expeditions along the lake shore, east and south, to survey his domains, catch a few lake trout and knock off a few young geese before they migrated south to sanctuary, maybe a moose or two for the freezer. (Being well attuned to the use of the correct, appropriate-sounding terminology of the federal civil service, Bill never actually just went hunting or fishing as other regular folk did. He was always "conducting a resource survey.")

This necessary preamble of course delayed the opening of school away beyond the official date but there'd be plenty of time to catch up later. In the meantime, people were hungry back there and he had to familiarize himself with the territory and its possibilities. When it came to the skills of survival in the harsh sub-Arctic wilderness of Great Bear, Wild Bill tried hard to show that he could out-Indian the Indians. He couldn't of course; he was far too inexperienced and out of condition, too dependent on his imported rations and luxuries, and his Man Friday, the school janitor, to actually manage on his own but appearances were what mattered. The local men needed a good example to encourage them to bestir themselves and fend for their families. If Wild Bill got out there and showed them the way, who would not follow? But if, on the other hand, they insisted on hanging around the settlement so much, then that was fine too, but in that case they had to be governed. Kindly of course, but firmly, and they would find he was no easy pushover if someone should come whining around asking for welfare.

Eventually Bill ran out of excuses for not opening school, and with his usual flourish he trumpeted the tidings throughout the settlement, tomorrow morning (at last!) at nine. So all the kids showed up, eager and on time, and their education began.

In typical style Wild Bill threw himself into his teaching for a week or two, spurred on both by innate (if temporary) enthusiasm and possibly too by the reminder of school superintendent reports dating from previous terms that had threatened him with firing unless he "pulled his socks up," and confined himself to only two or three projects at a time, "preferably teaching."

It was a little difficult for me to reconstruct, subsequent to Bill's departure, just how he managed to teach, his materials, his style and methodology. He was almost never inspected and with the school being almost a brand-new institution in that little collection of log cabins, the people themselves had no clear idea of what should be happening inside the classroom, and even less concern, so there would be no reaction from that quarter.

Bill got along fine with the kids in a good-natured sort of way, when he happened to be actually in the classroom. He would generally start things off by rambling on to the kids about this and that, telling them about the things he had done or about all the changes he was going to make to Fort Franklin, and so on. This was his period for teaching English as a second language, learning by a kind of osmosis. Bill could certainly talk enough for such an approach. Then, bored with that, he would set them to a reading assignment, handing out materials more or less at random without too much regard for their suitability. Too easy, too hard, no matter, just read it. Then might come a written assignment, filling in responses in a workbook, writing a story or just copying text, anything to get them all busy, heads down doing something, anything.

Once he had reached that stage, he was free to step off the teacher's treadmill and turn his energies to other, more important matters. A word to the teacher next door, I've been called away; would you just keep an eye on my kids for a little while? Or the wife upstairs might be called down to help. Or one of the 16-year-old girls could look after the sixes and sevens in the other room while the teacher from the junior class was switched into his own room. Failing that, the (uneducated) school janitor might be inveigled into the classroom to maintain some semblance of activity and law while Bill went off to attend to the latest crisis. "They can draw pictures when they are finished their work and if I'm not back by 11:30," (he wouldn't be) "no use keeping them, just send them home.'

And off he would go, marching through the little settlement, setting grand projects in motion or saving people. "I have to get down to check on that Betsedia baby," I once heard him say. "The medicine that the nurse at Fort Norman has prescribed is not going to do any good. She doesn't seem to have any idea, that woman. That baby's going to die if I don't get down there right away." Wild Bill was happiest when he was indispensable, which in Franklin was nearly all the time except when he had to go hunting.

I met Wild Bill in '57 when I was attending my first teachers' conference in Yellowknife. He was regarded as one of the local experts in the field of native education and a shining light to the rest of us, most especially in the then-important role of welfare worker in the community. He would stand up, white shirt and tie and a natty dark suit tailored to contain his generous girth, and expound entertainingly on the many great successes he had had in various places with his bold, innovative approach to everything. But Bill's involvement in that conference was cut short when word came through that a young Fort Franklin man had been drowned in a boating accident on the lake.

Bill was upset of course when he got the news and confided to some of us later over a couple of beers at the Yellowknife Inn that "this would never have happened if I'd been there," blaming himself and subtly implying a certain local omnipotence in all things.

"The situation at Fort Franklin is out of control," he announced to the superintendent next day. "I've got to get back right away to my people." (He always referred to the Sahtu Dene as "my people.") And with that, indispensable as ever, he caught the DC3 north down the Mackenzie Valley, leaving the superintendent shaking his head.

Bill may have been well turned out whenever he reached civilization, but his suit and tie never saw the light of day once he returned home to the settlement. There he reverted to another uniform, one which invariably evoked comments from everyone who went into Franklin in those years. Indoors, all he ever wore was a large, one-piece suit of grubby longjohns. When he was teaching in the classroom or at public meetings he did usually make the concession of adding a pair of trousers over the suit, but normally just the scruffy longjohns and a pair of moosehide moccasins was all he ever wore.

Being a military man, Bowerman believed in the character-building virtues of military training and discipline. This was at the height of the Cold War in the fifties when the radar antennas of the DEW line were aimed over the Pole at the much-feared skies of Stalin's awful Soviet Union. Canada's vast, seemingly indefensible Northland lay wide open for conquest by the Red hordes. We in the North were all enjoined in those years to watch the skies and report immediately by radio any sighting of unusual, unexpected or unexplained aircraft. How many? What type? Height? Speed? Direction? The visiting Canadian air force officers gave us each a little metal badge to show that we had been taken on officially as Ground Observers.

But the years went by and we never observed anything, and Wild Bill found this role far too passive. With the Cold War continuing as bad as ever and an attack on North America via Canada's northern flank seeming an ever-imminent possibility, he decided instead to take matters into his own hands. With material and logistical support from the Canadian army, Bill organized a small Company of Rangers, recruiting all the able-bodied men in Fort Franklin and parading them up and down with rifles over their shoulders, left, right, left, right. A couple of lectures in the school about winter combat, camouflage, first aid. (No school today, kids!) A few target-shooting sessions, and Wild Bill had put together his own little private army. Canadians could now sleep a little easier in their beds.

Bill got the janitor to build some large plywood racks on which all the 303 army rifles could be stacked in orderly fashion, and this armoury was kept in the upstairs apartment for all of his time there, and for all of mine too. Normally Bill's enthusiasm for a pet project only just barely survived the initial phases, and so it was with his Company of Rangers. But for a brief time anyway, a period of glory never again to return, the frontier militia of Sahtu was practically all that stood between the might of the Red Army and the edges of civilization in northern Alberta. Fortunately, of course, as history knows, the Kremlin's hordes never had to suffer the sting of Bowerman's frontier militia.

Throughout those Bowerman years at Fort Franklin, the people always knew when a meeting with the teacher/administrator was being scheduled and who would be expected to attend. Whenever Wild Bill wanted to call the chief and councillors together for a parley at the school (Bill actually used the term "pow-wow") he would grab one of those army rifles, clip a magazine into it, throw open one of his upstairs windows and fire off four shots in rapid succession. Two shots meant that he wanted to meet just with the chief alone, and one, the school janitor. On the other hand six shots were the signal for everyone in the settlement to down tools and show up at the school within the hour for a meeting of the general public, all 180 of it.

Apparently, this signalling system of Bill's got started in the following way: Jerry, the janitor at that time, was late for work one morning. His little cabin was down by the lake shore almost directly in front of the school, but though it was close by, Bill was damned if he was going to put on parka, pants and mukluks over his longjohns just to go out and stir up that cussed janitor. Jerry was obviously awake because smoke had been coming out of his chimney for an hour. So after giving the guy another five minutes, Bill grabbed one of the army rifles, aimed it out the window and put a bullet directly through that chimney. Jerry appeared almost instantly, hauling his parka on frantically as he ran up to the school. (So Bill said. In all my years in the North I can scarcely remember any occasion when I ever saw any adult actually running, especially running on his way to work. But Bill apparently did. Still, Bill was always spinning yarns, and the trick was to know whether or not to believe his stories as much as he believed them himself.)

Wild Bill bawled Jerry out a bit, bought him a new chimney pipe at the trading post using a government local purchase form and never had any further problems about punctuality. But from then on, that one shot out the window, into the air of course and never again in anger, meant that the janitor was needed right away at the school. After that it was not long before Wild Bill decided to extend the system to two, four and six shots so that everybody in Franklin might know what was on his mind. Bill's ammunition of course was supplied by the Canadian army and it needed to be, for his meetings were as frequent as they were colourful.

Actually Bill did occasionally have a few bright ideas, and some of the projects he got going on behalf of the people of the settlement, "his" people, were excellent. If he rated low as an educator, still he rated very highly for his welfare work, especially in the starry eyes of distant administrators, and he was always being held up as an example and inspiration to the rest of us, so long as it was agreed not to look too closely into how he contrived to get things done, or, for that matter, whether.

Bill was the de facto Indian Agent, and as such he had to concern himself with the general well-being of every family, every individual in the settlement. A casual stroll through the little place back in those distant times might have suggested a project or two to anyone. As in all the native communities of the North through the fifties, the starkest of all needs perhaps was decent housing. Those cabins were small, dark, drafty, crowded, badly constructed and riddled with dirt, lice and disease, and if the people didn't complain it was simply that they had never known anything else. There was no electricity or running water, mighty little privacy, no toilets inside or out, and never enough firewood. Almost every household had some tubercular old grandparent coughing over the kids, and the crowding was such that any kind of disease, colds, measles, flu, once introduced, spread like the plagues of old, till every household was infected. Wild Bill wangled a diminutive yellow tractor out of Indian Affairs, and the following year a small sawmill, wonderful assets to a place like Franklin in those days and yet in the light of more recent times when money in the North flows like water, what modest little concessions they were! There were some good stands of spruce down the Bear River away from the cold lake shore, and Bill could see that down there he had the makings of a house-building program. But it would need the co-operative action of a number of men to construct just one house and he had no funds to pay anyone. However, Bill was responsible for issuing welfare rations to families in times of need and for every dollar's worth of welfare they received, he wrote down, "You owe me one dollar's worth of labour." This would have horrified all the correctly indoctrinated social workers sitting in their offices at HQ if they had known. But they didn't and it worked for Bill, and he always had a willing little group of men industriously hauling logs across the lake, ripping planks on the mill, squaring logs, and in due course sure enough up went the houses.

Another of his better ideas was the building of outdoor privies. There were no toilets as such in the settlement nor had there ever been since time immemorial. So there was a huge sanitation problem, especially in the springtime when the spring runoff drained down to the lake, where of course everyone went to bail up their drinking water.

So Bill set up an outdoor toilet factory at the school, using lumber cut on the sawmill and "volunteer" (welfare) labour. A total of 19 toilets were needed throughout the little settlement. Bill got all the lumber stacked outside the school and organized his workers on assembly-line principles. (Some of the work had to be brought inside and done in the classroom. This rather disrupted teaching a bit and the kids had to be sent home. What a shame!)

By early summer the actual construction was finished (no mean feat!) and all the 19 one-holers were set up in the playground behind the school for painting. White walls and doors. Red trim. Tar-paper shingles on the roof. Everyone in the settlement was then ordered (following the usual volley of six shots) to dig their own hole behind the house now that the ground was thawing, and while the paint was drying, Bill and his janitor went off down the Bear River for a well-deserved break, hunting for moose.

While he was gone, a plane dropped in briefly (an unusual event in those times) bringing an official from Ottawa who was flying from the Mackenzie Delta to Yellowknife. The official was in the process of examining the state of government buildings and equipment in various localities, and at the last minute had decided to include Fort Franklin on his itinerary, it being conveniently on his route. In his report he wrote, "I was unable to meet with the teacher at Fort Franklin, but the school was unlocked, and I was therefore able to carry out a brief inspection of the building as well as diesel generating plant and other existing facilities, all of which appear to be in satisfactory working order. The only adverse comment I would make is that Mr. Bowerman seems to have been unnecessarily zealous in attending to the sanitation problem at the school for he appears to have provided in the rear playground a separate toilet for every child."

School in Summer

One winter I had a party of officials from Inuvik fly into Fort Franklin on Great Bear Lake for one of their brief and rare visits, and there being nowhere else for them, they all dossed down at the school. Included in the group were the new school superintendent and the regional superintendent from the Indian Agency. I knew and liked both these two men well so I was happy to have them staying overnight for a good long visit and a bit of gossip from the grapevine. They worked for two different federal departments. Northern Affairs ran the school system, the fish and wildlife administration and various other things, while Indian Affairs concerned themselves with the well-being of the Treaty Indian people. In the course of the evening, as the three of us discussed the deplorable economic conditions in so many native communities, and of this one in particular, the Indian Affairs official became carried away with the conviction that this new education system of ours was preventing the local families from following their ancient seasonal lifestyles in the bush. Increasingly, only the men camped on their traplines in winter, leaving the women and children behind in the settlement. And meantime the trappers themselves were spending less and less time in the bush. If only the school year could be changed, he argued, the kids would get their schooling through the summer and entire families would then be free to travel in midwinter to their old traditional lands as they had always done. The old patterns would continue, the people would be better off, and there would be much less need for welfare assistance. (But I think what he meant was less *demand* for welfare assistance. People don't come knocking on your office door bothering you for handouts when they are camped 80 miles away in the bush.)

The school superintendent was heavily sceptical about all this, and they argued back and forth for some time on this theme. I kept out of the argument for I was rather new to the North and I really had no clear opinion, though I did allow that I would be prepared to teach through the summer, if the kids could be persuaded to show up. Oddly, neither of these officials thought to consult the chief or any of the other local parents on this rather important matter, but in those days that was par for the course. North of 60°, government was of the people, for the people. By the people had still not been invented. The chief happened to be a very fine man, a well-respected leader and an exceptionally impressive orator. His counsel might have been of great interest to these two superintendents, but you had to live there to understand that.

The upshot was that the little two-room school on Great Bear Lake was chosen as a pilot project to test out the Indian Affairs' superintendent's theories, and I had to plan a summer teaching program for my 29 kids.

When I was a child, I held my blissful summer holidays to be quite sacred. After many long months of three Rs drudgery they were the high point of every year. They were our glorious days of sunshine, days of freedom from the usual tyranny of a demanding, unfeeling, indifferent adult world (as I saw it). I still remembered quietly promising myself once, when I was a small boy, that when I grew up and became one of *them*, I would never allow myself to forget how it felt to be a child.

So, I felt a little sorry for the kids and I determined that I would try to keep that childhood promise. I ordered a couple of large canvas tents for the school as well as a new outboard motor to go with our freighter canoe. We would take our reading books and go off when we felt like it, camping in the bush. I got hold of an old ice-cream churn, laid in stocks of popping corn, wieners and other supplies from illicit government sources, got half a dozen fishing rods from the Company store, some snare wires, matches, axes, fishing lures and other things, using Local Purchase Order forms purportedly supplying the school with other innocuous materials, tile cement, fencing nails and light bulbs. Today this is known as creative financing.

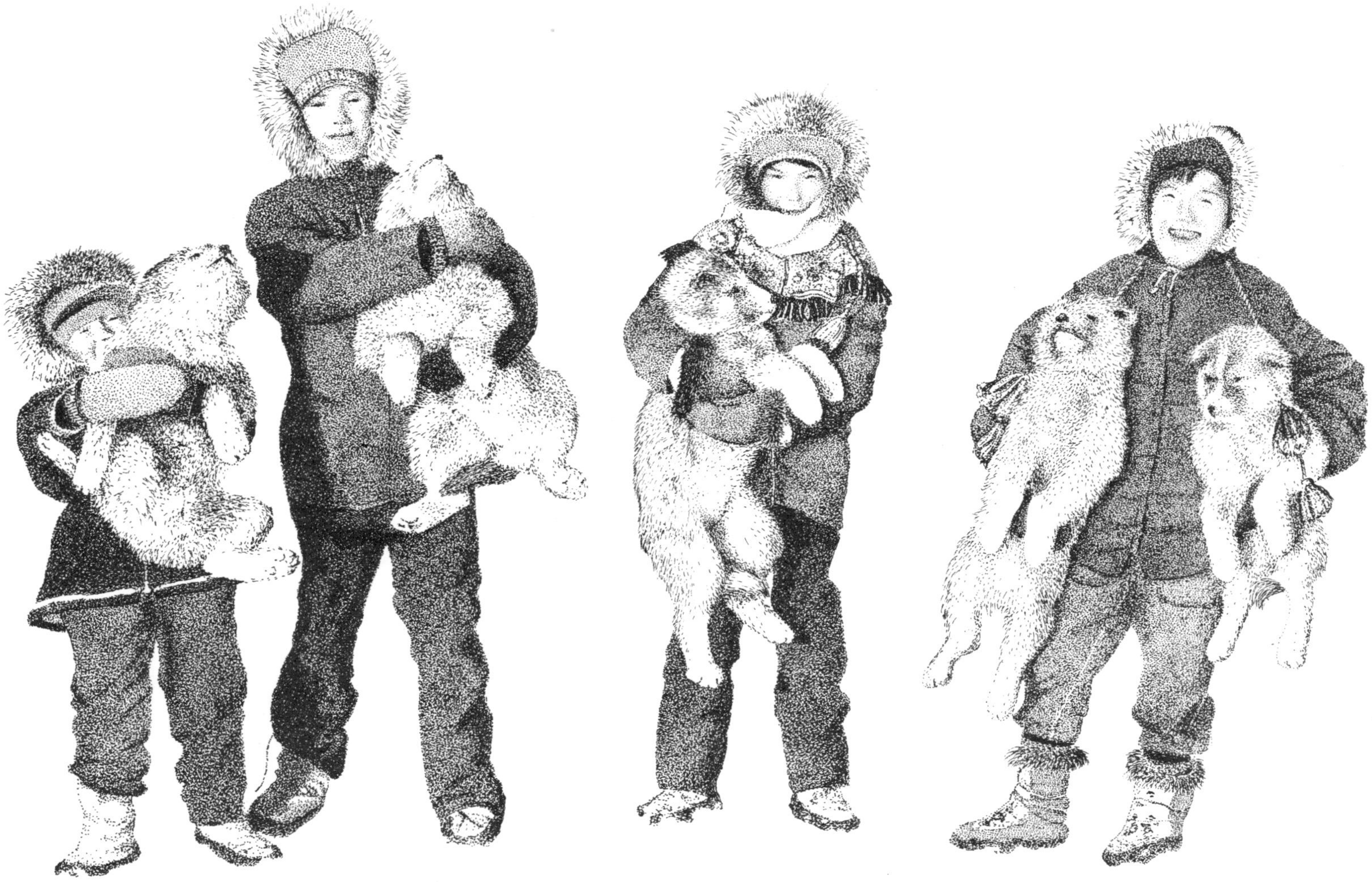

Dene children with puppies.

Now it was well known that the great mega-lake in front of the settlement, an inland sea stretching far out of sight beyond the horizon, was a deep, bitterly cold body of water even in midsummer, losing its ice only once July was well established, and never rising to more than about two degrees above freezing. Some of the kids did splash around the edges on warm days, but generally, the deep longing that all children have to cavort in water had to be satisfied here in the dark brown muskeg waters of little streams in the bush, away from the cold lake winds. There they threw their clothes aside and scampered about in the early summer, before the mosquito hordes arrived, in and out of the swampy water, screaming in wild delight. But nobody ever learned to swim.

Just the year before, one of the younger men of the settlement, newly married, had drowned not far from the shore in an unhappy, long-remembered boating accident. Despite the cold, he might have survived if he had known how to swim. But this was something that nobody had ever really learned, nor had anyone ever learned how to apply artificial respiration to a victim. Perhaps during this summer of teaching I could launch a learn-to-swim program? In New Zealand, even little one- and two-room country schools where I had taught had concrete pools in the playground, or a beach nearby, and swimming was a normal part of the phys. ed. program. Why not here?

"What we need," I said to the chief and two or three of the more interested parents, "is a swimming pool."

"What's that?" they asked.

So I referred them to a Sears summer catalogue, and showed them a picture of one of those cylindrical, steel-walled, blue-plastic-lined affairs shown in the setting of a nice green suburban garden with a nice White suburban family enjoying their nice blue pool.

"The kids could learn to swim properly if we had one of those," I pointed out. The chief didn't actually say "Crazy White Man," but doubt and amusement flickered briefly in his eyes. But he looked at the picture again and then said "Good idea!" in his own Slavey way, and "Good idea!" agreed the parents, the priest and the guy at the trading post. My creative financing of course didn't stretch to buying a swimming pool, but there was a healthy balance from funds collected at the classroom door when movies were shown at the school, so it was generally agreed between the councillors, the chief and the priest that we would have one sent in. This was the beginning of the sixties and it was very probably the first contraption of its kind ever to be shipped north of 60°.

The end of June rolled around, and the other teacher, unavailable for this summer teaching program, took off, leaving me with a total enrolment of 56, a hopeless number. I decided to try teaching my own senior class Mondays, Tuesdays and Wednesdays, and to bring the little ones in on the other two days, maybe Saturday morning as well. This plan was given the nod at headquarters. There were no native classroom assistants in those early days, and the load was mine alone (though the following summer, when the experiment continued, there were two of us on hand).

So, the first weekday of July, to sweeten this plundering of the sacred summertime of childhood, I spoke to William Sewi, the school janitor, and we levelled off a bit of the grassy playground behind the school, and set up the strange new pool, a thing as novel to me as anyone else. It gleamed, shiny and new, seeming oddly out of place in this great Northern wilderness. The kids swarmed around us in great excitement.

"Teacher, we gonna swim today?"

"Not today, Little One. First we have to build a house over the pool."

"Why?"

"To make it warm. And keep the mosquitoes out."

"Aw, we wanna swim."

"Not yet. The first person to finish his work, go to the lake and get some ice, and I'll show you how to make ice cream."

William's English was rudimentary but he always understood what I was getting at, and he had great skill and ingenuity in tackling anything new. He constructed a square plywood wall right around the pool and put a little padlocked door on one side to control entry. He then added long spruce poles extending from the walls up to a central gable and we covered this skeleton frame with long strips of clear, reinforced plastic sheeting, forming a cozy enclosed greenhouse.

"Teacher, we gonna swim today, right?" they demanded.

"Not today, kids."

"Why?"

"Cause we haven't filled the pool yet. When your reading is finished we'll go to the point and catch fish."

William dug a little channel across the playground from the big plastic plug in the floor of the pool liner, to carry away the water when it needed changing. We had no filtration system, only a jug of bleach, and I knew what the water would look like after a short time, especially since nobody had swimsuits to change into, and, if anything, their own underwear would have to serve instead.

The days were getting warmer, and the sun beating down through the wide expanse of double-glazed windows turned the classroom into a stifling cage.

"Teacher, when you gonna fill the pool?"

"This morning."

On the school dock at the lake edge, William set up the big gasoline pump, a huge noisy thing intended for fighting forest fires, and connected canvas fire hoses all the way up behind the classroom to the pool while we did mathematics inside. The roar of the pump began and everyone looked up happily. After a few minutes the sound of the motor died away and William, splashed with water, looked into the classroom.

"Water *strong*," he said. "I need kid," and he rattled off something in Slavey to the class. At the pool end, the hose had flailed around under pressure like a demented snake, and had to be held.

"Me!"

"No, me."

"Me, Teacher." Me, Me, Me. A forest of hands.

"The first one to finish," I replied. They were learning to "carry" in multiplication.

Matthew, the chief's son, nine years old, was good at maths. He was one of those quiet, polite, unobtrusive, happy kids, always smiling, or on the point of smiling. Matthew had finished first and his broad grin proclaimed his triumph. I looked up to say to him, "Don't get your clothes wet, Matthew, and you must have bare feet if you go inside the pool."

I returned to helping a small group and looked up a few minutes later to see Matthew the smiler marching happily from the classroom, all his clothes piled on top of his desk. The others gazed at his triumphant exit in envy, and then reapplied themselves to their work, since I had allowed that three or four others might be allowed to help him if they got their work right. The result was that within a few minutes first Maria and Patty, and then two of the boys, Harry and David, all happily departed the classroom in the same manner, to help control the flailing demon that delivered the chilling flood.

So from the day after Matthew and his friends had filled the pool, swimming became the highlight and the great joy of every school day. The greenhouse worked nicely to take much of the chill off the ice-cold lake water, and this was augmented with buckets of hot water drained from the school water heater. They splashed and cavorted and yelled their heads off once each morning and once each afternoon, and soon, with guidance, with being taken step by step through a progression of skills I had learned and taught in New Zealand, they began indeed to swim.

All this actually seemed to enhance the all-important three Rs just as all happy activity can be made to do by being interwoven into it. All practice had to be done, every assignment completed before there would be any swimming and they tackled these things with redoubled energy and new-found enthusiasm. They wrote little stories about their pool and sent them to their Maori counterparts (for we had twinned this little school with a similar two-classroom school for native children on the shores of the South Pacific). They learned to measure temperatures and graph the changes from day to day. They began to think and measure in gallons (of hot water) and seconds (of underwater immersion) and ounces (of bleach). They learned about oxygen and the difference between lungs and gills. They learned how to revive someone unconscious, and they listened to fabled yarns of mermaids, mermen and water babies. They learned English!

Before July was too far gone, before we grew weary of the hot, stale, old classroom, I spoke to some of the hunters who were preparing to go hunting for moose down the great cold river draining out of the lake. Could they drop off these tents, these grub boxes, this bag of books on their way past the Porcupine River tributary? A sheltered campsite lay there above the banks of the Porcupine, and a nice yellow sand beach extended far upstream from the confluence where pickerel and grayling lay in the shadowy pools beneath the overhanging spruce and willow. A perfect place to take the kids for a short time.

I took only half the class, 15 kids at a time, and the little Oblate priest helped me to ferry them in our two big canoes from the settlement.

"I'll come back for you on Saturday," he called, leaving me and my 15 on the beach surrounded by piles of sleeping bags, and the tents and equipment that would be our school for the next four days.

"Teacher," they cried before even the tents were up, "we can swim?" And so, clothes scattered all about as if to the winds, they raced and splashed in the silky waters of the Porcupine, water far warmer and cleaner than our pool, ran up and down, jumping over the banks in the sunshine, and then lay in the sand while I read to them the hilarious shenanigans of Hans Andersen's Big Claus and Little Claus, translating, rewording carefully all the while into simpler English. And when the sun retreated slowly westwards taking with it the heat of the afternoon, and the mosquitoes began moving in onto those acres of golden opportunity, they scrambled quickly for their clothes, the matches, the axe, for birch bark and the dry lower branches of the spruce to start their fires, and then soon in the billowing blue smoke up went the tents, a large one for the eight girls, a bigger one still for the seven boys and myself. Then out came the pots and frying pans and roasting sticks.

"David, get a bucket of clean water from the Bear River, please. Harry and Elizabeth, would you put all the sleeping bags inside the tents? Maria and Janine, you mix the pancake batter in this bowl. Sandra, spread the cloth on the grass over there, and put the plates and forks on it. Timmy, would you hang those wet towels to dry over the willows, please. And then mix the milk.

"Billy, you have to keep the fires going, okay? Edith, can you open those tins of beans? Judy can help you. Who wants to make the bannock? You Matthew? You know how to do it? You could put some cranberries in it if you like. Shirley can help you. Did anyone see that bag of wieners?..." and so life, and school, began at Porcupine River.

They had to say grace before their meals, kneeling there so innocently in the sand, and, with hot chocolate inside them, their little Catholic prayers before going to sleep, for even if I didn't expect such things of them, others did. They had to wash at the river before breakfast and scrub their teeth before lessons. They had to do their reading assignments before their swim, their math before gathering berries, their chores before the baseball game. They caught fish for supper and went exploring in the bush, swam again, drew pictures of camp life, listened to stories, sang around the fire as twilight fell at midnight, and slept as long as they liked.

Their days were full and happy and before anyone had a chance to get homesick, I took them back to the settlement, released them to their happy anarchy and prepared for another group.

* * *

The experiment failed, of course. The Indian Affairs superintendent's nice theories about the family migratory patterns of the local native people didn't work out at all. The following winter only two families left in their entirety for their distant winter traplines. They would have done so anyway, regardless of any rescheduling of the school year. For the rest, the kids merely ended up moping around the settlement for two months in the middle of winter with nothing much to do. At all events, looking back, I felt I had kept that old childhood promise of mine, blending adventure, novelty, freedom, excitement and pleasure, in with the imperatives of a basic education.

They came to us at that school from humble little log cabins where poor simple folk lived an almost incredibly hard-scrabble existence, devoid of the slightest luxury nearly devoid all too often, as it was my business to know, of the absolute essentials, a bag of flour, lard, tea, enough wood to get them through another day. Perhaps that was why, every day, they came so willingly to school, those kids, and because they came they continued to progress. The happy, cheerful, co-operative spirit that pervaded that generation of children in that little place, their openness, their absence of reserve or artifice, and their so-endearing innocence made them a great joy to teach, and a privilege I will never forget.

The Bush Man

School opened as usual one Monday morning at Fort Franklin in midwinter, but not one solitary child showed up. Exactly the same thing happened on Tuesday, and again not even one child came on Wednesday either.

Normally our attendance there was excellent. The kids started gathering in the corridor in a happy, noisy, swelling swarm starting any time from 8:15 on. The stragglers dribbled in perhaps half an hour after the nine o'clock bell, for many of the homes had no clock and they depended on kids from other homes to come in and wake them up on their own way to school. Tardiness was never scolded, I suggested to Jack, the other teacher, who was a bit inclined to make a fuss. But attendance was praised, and so was punctuality.

Absenteeism is the greatest single factor explaining the sometimes catastrophic shortfall in academic standards affecting native children, and I had been mostly delighted with the record in that settlement, and very happy, under the circumstances, with general progress. Certainly kids were absent from time to time, but there was always a reason — usually having something to do with temporary domestic responsibilities in the absence of one or other parent. It was no big deal.

But this was something new.

We still had families living in winter tents there, as there were still not enough log cabins. Some of our school kids lived in these tents. How those poor people managed through those long, bitter, Arctic nights with nothing but a piece of canvas or animal hide between them and the stars I do not know. But they had been doing it for countless thousands of years. Incredible!

On Sunday night, two women from one of those tents were trudging back home from the bush loaded down with bundles of dry firewood, and a bag of fresh green spruce boughs to spread over the snow for padding and insulation on the floor of their tent. They had a dog with them, a starving little thing, and the dog too had saddle bags of spruce boughs.

The school was at the far eastern end of the little settlement and it was while they were snowshoeing their way home in the advancing darkness away back behind the school, that they noticed the dog acting strangely, hurrying forward, looking back quickly, hackles rising, staring wild-eyed and growling softly, ears back, slinking on, tail between the legs, turning again and growling. It was a clear night, but cold, with a cutting wind off the lake ice, and they were close to the edge of the forest. The women, imaginations racing, looked fearfully behind them, stopped for a moment and thought they could hear a low, continuous, grumbling sound, almost human. No animal made that sort of noise. It could come only from one truly awful thing.

They hurried on and the sound stopped. Then on again quickly, looking back constantly and fearfully, and then suddenly one of them cried out in hysterical terror as she saw (she said she saw) a large, dark shape, an almost erect, nearly human form, but bigger than a human, a dark, wild, evil thing of unspeakable malice slipping silently across a snowy gap between one clump of spruce and another, parallelling their own trail, stalking, moving in towards a point of ambush.

The Bush Man!

Many times, the children had spoken to me, wide eyed, of this lurking, malevolent monster. "Yes it true...."

"He real, and he done a lot of thing. Awful thing...."

"He very scary thing, and everbody scare of him."

"Everbody say he bad."

"Sometime he come in a winter...."

"No, I never seen him. But my brudder he seen him one time when he on trapline. That why he come back quick, my brudder. He not stay on trapline cause Bush Man he come."

"All a peoples, he really scare for Bush Man, you know."

"Yeah he alays hurt peoples."

"Me gran'mudder, she say me Bush Man take peoples away, old time ago, he stealing peoples she say."

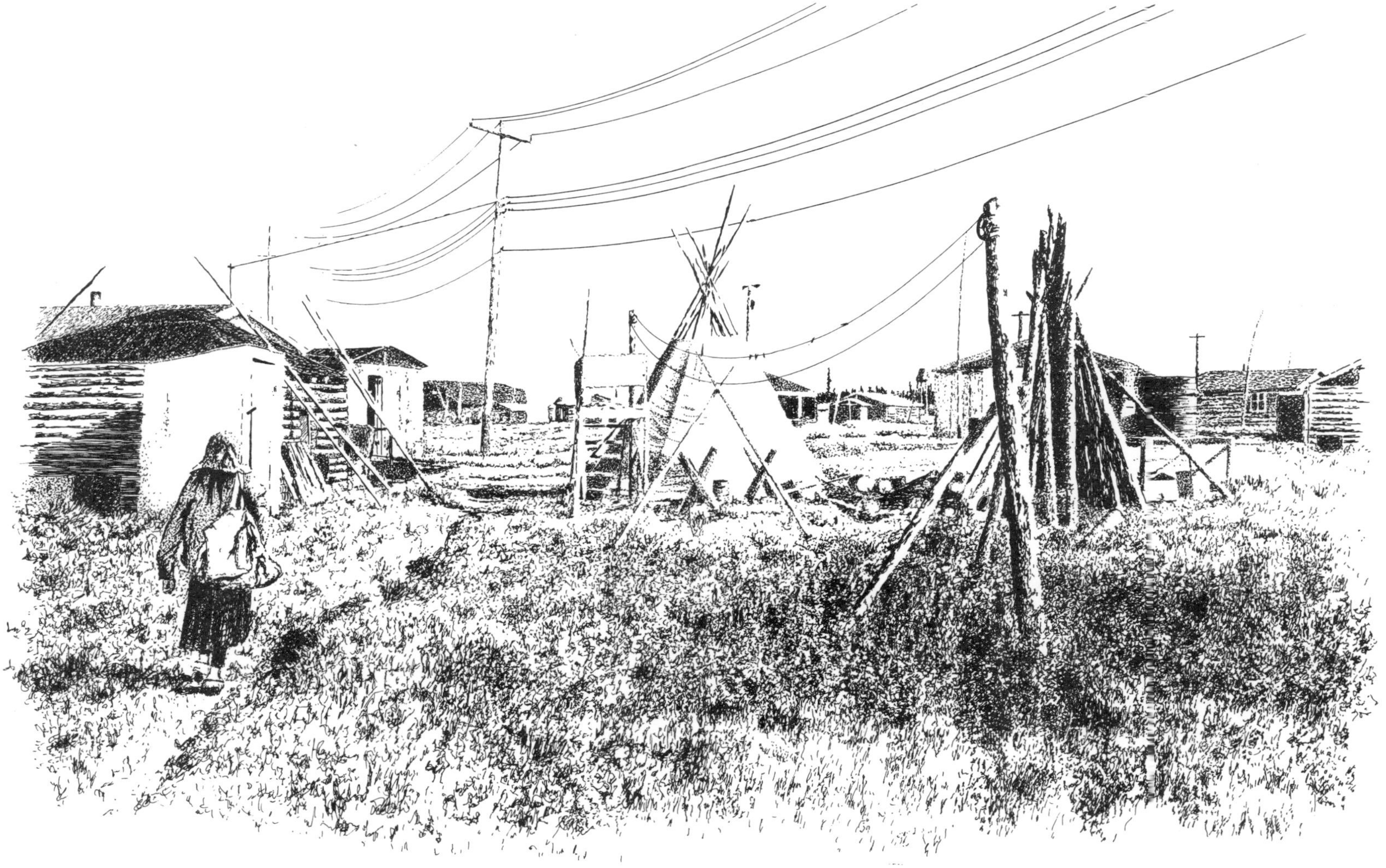

Dene village.

"Sometime he stealing baby."

"He eat peoples too."

"No, he not eating peoples. He just killing peoples."

"No he eat peoples."

"My father, he say me Bush Man steal womans."

"Your father don't know."

"Yeah, he know."

"Yeah it true, you know. Old days loooong time, womans pickin' a berries in a bush, two womans, and he never come back. Man look and look and he can't find nothing, and he never come back that womans. Bush Man he catch womans, that why."

"Maybe for kill womans."

"No, maybe for make baby."

"Yeah?"

"Yeah."

"You know what? One night old woman Napati she go toilet outside for shit. She see Bush Man. He come. She close toilet door and she *cry*, *cry*, *cry*, really loud, you know. Old man Napati he come. He say, 'What for you crying too much?' She say, 'For Bush Man, that why. He come for catch me.' Old man Napati he lookin' around. He say, 'Don't worry, Bush Man he go now.' So old woman Napati go home. She running running fast. She really scare you know."

(Everybody laughed.)

"Sometime Bush Man he kill dog too."

"My mum she say me dog get sick if he see a Bush Man. He get crazy that dog and he die, that why cause Bush Man he come."

"Yeah, lotsa dog get crazy."

"Dog sometime she cry and cry. That why she scare for Bush Man, that why."

"My mum she say me Bush Man steal a clothes on a line too."

"Who clothes stealing a Bush Man?"

"My gran'mudder, long time."

"He just liar, your gran'mudder, that why. Bush Man he don't wear no clothes."

"Sure he wear clothes."

"No he just hairy, that's all, he lotsa hairy."

"You don't know."

"Sure I know. You don't know."

And so, arguing and swapping yarns in the classroom (in my language instead of their own for I was feeding them with occasional prompts, egging them on) they filled me in on this dread sinister menace, this lurking, evil thing forever haunting their dreams and their wilderness.

Whatever could be said of the Bush Man, the fear of him was a very real thing, not only amongst the kids but many of the adults too. Perhaps in time, as people examined their old legends with the perspective of a more modern eye, the dreaded Bush Man would fade from being a living horror to something more like our bogey man, no longer anything more maybe than a silly device to frighten small children into compliance.

I offered no opinion. I just listened to their tales, and shared in the fascination they had for the subject. The other teacher scoffed openly at these stories, the product of the illiterate uneducated mind, he said, but I pointed out that the many people of British Columbia and the states of the Pacific Northwest who honestly believed in Bigfoot, or Sasquatch, were mostly educated Whites. (Or at least literate; the well-educated mind is not gullible, but questioning and sceptical.) Just as literate and just as White were the people who believed in the Loch Ness monster, the Bermuda triangle, flying saucers with little green men, and an endless litany of other fancies. Humans are always intrigued by mystery, and they love being shocked or scared, so they tend to cling to their fantasies, and in a humdrum world the more shocking or scary they are, the more they want to believe in them, and reason be damned.

Anyway, these two Bush Man-haunted women did make it back home, without their loads (I could imagine those snowshoes flailing!) and so did the little dog with his. Forthwith, they abandoned their tent and moved into a cabin with other people, and their ghastly vision, their horror and fright, their fortuitous escape, had enlivened the little settlement, given everyone something to talk about, dwell upon, exaggerate, and it served to scatter everyone's dead-of-winter blues.

Including mine. A nice, long, undeclared holiday, just when I needed it.

But it was going to be over the next day. People were running out of firewood, so someone had to be the first to get back out there to the bush. And the chief and a couple of others came by on Wednesday to mention that he thought it would be safe for the kids to return next day to school. They had had their three days. Would that be all right? he asked.

"Of course," I said, "they could have come back anytime. It doesn't have to be after three days."

"Oh, but old teacher Bill Bowerman he say me three days for no school," said the chief.

Ah, so that was it! That crafty old rascal Wild Bill Bowerman, my predecessor. I soon had it all worked out. Bill relished being the Big Cheese, but teaching bored him to distraction, and he would use any old thing at all, ruse or excuse, to get out of it. "So," says Bill, "whenever a Bush Man is seen around here, the most important thing is we'll have to protect the kids. School will close for three days after every sighting!"

An old chap came down the Mackenzie during the summer and passed through Fort Franklin with his dogs and canoe on his way to Grizzly Bear Mountain away across the lake to the south-east, a place he apparently had known well, long decades ago. He was one of the dwindling remnant of White men who came north between the wars to trap, and he still had his general hunting licence which gave him the same privileges as native people. He had lived in retirement at Hay River away to the south for many years, then suddenly he decided to return to his old trapline.

Now why on earth would an old man do a thing like that? Nostalgia? Intimations of mortality? I don't know; I just met him briefly and then away he went on his final lonely way across the lake in the late fall.

The Mounties from Fort Norman flew in some months later to check on the old fellow, landing on the lake ice near where they understood his camp to be. A few dog tracks, nothing more.... A couple of scrawny dogs skulking out of sight.... Then, there was his camp!

All they found there were a part of his skull and one leg bone, a femur. They searched all around and there was nothing more. Death for some people must be a lonely business.

The Mounties shot the two dogs. The two human bones they put into a bag, and then flew these sorry remains back to Hay River for burial. Case closed.

"The wolves," said the game warden from down at Fort Norman.

"His own dogs," said the Mounties.

"The Bush Man!" said the people of Great Bear Lake.

Discord and Harmony

In those earlier times, when the Northern school system was still in its infancy, communication over long distances was a difficult and uncertain business, especially with the "Outside," as populated "civilized" southern Canada was called. (This shortened form of the term "outside world" was one shared with Alaskans who used it, as they still do, to refer to the lower 48 contiguous states.) Our federal department provided each teacher residence with a shortwave radio, to keep us in touch with our own world, but no matter how long or how high the antennas, we seldom coaxed much more out of those useless radios than the background static they seemed to have been built for. The CBC Northern Service came and went (but mostly went), occasionally the excruciating Voice of America came in loud and clear, and we could usually get a generous dollop of the wearying propaganda that Radio Moscow, not all that far beyond the Pole, served up to us daily as news. Normally, the frustrating radio was left turned off.

This meant that the whole wonderful world of music — modern, ancient, classical, folk, jazz, country, pop, and everything else — was still beyond the reach of the people of the North for whom, by and large, the old drum dances, the dirges, the two- or three-note chants and the usually doleful intonations of the church still lingered on as the repertoire of the people. Actually, wherever Scottish traders of the Hudson's Bay Company had been posted over the centuries, or wherever the coureurs du bois had frequented, there was also a nice tradition of square dancing or jigging to the fiddle, and nowhere more so in our experience than in Split Lake in northern Manitoba where Katie and I kicked up our heels endless times to the resinous sawing of an old Cree fiddler.

But mostly those outside influences had not taken firm root. There was no radio, there was assuredly no television, there were hardly any musical instruments, and music other than the tedious once-a-week church liturgy and the occasional traditional drum dance seemed to play only a minor role in the lives of the people. And indeed, so it did in the suggested curriculum of the school system. For 30 years I was always puzzled by the almost-absence of music in the smaller schools. Officially the line was, "Do what you can and don't worry if you can't. It isn't very important." The music curriculum was about that simple.

But children *love* music! Surely it well deserved to be taught, heard and made for its own sake alone. More than that though, in song, music is also the joyous vehicle of language and nothing can possibly compete with song as a sure-fire way of implanting, nourishing and reinforcing language, and a love of language. We were in the business of teaching a difficult, alien tongue to these kids and even if for no other reason than that, we should have been encouraged more to bring music into our classrooms.

Still, if the curriculum was written for the musically deprived by the tone deaf that didn't really bother me very much. One of the great things about teaching in those little settlements was the freedom we enjoyed to achieve our ultimate goals by doing creative, innovative things in our own way. That freedom made me a much more effective teacher than I could possibly have been otherwise. It was a freedom that was not always intended, but we took it anyway.

I got myself a guitar. I practised a few basic chords in each of three or four different keys, and every day in those earlier settlements in the bush, we would light up for a short time with "Red River Valley," "Camptown Races," "She'll be Comin' Round the Mountain," "Old MacDonald," "Go Tell Aunt Rhody" and other folksy favourites of North America.

At first the kids couldn't sing worth a darn, but they didn't know that and I didn't care. Grinning happily they bellowed away with gusto and that's all I wanted. Where nothing exists except enthusiasm, all other things can follow. They enjoyed it. So far so good. In that case, they would not only learn to sing better, but I could easily come up with songs that would more or less match the primitive level of their English. If these were hard to find, I picked a bright, happy melody and made up my own words on a local theme, using expressions and grammatical forms that I wanted to teach.

In this matter of language I had to be careful about not assuming too much. In one little Dene school I experimented with a discreetly placed tape recorder mike to find out just what it was that individual kids were singing in the midst of the droning hullabaloo. I then wrote down later an approximation of what came over on the tape:

Twinkle Twinkle Little Star

Teekoo teekoo leetoosh dah
Awawata washua
Apapafa wasowai
Laka dama eenoosh kai
Teekoo teekoo leetoosh dah
Awawata washua.

The kids loved this song, this delightful, child-like little hint of Mozart, and were forever demanding to sing it again, but clearly the words meant nothing to them. They were just gobbledy gook.

In another school I once recorded in the same manner the following version of Canada's national anthem:

O Canada

Aroma nutty flan
Do baseela
Eenorkai sunky mad
We gowia, We sitiai
Tanuno songafee
We sand o god O Canada
We sand o god for tea
O Canada gollias a pea
O Canada we sand o god for tea
O Canada we sand o god for tea.

But if this was so much nonsense to the Indian kids, it was hardly more so than is the actual English version to English-speaking children of tender years, for whom singing the anthem is a ritual like the Latin mass, done for its own sake without understanding.

So I began to make up my own repertoire of songs using either borrowed melodies or my own compositions. The words had to be very controlled and chosen carefully, keeping in mind the children's limited level of English, for the songs were intended to augment and reinforce the English language program. But they also needed to be fun, happy or hilarious. They usually had to do with local people or events, or perhaps amplified stories from the reading program or other bits of our school day. These jingles and ditties quickly caught on with the kids. They clapped to the rhythms and bashed away chaotically on percussion instruments while roaring their hearts out happily at the silly stuff I fed to them.

Still, my songs were not all just subliminal English language lessons. Throughout my Northern years in all those little settlements, I tried to give the children a perspective of their own unique position as aboriginal people on a continent engulfed by a flood of uninvited aliens from other parts of the world, myself included. But I tried also to open their eyes to other similarly inundated groups around the world, and to show how these other indigenous peoples and cultures were adapting (or not) to the altered circumstances of their own suddenly changed world. So I told my classes all about the Incas and the Maoris, the Bushmen of the Kalahari and the Melanesians of West Irian, the Tibetans, the Lapps, the Masai, the Micronesians and the Ainu, showed them pictures and told them stories, and as much as I could, introduced them to the music of some of those faraway cultures.

At Fort Franklin, we twinned our little school with a two-classroom school of northern New Zealand, all Maori pupils except for the teacher's own children. We sent them pictures of snow and snowshoes. They sent us pictures of green pastures, horses, and the long, golden beach in front of their classrooms. We exchanged legends, how the world was made and who did it. They described their foods, their language; we described ours. I taught Maori songs to my kids, and once, after a brief visit by the superintendent from Inuvik, he having overheard us singing the traditional "Pokarekare Ana," he added a note at the bottom of his report suggesting that I have the children singing in English, please, instead of their own native Slavey language.

All children, of course, love to make noise, as anyone knows who has been brave enough to pass around indiscriminately a full set of percussion instruments. The kids had to sing along in the midst of their own racket, or they lost their instruments. Gradually the chaos of the rhythm band came under control as I selected the better talented to take charge of the more popular drums and castanets, and assigned the sticks to the mere noise-makers. Meanwhile, I kept them more or less on just one key at a time by strumming away steadily at the guitar, and inspiring them to sing along.

What noise! The teachers who had the bad luck to work in an adjacent classroom were usually tolerant and good natured about it. They would make their own noise, after all, just when I would try to teach long division or have my kids writing a story. For these reasons I liked to claim a classroom separate from the rest of the school if such a thing existed. But ideally, what I liked best of all was the little one-room school, all ages together and no other classes to worry about. Those were the happiest schools of all.

Gradually I moved from mere percussion to the reading and playing of actual music written out on staves on the blackboard. I was surprised by how quickly young children learned to stretch their short fingers along onto all the holes of a recorder, to associate each position on the staff with a given set of finger combinations, and eventually to produce melodies. They were harsh, squealing, excruciating noises at first, but they learned to control their breath and gradually they all came under control, playing at last in unison. The kids derived enormous pleasure from these squeaky, high-pitched little instruments, and from the ukuleles that I later introduced in some schools.

Up on the Arctic coast in the sixties things were a lot different and my erstwhile career as music teacher went over some bumps. Those happy, delightful children grinning up at me seemed to relish every moment in school. To them the world was new and everything in it was fun. They had, almost all of them, been born in igloos, or summer tents or shacks out at the traditional hunting camps, and out there the ancient chanting to a sealskin drum was practically the only music they had ever heard and even that was seldom.

As always, I wondered about what I was doing. I was on the edge of the Ancient Days! These kids were the direct inheritors of traditions slowly evolving on down through the millenia from pre-history. Was I now going to mark the beginning of the end of all that by getting them to sing "Three Blind Mice"? Teaching them to play recorders? With my guitar, I could begin an inexorable process that might well within a few short years or a generation kill those old drum dances stone dead.

Well, but change is the eternal condition, and the survival of the old ways (which I so earnestly hoped for) was up to the local people. My job was to add on to the culture, not supplant it. Get on with the job.

So I began making up silly jingles about those two white ninnies Dick and Jane (since they still lived on in the required reading program) and about why Ooleesee was taken away on the ship (she had TB) and how Joopee's pet lemming died (it fell into the school bathtub) and why the sea goes up and down (it's pulled by the moon).

But I was disappointed. The kids seemed to have no musical talent, no flair for melody and not much more even for rhythm. They gazed at me in puzzled fascination as I sang my little songs. Clearly they enjoyed hearing them. "Ilisaisi," they would call at any inopportune time, (the word itself, meaning "teacher," was applied to me by the whole community) "Ilisaisi, make sing, okay?"

Fine, I would sing. Then I would encourage them to try singing along with me, words on the board. Most gave it a half-hearted try, droning along tunelessly on any old note, almost as if mocking my compositions. I was about ready to give up.

But what about the drums? This was probably more along their line. Wouldn't they put some heart into it if we could get a drummer to inspire them and stir their latent atavistic passions? As it happened there was an old sealskin drum gathering dust on top of one of the storage cupboards, one of a collection of old artifacts in the school, and a small bone club to pound it with. Can anyone play the drum?

Well, of course, Kaminerk could. Twelve-year-old Kaminerk was the class clown. He had come in only recently from one of

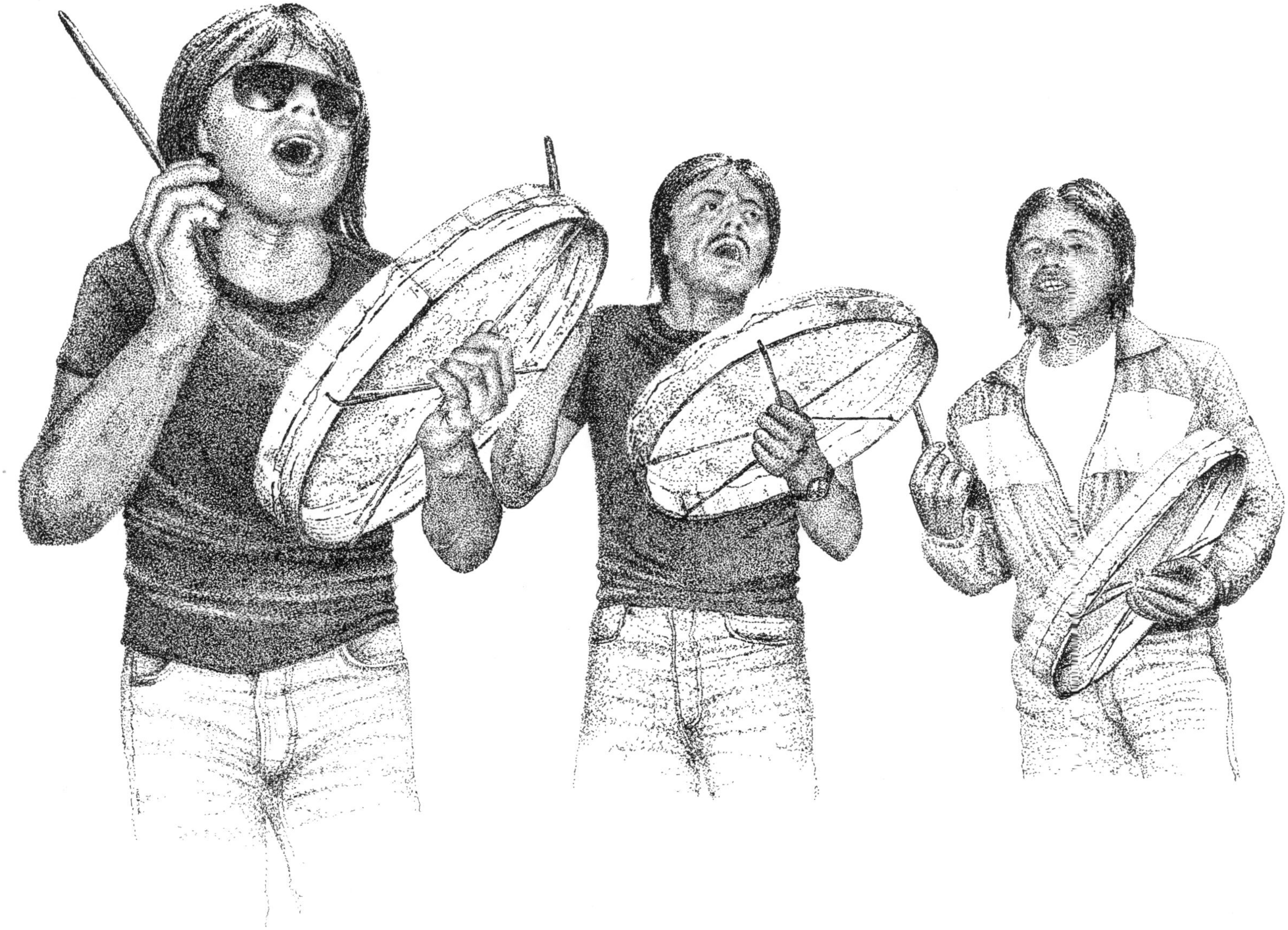

Dene drummers.

the camps where he had always lived previously, and although his English was still rudimentary, it was improving rapidly, mostly because he had no qualms about using it, just as he had none about almost anything else. He was always good for any enterprise and was always enlivening things with some trick or other.

Kaminerk swaggered to the front of the class with a grin on his face. He took hold of the drum, and to add drama to his performance he stood up on a chair and began pounding lustily to my little song as I led things with the guitar. The class joined in, singing along softly to the ludicrous performance, but their voices tapered off and turned to giggles as Kaminerk started swaying his body this way and that way to the rhythm, just as the old traditional drummers did.

Encouraged by the appreciation of his audience, Kaminerk's performance became gradually louder, wilder and more exaggerated until, towards the end of the song, I thought he might fall off the chair. The class loved it. And then, right at the end, to cap all this off with his own personal cadenza, the culminating flourish of the maestro, he held his drumstick high over his head, one foot lifted from the chair, and concluded with a perfectly clear, perfectly timed, perfectly syncopated fart! I was astonished not only that he had the wherewithal to produce this one final triumphant note, but that he knew how to time it to perfection. Here was a boy with a superb sense of rhythm!

The class exploded in happy uproar as Kaminerk set the drum on my table and marched proudly back to his desk. Little seven-year-old Komangapik and her friend Enoya rolled on the floor in helpless mirth. As Kaminerk passed by, Komangapik lashed out at him with her feet in mock disgust.

"Ilisaisi," she cried out, "Kaminerk he too awful!"

Don't tell me, Little One, don't tell me.

I took beans off the school lunch menu and tried the guitar/drum combo again once or twice, but after Kaminerk's brilliant performance no one showed much interest in trying to match such talent, and the rest was anticlimax. Life went on for a while, musicless.

But to my surprise it was the kids themselves who brought me back to the songs. They hardly put any effort into singing themselves, but they seemed to enjoy just listening to them. "Play guitar, Ilisaisi," they demanded. So music again came into the classroom. On the few occasions when I had the entire 30 or so all busy on their various projects, and none of them in any immediate need of attention, I would fill the void with a song, leaving them to carry on with their work and to listen if they wished. They kept busy, but their talking seemed to become softer as I played some old familiar tune.

There was a shy little girl called Apitak. She was about eight, and her family had moved to the settlement from one of the camps the previous summer. Apitak had never spoken a word of English to me, and seldom even much of her own language to the others. She lived in her own little shell and all the others left her to emerge from it in her own time. But one day Apitak broke her silence. On her own initiative she went back to the furnace room, took my guitar down from the top of the water tank and brought it back to the classroom. She then passed it to me and said, "Ilisaisi, Somerset!"

Now, Somerset Island is one of those large islands that make up Canada's Arctic archipelago. It lies far away to the west of Arctic Bay and to the south of Resolute Bay, and families from both these settlements used to travel there in the late winter by dog team or *sikidu* (snowmobile), or plane, and stay there for the lovely spring hunting season. The children of these families were forever telling me about their happy hunting days on the coast of Somerset. So I made up a little song based on their stories. The first verse went like this:

Somerset Island is a lot of fun,
Where the walrus swim and the caribou run;
My father takes me there to camp in the sun,
I'm going back to Somerset Island.
Where the ducks and geese and caribou are,
We all eat fish 'cause we catch a lot of char
By plane or sikidu it isn't too far
To my camp on Somerset Island.

I printed the words out on a large sheet of paper on the wall, and I had some of the children surround it with pictures of caribou, bears, tents, fish racks and so on, and I would sing this at any opportune moment over a period of many days. They seemed to love listening to it. Again I tried to get the whole class

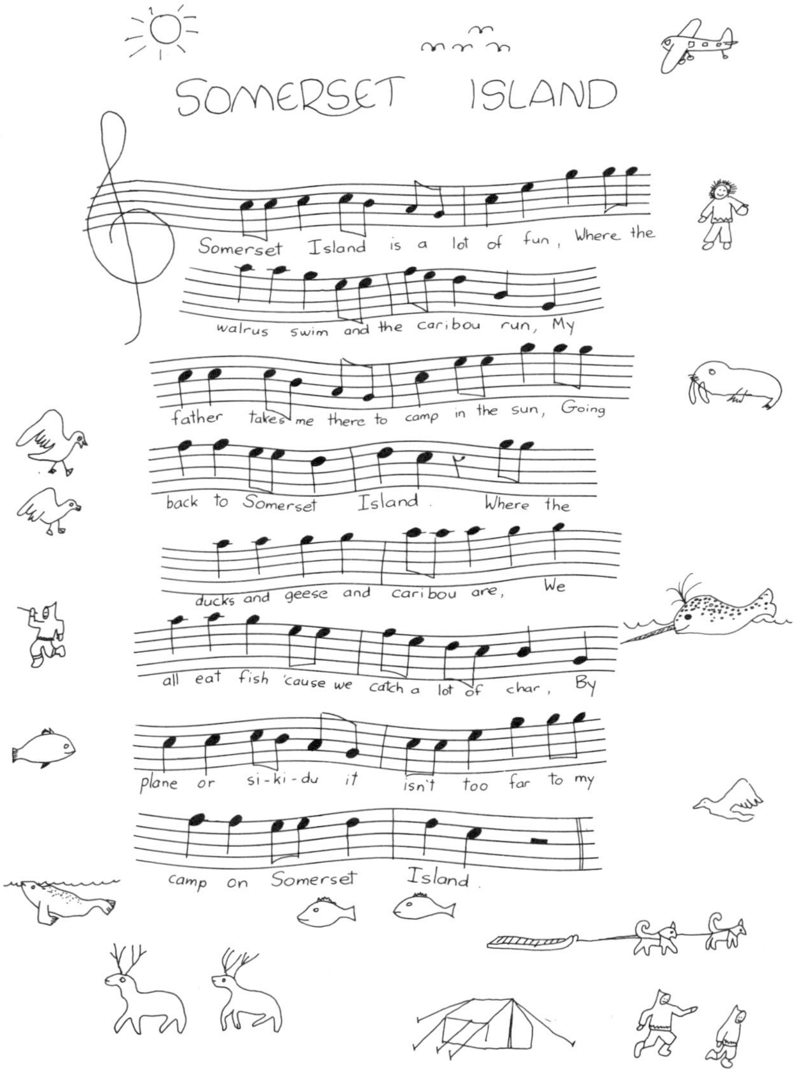

to sing along, and again I was rewarded with a few shy efforts, tremulous and tuneless, that generally faded away halfway through. As with the other songs, I persevered until I was sure that the words and music were more or less memorized.

But to have those kids actually sing? Forget it! Though they were about the most delightful children that it was ever my pleasure to teach, musically they were tone deaf and hopeless. Their half-hearted droning was all that could ever be expected of them, and I might as well accept the fact. Perhaps in another generation, I thought.... Or more likely, make that two!

And then one day something happened. It was something that seemed at the time so astonishing, so unbelievable and so unexpected that I was left wide-eyed with surprise and wonder at the recollection of it for many days after. Nothing quite like it had ever happened before, or ever happened again in all my years of teaching and I still recall it years later with a smile and a shake of the head.

My 30 or so kids were all intent on their various projects. I was with a small group of nine and ten year olds working on the floor with flashcards and pictures. The older ones, the teen-agers, had a small math assignment to complete. Three boys, Kaunak, Gutserk, and Uvuatatiε, were emerging from the shower and drying their hair over the space heater. Two girls were trying to make fish-head soup on the stove from a recipe I'd given them. A group of beginners was making plasticine seals by the sand box, and some other little ones were drawing a narwhal hunt. The room had that nice, happy, buzzing sound that means that everyone is busy and everything is running smoothly. No fuss, no raised voices. Experienced teachers love that sound. When you walk into someone else's classroom and you hear that soft, busy sound, you know instantly that here, for the moment anyway, is a well-ordered situation with everything running as it should. If only it would stay that way!

Anyway, while I was watching over the flashcard game, I became aware of a soft, beautiful voice wafting lightly over the general buzz of the classroom. It was Oodlateeta, *singing*. It had been unknown, to me, for Oodlateeta ever to sing. She was actually staying in key too and her friend, Kigutikajuk, soon joined in with her as they stirred the soup pot.

"Somerset Island is a lot of fun...," they intoned.

I paused for a moment, but betrayed no surprise or undue interest lest I frighten away this unexpected chimera, just kept on with the flashcards. The half-dressed boys at the space heater then joined in while they huddled over the hot air.

"Where the ducks and geese and caribou are...."

While the rest of the class carried on unnoticing, these five worked their way on into the second verse where they were joined, again quite unselfconsciously, by one of the seniors. Some of my own group joined in when they returned to the first verse, and, I noticed, two or three beginners as well. Nobody paused in what they were doing. They were as intent as ever on their own little projects but they sang along as if this was the most normal thing in the world, like singing in the shower. Before long, to my well-concealed astonishment, the entire class had joined in (all, that is, except for my two little deaf ones), singing happily away on key in clear, sweet voices that I had never heard before.

I was quite enchanted, secretly beside myself with pleasure and delight. The volume swelled up a bit as they returned again with greater confidence to the first verse, and they held it boldly for a short while. And then the boys went to put their shirts on, leaving the rest to carry on, and then one or two others stopped, returning with undivided concentration to their tasks, and gradually the wonderfully spontaneous song faded until only two little beginners were left trailing off at the end, "going back to Somerset Island."

To me, nothing could have been more beautiful or less expected than this sudden, magic song out of the blue. It seemed to have appeared like a miracle just when my faith was fading, and when it was over, only the recurring sound of it ringing fresh in my memory persuaded me that it had actually happened.

I shall never forget it.

The Flicks Go North

Many of the Indian communities along the Mackenzie River back in the fifties boasted a so-called Community Club, and Fort Norman was no exception. But it was usually the small White contingent that ran these things. There was not a single native person in Fort Norman's Community Club nor, apart from the priests who wisely kept themselves aloof, was there any White adult who did not belong. I once suggested that we might do well to invite local people to join our club, but the suggestion was greeted by a very slightly pained, embarrassed silence and there being no seconder, our chairman rather quickly hurried on to other more important business. So there was just a little irony in the term, although it was quite lost on the Quite Whites.

Nevertheless, the club, apart from providing the Whites with endless opportunities for bickering and finding fault with each other, did serve many other useful purposes, ensuring, for instance, that every child in the settlement got a Christmas present, organizing sports days, square dances and so on for the whole community. Its source of revenue was movies. Each year we used to order 25 or 30 full-length movies from a distributor Outside. Of all these, Westerns of course were by far the most popular. Language barriers hardly mattered when there was as much richly virile action going on as there always was in a Western. The local native people loved them, cheering on the cowboys, the "good" ones, and yelling joyfully each time a "bad" one, or an Indian (!), was shot off his horse.

These 16-mm programs were sent down the river by barge in the summer shipping season. They were held by the Community Club at the school all winter for public showing on the school projector, and returned by river barge to the distributors in Edmonton the following summer. (There was never the slightest possibility that we could have afforded to fly these in or out. It was the river or nothing.) We paid between $18 and $25 rental for each program for the whole 14-month borrowing period.

Every Friday night, not just at Fort Norman, but also later at Fort Franklin, Split Lake, Grise Fiord and other isolated little settlements of earlier times, long streams of people, everyone from babies strapped behind mothers' backs, to ancients hobbling along with a stick and a tobacco tin spitoon, came up to the school, paid their money at the door (or "borrowed" it from me if they couldn't) and sat in to gaze through the tobacco smoke in wonder at the remarkable flickering screen. The local appetite for these movies was quite insatiable. A new, exciting wonderworld of adventure, romance and exotic splendour was revealed to everyone's eyes. Over and over we repeated the favourites to local demand and for days afterwards people talked about the exciting events that had taken place before their very eyes on Friday night. I was forever reminding the children that what they saw was not really true life; it was just people acting, pretending to do all those things. Those bad guys weren't really bad, they were just acting like that, and when they died they didn't really die, they were just pretending to be dead. But it seemed far too real to be pretending and for a long time I was not believed. More than that, it was not *wanted* that I be believed.

In Grise Fiord there happened to be a clear precedent to prove that movies were not pretending at all, as the teacher claimed, but real life itself. While I was a student at university in my native New Zealand, I joined a film club, and the one movie above all others that really gripped my attention and left a lasting impression, was the old classic documentary "Nanook of the North," filmed by Robert Flaherty after the First World War on the shores of Hudson Bay. This fascinating old movie portrayed with graphic intensity the lives of the Eskimo people around the Port Harrison area in those distant times. I could never have imagined, as a callow student in southern New Zealand gazing at those astonishing images of the Arctic on that absorbing screen, that I would actually meet some of the native people who had appeared in that film, but Pilapusie, the oldest of the original

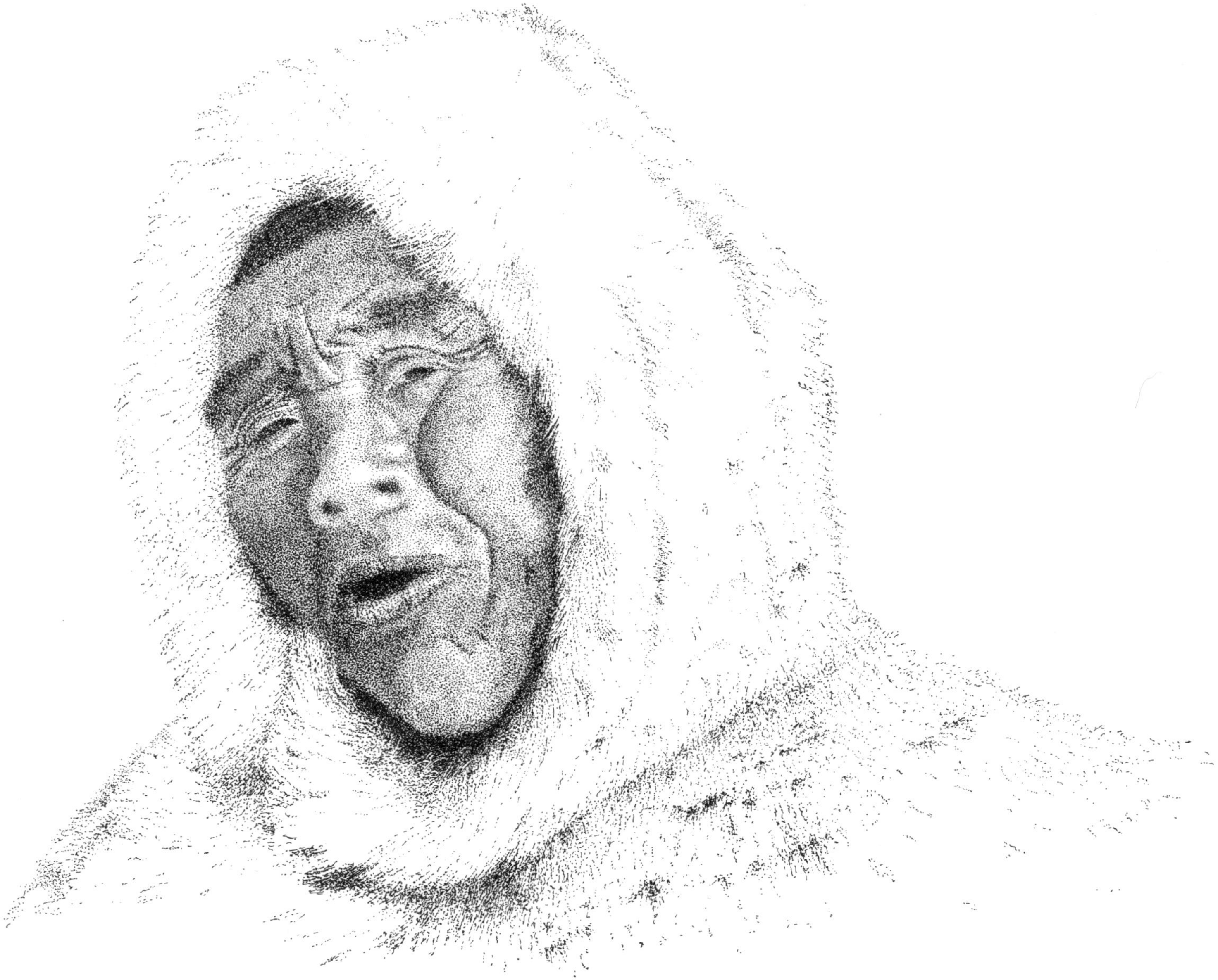

Pilapusie, pioneer of Grise Fiord.

people at Grise Fiord, had appeared as a boy in the film. Pilapusie was able to tell stories about every detail in the whole program (we had a copy in Grise Fiord) and of course was proudly insistent that this was not acting at all, but the real thing.

During the winters of his film-making, Flaherty happily availed himself of the agreeable company of a young native woman, and left behind some offspring including Josepee, who as an adult joined the historic exodus to Ellesmere Island. Josepee once proudly showed me a photo of his mother as a young woman, a photo taken and printed by his famous film-maker father. She was very beautiful. Some of Josepee's own delightful, happy children attended the school at Grise Fiord while I was there and in later years they adopted their grandfather's Irish surname as their own.

My first winter in Fort Franklin ended up with a healthy pile of loot in the Community Club fund at the Hudson's Bay Company store. It all came from the weekly take at the classroom door as everyone trailed along to see (or re-see) one of the first batch of movies ever to be shipped in there. After each showing, the cash was all counted out by the doorkeeper in the presence of the chief or myself or some other village worthy and then next morning it all had to go to the trading post as a credit deposit because there was never enough cash to go around in those little places and it would have been unsociable to accumulate it under the mattress. Somebody else would get a pension cheque in the mail, or a family allowance cheque, and if they were not already deeply in debt to the store, they would ask for cash, the store acting as a bank, and if they *were* deeply in debt, which was normal, they would hand their cheque over and hope to borrow against the arrival of the next one. So cash was passed out from the store as much as it was passed in, and it all derived from the same settlement cash pool. There was never enough of it to go around, and what there was, was dirty, worn, greasy and almost unreadable, like low-denomination *piastres* in Egypt.

On movie night, one of the local adults would volunteer to take up position at the classroom door with a school desk and a tobacco tin containing five dollars change. This could have been anybody at all, and was. It was a popular job because the volunteer got a free movie out of it. The people were all very honest and I never knew anyone to abuse their trust with that cash. Personal debts, once established, could go on unpaid for years, eventually to be abandoned (if never quite forgotten) but no one ever stole from anyone else, or locked their doors against each other.

Some of the movies bored the poor people to distraction. These were usually ones with convoluted plots and long, tedious conversations that nobody understood, or 1940s Hollywood romances that were interrupted every five minutes by the heroine with yet another love-sick song. All through these tiresome shows, everyone had to go to the bathroom, babies squalled on and on, older folks turned their chair backs to the screen and gossiped with the people behind, young lovers had to be chased out of the furnace room and kids ran everywhere.

But the cowboy shows! The saloon fights, the quick getaways on horseback, John Wayne taking no nonsense from those sneaky cheats in black hats, and Gary Cooper, upholder of law, facing his sworn enemies alone on the main street of town; how everyone loved them! When a Western was advertised at the store, no one came late, and everyone already had their 25¢ entrance borrowed from somebody else well beforehand. Everyone's attention was riveted on the screen and all the hubbub settled to a low buzz as people discussed in their own language what was going on, or kids eagerly relayed to the older folks what John Wayne had just said. And then the cheerful uproar as another villain fell off his horse, or as another saloon chair disintegrated over the head of one of the bad guys. And the screams of Athapascan horror coming from those Dene, Dogribs, Cree, as a silent, menacing band of mounted Apaches (dozens of them, hundreds!) suddenly appeared in silhouette on the surrounding ridges. Then small children ran to their parents, and hysterical teen-age girls wanted to hide. The audience was sometimes as much fun as the movie, so carried away that they quite forgot to light up all those hand-rolled cigarettes. The more gunsmoke, the less tobacco smoke, this of course being in the good old bad old days when nobody, including myself, gave a hoot about fire prevention or had any concern for public health.

That first winter at Great Bear Lake, I was concurrently grappling with half a dozen hats. I was of course in charge of the little school. But in addition to looking after various other extraneous things, such as setting up this embryo Community Club, I was also the dispenser of medicine to the local people (God help them), radio operator, diesel-power-plant operator, Indian Agent and the all-important dog officer, and most of these things combined to keep me on the run once school was over each day.

I tried to take the Indian Agency work seriously and it did entail a great deal of work and worry. There was a lake trout fishery to organize in the fall using a large old scow and ten or 12 men. Some of the families were still living through the savage winters in tents, so the house-building program had to be kept running, logs being dragged across the lake by our one small tractor to the little sawmill at the end of the village. There was a constant demand (and *need*) for welfare assistance, not only from widows, families ravaged by TB, and the like, but from the able-bodied as well because, apart from the fishing which was nearly always good, fur prices were poor and times were generally hard.

That first fall I had issued to most of the men who had asked for it a grubstake, using Indian Agency funds, to help finance their departure for the winter traplines. This took the form of a credit advance at the little Hudson's Bay store where they could get all the basic supplies and equipment needed for the long months in the bush, the traps and tents, flour, sugar, matches, tobacco, ammunition and a hundred other things, as well as food for their families while they were gone. Theoretically this grubstake would be repaid out of the profits of the trapping season. But that was just theory. There was no employment whatever in the settlement, and as far as I could see the sooner they harnessed up those dogs and got out in the bush to their traplines the better.

Still, the weeks went on and nearly all the men lingered around the settlement, moping about, occasionally drinking each other's home brew and raising a bit of a ruckus, not even stockpiling the firewood their families would need while they were gone. So I began to feel a bit frustrated, annoyed with myself that I had been so gullible as to issue all those grubstakes, just as was the Indian Agent every winter at Fort Norman for the same reason. But there the problem was put down to a reluctance on everyone's part to be the first man to leave, because this entailed breaking trail with snowshoes ahead of the dogs through the soft, fluffy snow of the deep bush, hour after hour, mile after weary mile. Once the first trapper had gone through, it was easy for the rest. So everyone waited for everyone else.

Life was often rather like a game of cards, and towards each other, towards me, the priest, the trader and everyone else, many of the people were full of little tricks, harmless enough mostly, but you needed a sense of humour. In Fort Norman a trapper would make a big ostentatious performance of assembling all his equipment, purchasing his gear at the Company (as some of the people called the Hudson's Bay Company at times) and over a period of two or three days let it be known that he was leaving to break trail at last to the traplines. But he would only cover a small part of the distance from the settlement and then make camp in the bush. Other trappers, thinking the trail was now fully broken, would inevitably follow along in a day or two, and once they reached the first man's detour they would be faced with having to break the trail themselves.

But I didn't think this was our problem at the lake. Everyone had very different destinations and those crossing or skirting the nearly frozen lake had no need to snowshoe ahead of their dogs. I grumbled about all these long procrastinations to Russ, the young fellow who was in charge of the Hudson's Bay trading post. Russ laughed and said, "I know what the problem is." He then pointed to my movie schedule. "Look," he said, "last Friday you showed 'High Noon.' Next week you're reshowing that one about the train robbers and the sheriff, and then you've got two John Waynes following on after that. These guys are never going to leave town."

So we took the schedule down, and instead I announced a weekend festival of three free Westerns, plus a matinee for kids on Saturday, and then slated in a series of Hollywood musicals for the several weeks following. Russ must have been right because within a week following our Cowboy Festival, nearly all the trappers who were going to go had gone.

I suppose those old movies rather disrupted the traditional rhythms of life for the people of that so-isolated community of the Sahtu Dene, as they called themselves, and probably gave them a false sense of the reality of life outside of their own tiny, closed, remote and frozen little world. But they also brought a glint of happiness perhaps, not just to the people of Fort Franklin, but to those of Split Lake and Arctic Bay and Grise

Fiord, for in each of those tiny communities, places far more remote and unsophisticated even than Fort Norman, we were able to wangle the same deal with Southern suppliers back in the fifties and sixties long before anyone imagined the advent of satellite television, or the possibility that video technology would bring movies straight into everyone's home.

In each place the school projector was called into service and the classroom became the local cinema for people who had mostly never seen a movie before, who knew little about the outside world, and who were only too eager to believe that what they saw on the screen was the way of everyday life in the White man's world. But gradually, in each place, my repeated assurance that it was all just pretending began to take hold, and then in a way I felt I had killed something inside them, snuffed out an eager little flame of hope that life somewhere could possibly be that exciting, that that was the way people lived in the exotic and tantalizing place that White people called Outside.

Faith and the Pursuit of Sin

I USED TO have many interesting conversations from time to time with the priest in Fort Franklin. He cared greatly and sincerely for the Indian people, this little Oblate clergyman, and despite the yawning unbridgeable philosophical chasm separating the two of us, I appreciated this gentle, caring man. He came along to the school every afternoon at three o'clock just as the School Ordinance said he might, to deliver himself of half an hour of religion to the kids at the end of their day, and he often then came upstairs to my apartment for a chat and a cup of tea. He was probably trying to figure me out.

Time was when the only form of schooling in the North was provided by the missions, the mutually antagonistic Catholics and Anglicans. There were not really all that many of those old mission schools but they cast their nets wide. They were nearly all residential. This meant that selected children could be scooped up from outlying settlements for a whole year at a time (their regular attendance now guaranteed by the sort of de facto capture that is inherent in any residential school) and fed on an educational diet that was defined and delivered entirely by the church authorities themselves. When the federal authorities decided in the late forties to take over existing schools, and eventually to establish a secular system serving the entire population of the North, the missions, jealous of the power and control they exercised in all those little places, did a lot of kicking and screaming before their grip was finally prised loose, finger by finger. But they did win a few concessions, and the awkward fact that teachers had to belong (in my case was *supposed* to belong) to the predominant local religion, and that the missionaries still had daily access to the schools for ten percent of every school day (fully a month of schooling each year) were cases in point, compromises won by the churches during their hard-fought retreat from the field.

Anyway, it was this background of change that the poor old priest had come upstairs to complain about one afternoon over his cup of tea. Things were not what they used to be. The people were going to the dogs. All these modern changes were not good for the people....

"In the old days," he said, "the people were so simple. They lived beautiful, innocent lives out there on the land. They had no education, but they had no need of education either."

They didn't? "No, Father, I'm sure they didn't."

"They were such good people, you know, always true to their faith. They were so devoted to the church in earlier years and we were always able to guide and help and direct them so that they would not fall aside from their duty to God."

And to the men of God? "Yes, I'm sure that's true, Father."

"Now everything is changing so quickly. It isn't good for the people. The outside world is encroaching more and more in the North and it is having a corrupting influence."

"I know, isn't it awful, Father."

"Even the new school system unfortunately contributes to the breakdown of the old values as new ideas from the outside world take hold on the minds of the people. They are not ready for it..."

When will they be ready for it, Father?

"...but I'm not blaming you of course."

Whew!

"It's just that I see these changes taking place so rapidly. In the old days people travelled on the land most of the year, fishing and following the caribou. The families were more cohesive and people helped each other more. Now, with schools and nurses and so many other facilities coming into the settlements, and better homes for the native people, they don't want to travel to their distant lands any more, like in the old times."

How annoying of them.

"So they just stay in the settlement all the time. And this leads to idleness and gambling and drinking and infidelity."

Exactly what you might expect when people get together.

"Things are not the way they used to be."

"No, Father, you are right. It's too bad. Things are never what they used to be."

And so on in that vein, the priest giving vent to his anguish, I keeping him at it with my perfidious sympathy. Basically, I suppose, he was grieving the final decline of that one thing so dear to the hearts of all missionaries (and all politicians) of all stripes, the simple, credulous minds of unsophisticated people, easily coerced, easily persuaded and easily controlled, a loss irrevocable for both people and priest, the innocence of the one, and the influence of the other. And I could appreciate how he felt, for what he said was perfectly true. The only difference was that while he deplored it, I, despite some of the sorrier social side-effects of current change, was much more inclined to rejoice. But the church was a powerful force in this land (and in any case I rather liked this priest, despite everything), so I rejoiced in secret.

Whatever my reservations about religion in schools, I was actually very happy about that last half-hour because it freed me at last to attend to a multitude of other administrative things, a check on the diesel generator, completion of forms for the Indian Agent, a word to the janitor, a radio message to the offices at Fort Smith, a packet of pills for Old Levi. However much I enjoyed teaching those kids, four and a half solid hours of dealing with 25, 30 kids or more, at a wide variety of academic levels, was a demanding, exhausting, draining business, and so I was mighty glad to see that black-cassocked figure, dear old Father, show up on time at three o'clock to pray and sing and bore them silly with another lengthy tirade about sin.

Sometimes I hovered in and out, in the vicinity of the classroom, and though I was hardly fit to enter Catholic kindergarten, still my own religious education got another little boost as more doctrinal matters were revealed to the rather-less-than-eager class, and to me also as I hurried around. I was amazed, both there and even more at my previous school, at how much time was spent dwelling on sin. It seemed a great preoccupation of the church, and I was quite staggered at the richness of the subject. The very business of being born into this sinful world appeared itself to carry with it the dreadful stain of sin, an idea so cockeyed, so bizarre, so utterly irrational and idiotic that I wondered if I was hearing right, but since I was supposed to be familiar with all this, I was far too embarrassed to ask for any illumination.

But being born was just the beginning. It was a sin to think certain awful unspecifiable thoughts, a sin to look at your neighbour's wife, another to neglect duties to God and family, to indulge carnal appetites and so on. It appeared to be tantamount to sin to die without the formal rites of the church. It was certainly a sin (as I learned one day at church) to take by stealth in the middle of the night firewood from another person's woodpile. (The priest at the time was seeing his own woodpile dwindling at a time when he himself was depending just on his diesel space heater.) A little earlier, it had also been a sin to take beaver from another person's traps, or fish from another man's nets unless dire and immediate need required it, and it would then be a debt to be repaid in kind. (Shortly after this exhortation, somebody did indeed remove a quantity of nice lake trout from the net maintained across the lake by the mission. But the trappers often used sardines as marten bait on their traps, and the sinner this time wired a tin of sardines into the net by way of compensation. This had happened to one of the previous priests whose own principal sin was not having any sense of humour.)

There really wasn't much in life that wasn't potentially sinful in some way, and the kids were not spared the whole long litany. It was dwelt upon every afternoon and reeled off to them almost like their daily bread, and listening to it all with one ear, as I often did, it slowly began to rearrange itself rhythmically in my mind into the shape of a mnemonic jingle:

Gluttony, hedony, sodomy, blasphemy;
Greed, sloth, pride, lust,
Envy, anger, falsehood, malice,
(Don't be selfish; Don't be jealous;)
Infidelity, fornication,
Sensuality, masturbation.

(These last four were meant only for the senior class who hadn't the slightest idea what those long English words meant, nor for that matter most of the others.)

There were sins of commission and sins of omission. There were venial sins and mortal sins, sins cardinal and sins original.

All the sins were there. They were catalogued and categorized, catechismed and castigated. To me, those children seemed the most endearing, the most trusting, affectionate, beautiful and innocent that I had ever encountered, and that they had to be fed this unremitting diet of guilt quite took my breath away.

My own Presbyterian upbringing suddenly seemed by comparison ludicrously inadequate. We had basically just the one kind of sin to worry about, and that was the *big* one. It was a God-given thing, oddly enough, yet it was so awful one would have thought that the invention of it ought really to be credited to the Devil. It was a secret, shameful thing, something almost unmentionable except in the very coarsest company, or only alluded to obliquely, something to be resisted very strongly and struggled manfully against, at least until you were both well and truly married. (To each other of course, otherwise it would then not only continue to be a sin of the same order, but of an even greater magnitude which one would hardly have thought possible.)

We teachers of course (despite our officially required adherence to the local faith) were expected to refrain from any sort of religious teaching in class, and I had occasion to dampen the ardour of one or two fellow teachers who wished it were otherwise. There was one lady in particular at Fort Norman who was appointed at the last minute as Welfare Teacher responsible for the junior class. She was new to the North, and almost as new to Canada as I was, a Transylvanian widow, "of a certain age" as the French say, with a small boy and a heavy accent. Accompanying the accent was a shrill voice that could cut glass and which she used a little too frequently to proclaim her devotion to the only true church and to recommend it to all and sundry, not excluding me, her principal. Did she smell a rat?

We got along fine. I felt a little sorry for her because she seemed, on this raw, untamed, alien frontier of the uncouth, uncultured New World, to be quite out of place, a fish out of water. She had no friends but she was always kind to me, trying to fatten me with cookies, and I appreciated her generous intentions, especially the ones with peanuts or raisins. Still, she got off to rather a bad start in the fall. The school had newly installed indoor toilets, a completely unaccustomed thing, I suppose, to the local children, and at recess time the boys were just as happy to pee outside in the snow, a perfectly normal thing to the kids, as to use those toilets. Little yellow stains lay scattered around, disappearing into the deep snow. Along would come a strong wind carrying away the upper layers of fluffy new snow and all those frozen little yellow tunnels would remain there sticking up as long hollow yellow stalagmites. I suppose such things were unknown in Transylvania, and their sudden appearance here drove the poor woman to distraction, so she took to parading the playground with a switch, recess time, movie time, any time, and with that shrill voice berating any boy in sight who looked like he might be tempted. So the local people laughed at her, and began to think she was a little crazy (although I suppose at least in that respect she was true to form, indistinguishable from the general run of Whites).

Engrossed full time with my own class as I was, I had little opportunity to know in any great detail what went on in hers, so it was only when I began to get complaints from one of the White parents that I realized that she was being quite free with her strongly held religious views, doling them out liberally to her little ones. Perhaps what was a proscribed vice for teachers in one place, or time, was a required virtue for teachers in another.

So I remonstrated gently with her on that occasion, and also again on the second, dwelling a little on the school regulations of the Northwest Territories as they contrasted with those out on Romania's Hungarian-tainted edges. I always have a little difficulty mustering up a good mad anger, even when it is called for, and although I should have augmented the parents' bitchy outrage and passed it on at about 120%, I could never manage more than 20% or so, if that. However, when it happened a third time I blew my top (just as had the parents, of course) and said a couple of un-Christian things that I shouldn't have said. But we got over that and things went smoothly with no more complaints for most of the winter.

Then suddenly in March the half-dozen White kids in her class and one or two others were yanked out of school. Oh dear, angry parents again. Now what? This time the lady had actually managed to rave on disparagingly to her class about "Protestants and other heathens" in the community. (She pronounced "heathen" like "headin'," as in "I'm headin' for the last roundup." I'm surprised anyone knew what she meant.) Anyway, all the little heathen children went home and told their heathen parents, happily no doubt... breathlessly, what their teacher had just said.

I suggested one or two things to her, at that stage, but what was the point? The damage was already done and all the little heathens stayed home for the rest of the school year. At least from that class.

So one way or another the poor woman had managed to offend or alienate almost everyone. Almost... except the then-priest.

Now it happened that those two got along just fine and the priest got into the practice of dropping by at her place most evenings for a visit. As springtime rolled around the poor man's return to the mission tended to get later and later, and the disappearance of darkness in that season ensured that all those gossipy Whites could observe his retreat homewards at their leisure; the mission lay at a distance from the teacherage, and he had to run the gauntlet of the mostly heathen Establishment on his way home.

"One o'clock in the morning!" they reported to me and each other, wide-eyed.

"Two o'clock!"

Eventually, "Four o'clock! Can you imagine?"

This exciting turn of events gave all the righteous Puritans something to chew over, behind their curtains. At last, at last! Scandal to brighten everyone's lives. Scandal exactly where everyone most wished to find it: at the very highest levels in the camps of the enemy. What an example to the natives! They were appalled. They were shocked and scandalized. They were thrilled!

They compared notes. "Did you see him go home last night?"

"No, we turned in at 1:30 and he hadn't passed our place by then."

And so on, and on, a rich field for the kind of vindictive gossip that most of the Western (or at least English-speaking) world seems so morbidly to relish.

As the school principal and an alleged adherent of the church to boot, my reaction was in some demand. But I disliked gossip, and perhaps I disappointed them by suggesting, in effect, that only the two people involved knew the truth of the matter, that only they were *entitled* to know, that if what was imagined to take place actually did, then I would be very glad for them and hope for their happiness, and that I would therefore in that case look forward in the future to a bit less preaching about "sin."

The teacher left in June, and the priest subsequently left the church, to marry... someone else.

What fascinated me about this mundane enough affair, apart from the malicious glee of the "heathens," was the extraordinarily different reactions to it of the local native people. Their amusement, or bemusement, was so very slight as almost to amount to total disinterest. Well, so what, who cares? was the basic attitude. Can't they do what they want? How much more mature than we puritans they were, to my mind.

Likewise, some time before all this, up on the lake, there had been a similarly delicate business when the good cleric of the time had become in the habit (out of the habit?) of surrendering himself, and everything he represented, to the undoubted charms of a number of the local ladies. But this was a purely native community, and when it was spoken of in passing by local people during my stay there (he was gone by then), it was done just in an incidental way, with perfect understanding, without any trace of puritanical malice or glee, with gentle tolerance, with a measure of affection even that he too had proven, for all his fine preaching, that he was a genuine human being after all, just like everybody else.

I very greatly admired and respected the Indian people for that, and I often longed that we of the Pale Face, and the frequently sharp, if not forked, tongue could somehow become a bit more like them, less judgmental, rather more charitable; indeed, a little more Christian.

A Sojourn among the Cree

I have said that absenteeism has been the single biggest factor contributing to the disastrous shortfall in academic standards amongst the native people of the North. But it has been by no means the only rotten apple in the barrel, and a visit to the school on the little Cree Indian reserve of Split Lake in northern Manitoba back in the early sixties, (a place where attendance wasn't really so bad) would have suggested at least half a dozen other abundantly obvious causes to even the most casual observer.

How I came to be in Split Lake in those years happened this way: Katie had lived her entire life in the suburbs of London, and when we planned to marry and to begin our lives together in the wilds of Canada, I had to reflect a little about the advisability of it all. Though life in the northern woods amongst what the English still called the Red Indians was an exciting prospect for Katie, realistically I doubted whether, with her big-city background, she could be expected to cope with the extremes of climate and long isolation such as I had so happily endured in the Northwest Territories. So I decided to compromise by trying for a situation a bit farther south, closer to civilization, an easier climate, a softer life, and I accepted the principal's position at Split Lake in the wilds of northern Manitoba between Thompson and Churchill.

Now as it happened, we loved Split Lake, and we stayed on there for three years, never once going south in all that time even for our summer vacations, because just being there through the long, lovely summers was holiday enough. But any fond notions I had entertained that life there would be easier, more comfortable, less primitive and less isolated than up in the Territories could not have been more utterly wrong. By a long way, it was worse. But luckily, Katie took to the life.

Except for the church, the nursing station and the ubiquitous Hudson's Bay Company, the federal Department of Indian Affairs ran everything in Split Lake, which is to say the school and the Indians, and the mark of their distinctive style showed everywhere. Our home was just a small, one-bedroom apartment attached to the school, and, like the school itself, it came with all the conveniences, the charm, the well-thought-out amenities of a rural teacherage dating from about 1910. Old broken linoleum covered the living room floor. White stuffing protruded from the holes of the upholstered furniture and half of the storm windows were cracked or broken. The insect screens never kept the mosquitoes or the bluebottles out, but they did keep them in. It was probably just as well that Katie was unaccustomed to running a kitchen. She might have rebelled at that old wood stove if she had known anything better. We had a smoky old fridge, run on a reservoir of kerosene. For a water system, Katie was provided with two metal buckets and a dipper; there they were indeed on the residence inventory, and I had better not lose them, the Indian Agent reminded me when he came in on one of his rare visits. The lake was 150 yards down the hill, and you were allowed to take as much water out of it as you liked.

Actually, we were never too sure just how much water we did like to take. The great Nelson River system flowed into and out of Split Lake. Fed by a thousand tributaries, the Nelson drained the country all the way from the Rockies, across the prairies and through Lake Winnipeg before flowing finally north and east to Hudson Bay. Our reserve was on a promontory where the lake narrowed to less than a mile across, and there was a small but noticeable current at the point where the school was located. This meant that we were immediately downstream of all the outdoor privies, and the dogs (alive and otherwise), and the garbage and litter of the settlement itself, but we tried not to think about that. In the wintertime Katie shared a chopped-out hole in the ice with four other families. The temperatures fell just as far as they ever did in the Territories, at times as far as minus 70°F, and the ice would steadily close around the hole

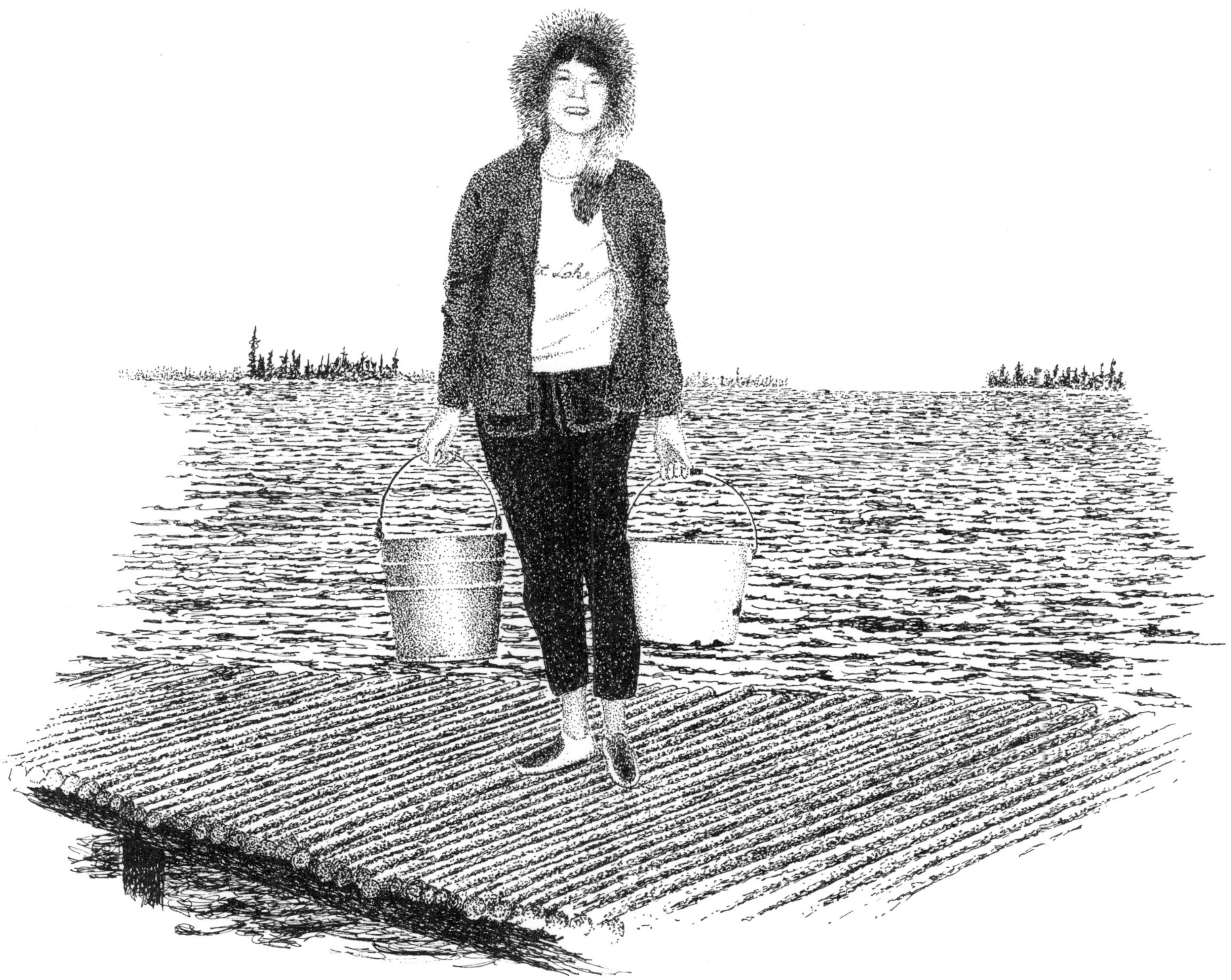

Katie at the school dock, Split Lake.

until only a cup could be used to scoop water out, or it would close completely, and it was always a silent contest, a subtle little waiting game of the Cree, to find who was going to end up having to reopen that hole, down through the five feet of ice.

Given all the arduous work involved in the ongoing pursuit of water, our employer had thoughtfully not provided us with showers or bathtub, nor for that matter even with a bathroom. Instead we had a cheap, round, galvanized laundry tub, and on Saturday nights, with much hilarity, we heated water up over the cookstove, stripped off in the kitchen, and by alternately sitting in the tub with feet on the floor, or sitting on the floor with feet in the tub, we managed to remove the week's grime and wash away our cares. But truly our cares were few, just as our dreams were many.

Physically the school was as neglected and primitive as our home. A passageway where the kids hung their threadbare jackets separated the tiny apartment from one of the classrooms. A second room was provided directly below it in the basement, with access only through the furnace room (a hideously dangerous firetrap if ever I saw one), and a third, of ancient vintage but newer than the others, had been constructed in the playground.

There was nothing appealing or exciting about this school. It was tired, dull and dreary. It had seen no coat of paint or any other maintenance for many years, and everything about it was absolutely rock-bottom basic. Four walls, blackboards, enough desks to fill the rooms to overflowing. A library shelf full of tired old books that were never read. Chalk, pencils, nib pens and inkwells, and cheap, newsprint-quality notebooks called, with unintended appropriateness, "scribblers." No washbasins, but an urn if somebody wanted a drink of untreated water. There was no gym, almost no science equipment (the shelves held two and a half feet of Bibles), no musical instruments, no audio equipment. There were no showers, kitchen, or workshop. There was no office, no staffroom, no typewriter. There was hardly any sports equipment, and hardly any place to store what little we had, a few ratty skipping ropes, a couple of baseball bats, a few balls and hockey sticks, a small assortment of old blunt skates, one puck.

There was no duplicator of any description. Instead we had a supply of gelatine pads, ancient turn-of-the-century precursor of the spirit duplicator. Using a purple indelible pencil one could write out whatever needed duplicating onto a plain sheet of paper. This was then pasted face down over a previously dampened sheet of gelatine and left for a minute or two. Once peeled away from the pad, the paper left its indelible ink behind as a reverse image on the surface of the gelatine, and it was then just a matter of applying blank papers, patiently, one by one, over the damp, inked surface in order to transfer the purple image onto each successive sheet. Each paper would curl itself into a tube as it was peeled away from the gelatine, and gradually the image faded to a faint shadow by the time the 15th or 20th copy was pulled laboriously away. You then gathered up all those tubes, straightened them out flat and sat on them. When I was first confronted by this boggling technology I was practically speechless with exasperation, but the other teachers, more accustomed than I to those Manitoba backwoods, appeared to think nothing of it.

Over against the fence at the side of the playground sat two small, identical and ominous-looking buildings, one for the boys, one for the girls. These of course were poised over deep holes dug far down into the clay as far as the permafrost would allow, and every few years they would be lifted and moved bodily sideways to other, newly dug holes a little farther along the fenceline, migrating slowly with almost geological deliberation around the whole perimeter of the school grounds.

Each of these two buildings was itself provided with two cubicles of standard design, a place for the roll of paper and a wooden platform with an oval hole cut out in the centre. Nothing more. I had occasion to write a number of complaining letters to the Indian Agent and the superintendent concerning those toilets during our stay at Split Lake, but the Indian Agent (whose offices were established at Ilford, 25 air miles across the bush on the Churchill rail line; he might just as well have lived in Tashkent) maintained that these facilities quite adequately met the needs of the children of the Split Lake reserve, and that was that. Nothing was ever done during those years to correct the problem, because there *was* no problem.

But there certainly was. For one thing the boys had no actual urinal, just the hole in the seat, and in the nature of things as anyone with any brains might easily imagine (how to put this delicately?...) when they pissed they missed. So it goes without saying that nobody, when the need arose, ever wanted to actually sit on those seats, soggy or icy, depending on the season, so they didn't. They squatted, again with disastrous results. The girls had the same problem. I suppose even a dry seat can be pretty uninviting at 50 below, and they didn't stay dry long. Attending routinely to this ongoing horror was the one job that my faithful old janitor, Jehu, hated.

But if the kids had problems, so did their principal. Our apartment had a small cubicle in which a plain white toilet seat was installed with a direct drop into a huge cylindrical steel tank in the basement. Theoretically, this awful thing was supposed to digest its contents and discharge out into a septic field. This was a simple enough concept, but nobody had ever explained it to the tank, and it was suffering from indigestion, literally constipated and solid to the brim when we first arrived, just the way the previous principal had left it. No wonder he transferred. It had to be emptied!

I like to fancy I have a strong stomach, but I admit I rather balked at what obviously lay ahead, cleaning up someone else's monumental mess. Luckily, the local people knew this problem at the school to be cyclical rather than unique, and one or two enquiries revealed that there was indeed one particular person on the reserve who was considered to be peculiarly qualified for this sort of work. He was a huge young man of enormous physical strength but also mentally handicapped. He always reminded me greatly of John Steinbeck's poor, tragic figure, Lenny, from *Of Mice and Men*. He was simple, and normally quite genial, but he was also widely considered to be exceedingly dangerous when provoked. No doubt he was teased at times in the village and, very literally, he was then quite capable of severe injury or worse. Well, our "Lenny," thank heaven, understood what was required of him (he had actually done this before) and was willing. I was so grateful. I provided him with the necessary equipment, and he launched himself into the unspeakable. Meanwhile, so as not to provoke Lenny, Katie and I discreetly removed ourselves from the premises and went off up the lake in quest of pickerel and pike. And clean fresh air. So many stories in the North centre around toilet arrangements, or the lack of them!

There were of course more than enough children for each of the three rooms, but somehow we squeezed them all in. They were nice kids, but I found them utterly different in nature from the Dene children I had been accustomed to. These Cree children were shy, wary, elusive, almost completely inaccessible at times. For a long time they wrapped themselves inside the protective cocoon of their own language, refusing to emerge, hating to be singled out, hating to be asked individually to respond in English to anything in front of all the rest, always distancing themselves from the friendly approach, clinging to their inbred reserve, the safe silence, the formality that they seemed to prefer and had been used to with and from their teachers.

Initially the kids spoke English only when they wanted something badly enough. I would stroll about the room, everybody working, and I would hear an urgent whisper, "Hockey!" Where did that come from? I would pretend not to have heard, though all eyes were glancing up at me. And soon again, always from behind, more urgently, "Teacher! Hockey!" All heads down, nobody wanting to be singled out for attention as the originator of this request. Anonymous, one-word English was about as far as they wanted to go. But the whole class wanted to play hockey!

I found this puzzling and frustrating but I knew that I would have to approach them on their own terms, not mine. If I were ever to improve their primitive English I had to communicate with them, and they with me. They had to feel as comfortable and confident speaking to me as to each other. The obvious inadequacy of their grasp of English wasn't the problem at all, but rather the emotional barriers that prevented them from trying. I had to break those barriers down. I knew that if I could just establish a relaxed, happy atmosphere in which they all felt at ease, unthreatened, allowed to remain themselves, the silent tension, fear and discomfort would dissolve and the distances would slowly close.

This would have been a lot easier if only the school had been equipped with all the facilities and equipment that I knew we needed and that I knew would never be forthcoming from the dead hand of Indian Affairs. I needed to get them, from time to time, out of those desks doing other things. I wanted them to ask questions, ask for help, enthuse and laugh. This would have come easily and naturally if they had had, perhaps, a spoon and mixing bowl in their hands, or a saw, or a brush, or a ukulele, or a developing tank, or a sewing machine, or a garden rake, or a loom, anything to absorb them, and rivet their attention. Creative activity could dissolve those harmful walls of suspicious reserve, and bring a measure of fun and satisfaction to their studies. Of course, it's a poor worker who blames his tools, but our problem was a dearth of tools, and a thousand times over I pondered why different native school systems should be treated so differently by the same federal government depending on whether they were north or south of the 60th parallel.

But quite apart from the many obvious inadequacies of that dull old school, overcrowded and underfunded, there was another, even more important key to the unlocking of the strange communications dilemma that we experienced in Split Lake, and we were well through our first year before I quite realized what it was. Casting my mind back to Fort Norman, I remembered how distant, withdrawn and resentful the children there had been made by the insistence that their own native tongue was outlawed in the classroom. I had done this myself. It was the policy strongly recommended to us all in the simple-minded fifties, and at first I went along with it. Of course you can lead a horse to water, but you can't make him drink. This almost mind-bogglingly foolish policy, so naively intended to force the kids to speak English, had, as I had rather quickly discovered, exactly the opposite effect, making all communication a slow, unhappy business, like pulling teeth. The Cree people had had their school for 30 years longer than the Mackenzie River Dene, and had endured for more than another generation exactly that same naive and hopeless approach. "Cree was not to be spoken in school." This fixed, invariable rule had dated from the school's very beginnings, and it had been assumed by everyone that it was to be my rule also.

I checked out this background with a couple of the adults. "Oh sure, all a time, teacher they jus' like that. They tellin' a kids, you don' gotta talkin' a Cree, you jus' gotta talkin' a English. Same ting every teacher you know. School always like that. We s'pose talkin' a English, but we never talkin' no fuckin' English. Some teacher they really mad to us, you know. But we don' care. We jus' whisper in a Cree all a time for make him mad all a goddam teacher."

Katie and I were not long in rounding up the equipment we needed to survive and enjoy our years at Split Lake: a transom stern canoe and an outboard motor, a tent, fishing rods, sleeping bags and a grub box, snowshoes and ordinance maps of all the surrounding country. The lake seemed endlessly complex, branching off behind islands and promontories into long, hidden inlets, nameless coves, little archipelagos and navigable tributary rivers that led winding miles away into new country and on to other lakes again. We were entranced, and we never tired of exploring this beautiful, magic wilderness of the Cree, naming all the features for ourselves out of our own adventures — Squirrel Beach, Pickerel Point, Sunburn Rocks, Blackcurrant Island, Thunder Cove, Lynx River and Black Bear Portage.

We lived on fish and passed our surplus to our neighbours back in the settlement, or fed their neglected dogs. We planted our own garden of greens and radishes (all that the climate would permit) and we picked wild berries and made jam for the winter. We camped in a hundred secret places and painted landscapes in oils and watercolours. We took kids out to swim at some of the beaches and we visited families at the summer fishing camps, or the men stockpiling firewood at the old bushfire sites.

I don't know, but perhaps all this made a small difference. The people of the reserve were accustomed to White teachers coming in from the South, putting in their necessary year, or two at the most, remaining in their own, silent little White enclave at the edge of the reserve and leaving as quickly as possible as soon as their time was over. They missed so much, it seemed to us, and at the end of their stay were almost as little known, and as little liked, as when they arrived.

Katie and I joined in the feasts at the community hall (caribou, duck, muskrat, roast haunch of black bear, with bannock) and the square dances, kicking our heels up to the sawing of the old Cree fiddlers, and we competed clumsily in the jigging contests, like a pair of old mules at the racecourse. We attended their funerals and shared their sorrows. We joined the canoe races and the Easter sports and went visiting other people in their houses, not with any ulterior motive but because we liked to do so.

The people talked to us at length about their life on the land in the Old Days (which were invariably happier, freer and better

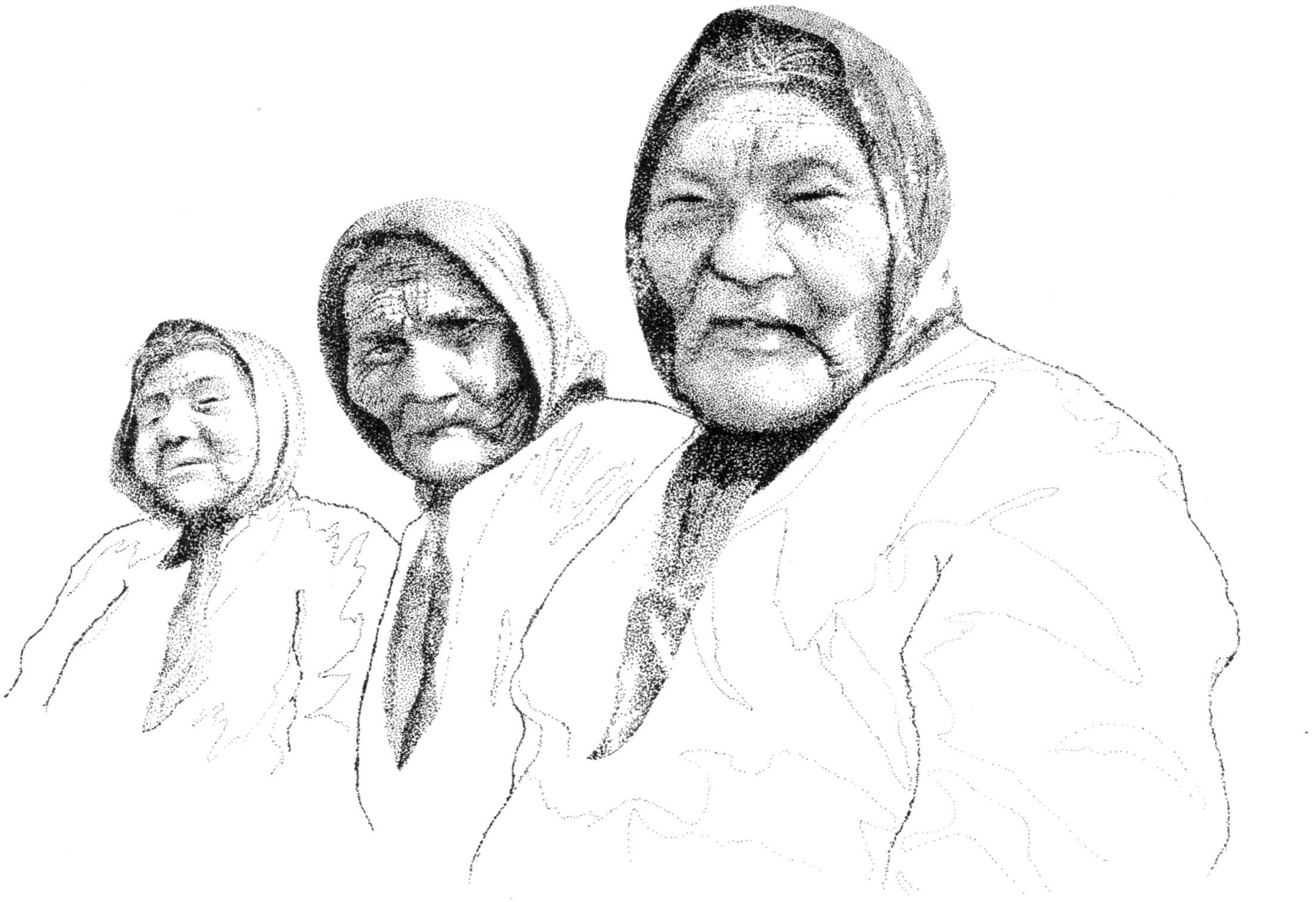

Elders of the Cree.

than the awful Present; it was the same everywhere, and always will be) and we told them of our own lives, travels, dreams, and of the sailboat we hoped to buy some day to carry us around the world to our faraway homelands, a perfectly crazy idea that made their eyes open wide when we tried to explain the sheer size of the monster ocean, not to mention the horrible taste of it, and the storms.

So gradually we became better known to the people, and the initial indifference and shyness of the adults slowly changed to smiles and knocks on the door. Old Woman Kirkness, with not a word of English in her, would seek me out at every public occasion to make a few loud, ribald suggestions, and call me "Metil," and I would respond in kind and call her "Mistos," both highly insulting terms that always sent her and everyone else around into paroxysms of laughter. And just as children everywhere reflect the adult world from which they spring, so also did those kids gradually cast off the protective, resentful shells that they had habitually hidden behind in the classrooms of the White teacher.

Mrs. Grey, widow of an old Swedish trapper from down the line a ways, took the junior room and did a fine job of it. She was the kind, motherly type and she was also an experienced, fully qualified teacher. (There were plenty in the system who were not. Mrs. Grey was replaced eventually by an experienced, fully qualified housewife. The school at Shamattawa at that time had an experienced, fully qualified hairdresser, while Nelson House got by with an experienced, fully qualified telephone operator. My predecessor, the principal before me, was an experienced, fully qualified Hudson's Bay clerk, and the guy who took over after me was an experienced, fully qualified CNR porter.) Like a broody hen, Mrs. Grey always seemed to be surrounded by her six and seven year olds, fussing over them, wiping their runny noses, telling them little Cree legends while she combed their nit-laden hair. The children came from

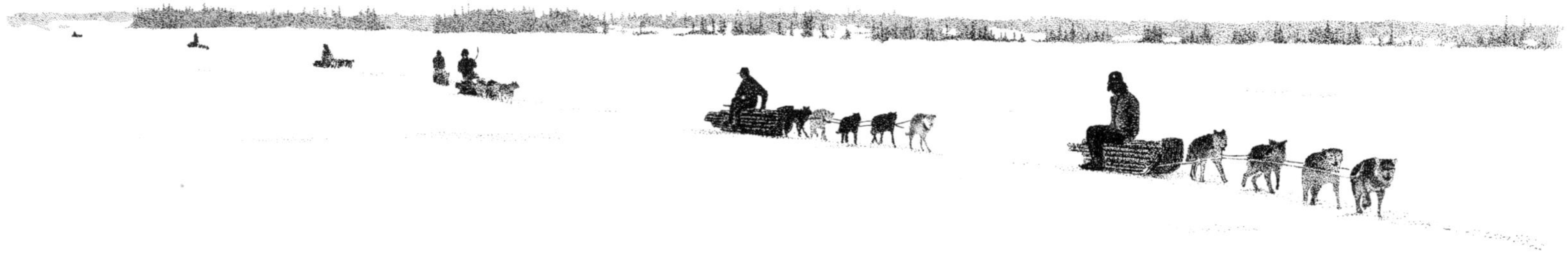

Dog teams bringing firewood from the bush.

sorry backgrounds of mostly unrelieved poverty where poor nutrition and indifferent health were the facts of everyday life, and she was forever fretting over their endless little ailments, cold sores around their mouths and nostrils, impetigo, snotty noses, body lice, sending them to the nurse for ear infections and so on.

We gave all the kids milk and vitamin biscuits every day, and sometimes cod-liver-oil capsules if the nurse provided them. I wanted them cleaning their teeth every day too, because they ate so much candy and other junk, and dentists almost never came to the reserve, certainly never during our three years there. So it was important to instill the habit, but of course the nurse refused to supply the toothbrushes, saying they should be provided by the Indian Agent. He in turn insisted that the school superintendent should buy them, and the superintendent said they should come from the nursing station. And though the Hudson's Bay Company that sold all the pop and candy also had toothbrushes for *sale*, they never actually sold any. So dental caries and stalemate prevailed and no one seemed to care. Some of those kids had not a single uninfected tooth in their mouths, and the pre-schoolers were even worse.

One day in late June, after the nurse had left on holiday, Mrs. Grey became exasperated with the flourishing population of lice in her class and marched the whole lot down to the sandy beach at the point below the school. Here the kids all stripped off and washed themselves all over, especially their hair, with an anti-louse shampoo from the medical supplies. Of course that gave them just a temporary respite; there were plenty more livestock waiting for them where that lot had come from. Better homes and higher living standards were the only real solutions to all these medical problems, but that seemed like asking for the moon. The children loved their afternoon at the beach anyway. They were not in the least abashed to be without their clothes down there since they never wore anything while swimming through the summer.

This contrasted rather oddly with the compelling attachment they normally had for their clothing at other times, especially their headgear. There was not a person of any age on the reserve who did not have the standard appropriate head covering, a baboushka or headscarf knotted under the chin for the women, a navy gabardine cap for the men, and these were worn compulsively by everyone, from the smallest tots to the ancients.

All the kids would have preferred to keep their headgear on in school. They seemed to feel exposed and vulnerable without it. They resented having to leave their gumboots in the porch, and there were tears each September when Mrs. Grey insisted of the new batch of little beginners that they had to leave their baboushkas or caps in the hallway. Being bare-headed was unheard of, seeming almost a shameful, unnatural thing.

We were given no government rations in Split Lake and depended for food on the meagre stocks in the local store. But once people discovered that we enjoyed their native foods they began bringing us whitefish for sale from their nets, bear meat and beaver tails, moose, ducks and once even a white swan. And they also sent kids to the door with notes. "Dear Maurice C. can you please borow me 5 dollar cause my baby real hungrey i gonna pay you for sure when check cummin necks weak pleese don say no cause i gonna pay you for realy sure Sarah Brightnose." And usually the five bucks came back in their own sweet time, but it was an ongoing pain, acting always as a non-profit credit bank, so sometimes I would say no just so I wouldn't forget how to.

The one person in Split Lake whose company and friendship we valued above all others was our old school janitor, Jehu Beardy. He was an exceedingly diligent, dependable worker, but also a gentle, humble man, always good humoured and kindly disposed. Jehu showed up every morning at 7:30 to light the fires and unfreeze the classrooms, and at the end of the day everything that had to be done was done, with almost never a word from me.

The Indian reserve was officially "dry," but the reserve ended at the school boundary fence, and that meant that I was free to brew and bottle my own beer, though even so I needed to be just a little circumspect, disguising my wickedness from common knowledge lest others should hope to acquaint themselves with my product. (More than once, in some of those Northern settlements, I had been asked at the airstrip by some curious and mystified native why it was that I had arrived with, of all things, a couple of cases of empties. "I already drank them all on the plane," I would reply, and my stock would rise.)

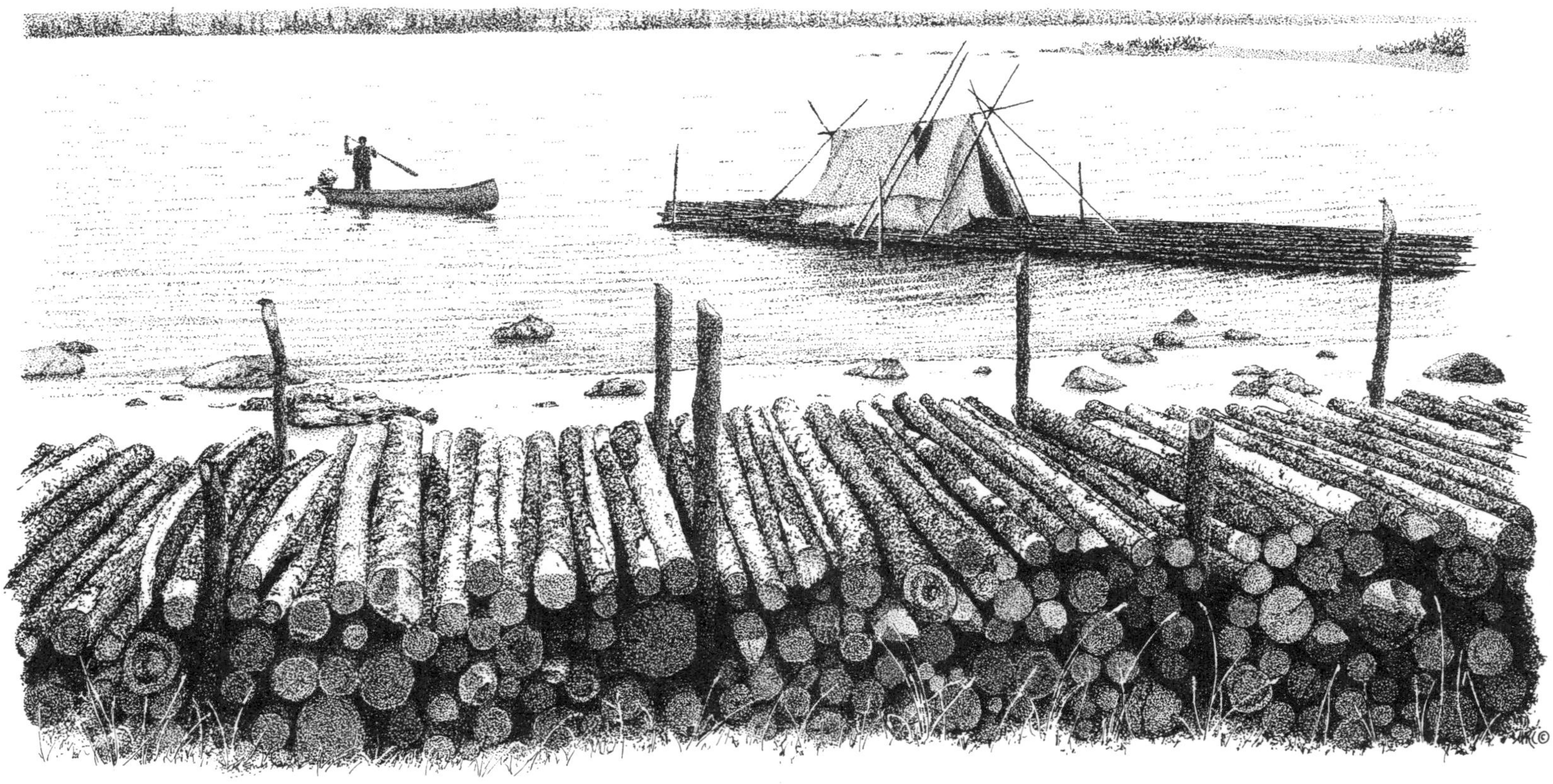

Raft of cordwood for the school arrives at Split Lake.

At the end of each day Jehu would come by for a short visit in our little apartment, and I would pour him a beer, an impossible luxury on the reserve, and maybe a second, and then he would get up before too long so as not to appear too presumptuous, say "Thank you beer," with a smile in his eyes, and go. At times Katie would ask him to have a bite to eat with us. So Jehu would sit down at the little table and share our meal, unable to contribute anything to our conversation because his English was quite as hopeless as our Cree. But when he was finished he would get up to go and say to Katie with an appreciative smile, "Good eat!"

Though the main economic activity at Split Lake consisted of waiting for the next welfare cheque from the Indian Agent, the Indian people did live off the land as much as their individual inclinations allowed. Jehu was no exception and from time to time he came by with some special little treat for us. He always liked to keep two or three large sturgeon tethered by a cord through their gills in a secret corner of the lake, and periodically Katie and I would receive a large slab of this quite wonderful, but illegal, meat.

From Split Lake, we transferred to Arctic Bay on the northern shores of Baffin Island, but for a long time we kept in occasional touch with our Cree friends, including Jehu, depending on them to use local interpreters. However, although Katie kept trying for a while, our correspondence finally ceased altogether. Northern folk are not great letter writers.

Katie and I spent a further three years at that time amongst the Eskimo people of the High Arctic, and we did eventually buy that sailboat, just as we had always planned. In 1969, three years after leaving Split Lake, we left the North to sail away, bound west around the world.

We never heard from the Cree folk again, though our hearts lingered long amongst the good people of Split Lake. Yet, surprisingly, 20 years later we found that we were indeed remembered. While living in Tungsten, in the mountains of the western border close to the Yukon, Katie and I became friends with the local public health nurse, Mary McMeel. Mary undertook a medical survey in the settlements of northern Manitoba after leaving Tungsten, and therefore had occasion to spend some time in Split Lake. While there she asked the local people if they remembered the Cloughleys.

"Oh yes," they replied. "He was our principal a very long time ago. He was tall, thin and kind."

Kind! I was so happy to hear that, so many years later. But then they went on, "When he punished us we deserved it."

I punished them? I have not the slightest recollection either that I ever did or that they had ever "deserved" it. Indeed, I am quite certain to the contrary. Like nearly all Northern kids, those children of the Cree never presented us with any behaviour problems whatever. They played and worked just as their parents lived, quietly, co-operatively and peacefully, not competitively or aggressively like so many children of the civilized South. "Punishment," apart perhaps from the very occasional sharp word, was unthinkable. But memory can be so selective, so treacherous, a thing never entirely to be trusted. Was it mine at fault or theirs? I could swear it was not mine.

Anyway, they continued, "They were nice people those two, but the trouble was they liked boats so much. They were always playing about on the lake with their little boat, and after they left Split Lake they got a sailing boat and they tried to cross the ocean with it. So of course they were lost in the sea, and they were never heard of again. All the people here were sorry about that, and we had a memorial service at the church for them."

So, just like Tom Sawyer and Huck Finn, Katie and I got to survive the solemn celebration of our own sad, untimely end. There are not many people lucky enough to be able to pull that one off, to go on living beyond their own Requiem.

Changing Times

After our lengthy but happy sojourn amongst the forest folk of the northern Manitoba wilderness, the so-called "Swampy Cree" of Split Lake, Katie and I felt in need of a change, and this we certainly got when, in 1966, I accepted the position of teacher at the one-room school at Arctic Bay, northernmost of the Baffin Island settlements, a tiny remote place far beyond the Arctic Circle. There was just a Hudson's Bay trading post there, and a small school building and power plant, and a collection of decrepit (but lived in) old shacks and tents above the beach.

The people of Arctic Bay and the surrounding area still lived largely at that time in the ancient ways, whole families travelling extensively on the land with their dog teams, heavily dependent still on their old hunting skills and the wildlife that had supported their ancestors from the dawning of their own time. Along with their more modern equipment, they still used and fashioned implements of stone and bone, antler and horn, obtained their heat and light from little yellow flames of burning seal fat, and preserved their language, traditions and values almost untouched by the great outside world which was poised at about that time to come flooding unbidden into their lives.

Arctic Bay was the community I had most wanted to live in when, as a callow bachelor, I first arrived in Canada, and now, eight years after the first opening of the school there, it was offered without my asking. Along with the teaching job came the impressive-sounding title Area Administrator, for all sorts of extraneous responsibilities came with the job and they had to send the two of us from Split Lake to Ottawa for a week to indoctrinate me in a multitude of policies and to outline my duties around the community, things familiar and otherwise. I thought the school itself would have more than filled my hands, as would any one-room school, and I was not wildly enthused over some of the other things that would demand my attention, but they threw in an extra thousand dollars a year for all that additional work and worry, an impressive sum which would help augment our slowly growing bank account and bring that sailboat of our dreams gradually closer to reality.

From the big jet runway at Resolute, Katie and I chartered a little single-engine Beaver with big balloon tires, and after long hours in the air crossing the ice-littered waters of Lancaster Sound and Admiralty Inlet, we finally circled over the little protected bay and flumped down onto a boggy bit of flat ground directly across the bay from the settlement itself. There it was at last, two miles across the water, the exotic little place of our imaginations, a few buildings of the Hudson's Bay Company, painted red and white as always, some small government buildings and a scattering of rough tiny shacks and tents by the beach, and high up on the mountainside behind, the name spelled out in white-painted rocks: ARCTIC BAY.

The native name was Ippiajuk, meaning "pocket," a perfect name for a circular, almost-enclosed cove, mostly cut off from the wider waters outside, and surrounded by high scree slopes and mountains. There was a cosy feeling of containment and security at Arctic Bay. Just like a pocket.

Panipuk, my hired help, was there at the shoreline near the landing site soon after we came in, and he took us by canoe and outboard with all our bags and boxes across the water to the settlement, and introduced us to our new home, a pleasant, furnished, two-bedroom house in stark contrast to the mostly plywood, canvas or cardboard-packing-case homes of the local people.

What lovely smiling people they were! One would have thought they had little to smile at, but I think they were the happiest, most cheerful people we ever met, anywhere in all the wide world, an example to all the rest of greedy, selfish, contentious humanity in the very highly rarified art of living with extremely little and yet preserving a spirit of abundant joy, generosity and good cheer. A case in point was our next-door

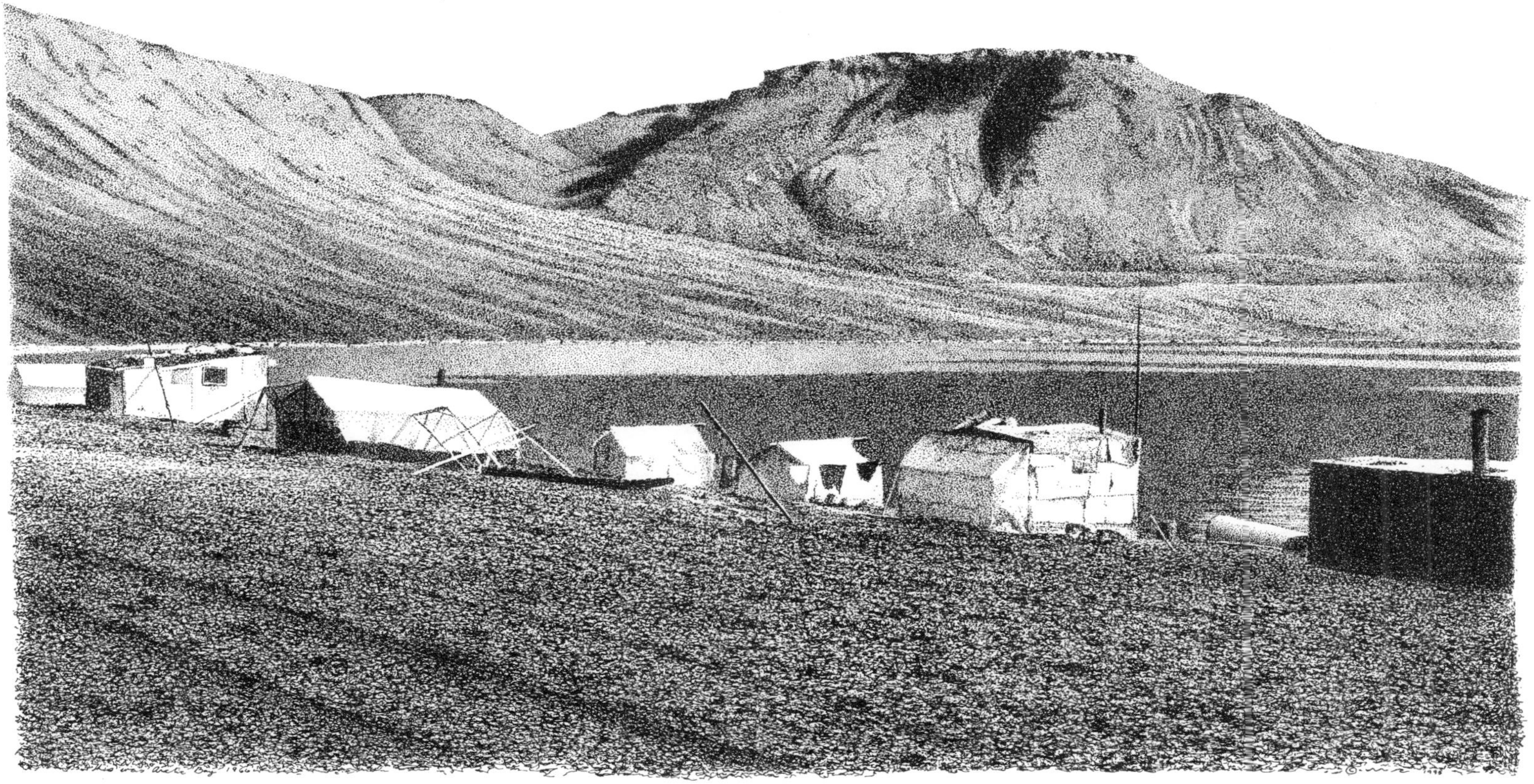

Arctic Bay, 1966.

neighbour, a plump old woman called Atoat, who came down to the beach to meet us, and grab us with her hands as we stepped out of Panipuk's canoe. Atoat was heavily tattooed in the old traditional way, on her face, all along her fat arms and on her hands. Atoat was enormous fun, always joking, and she shook like a jelly when she laughed, just exactly as she did that day at the beach when she apparently said something highly ribald in her strange, difficult language about what a long skinny caribou the new teacher was.

Up we went, following Panipuk, past a collection of old cardboard, plywood and sealskin shacks, and home-made canvas tents, snugly sewn together, with little wooden doors, and well anchored all around with stones, and on up past a horde of great, massive, brutish-looking dogs, to our little blue and white house. There we dropped our bags on the double bed and ran about in ecstasy from room to room, like children, excited at the perfection of our new home (a palace after our place in Split Lake) and the stunning scenery from every window.

In contrast to this multi-roomed mansion, the humble dwellings that spread around above the nearby beach all consisted of the one room. The floor might be the cold stones themselves or perhaps some bits of plywood rescued from a packing crate. The gloom would be relieved by the glow of a seal-oil lamp, or *kudlik*, the great, heavy, soapstone dish of antiquity in which seal blubber melted and burned through a moss wick along one edge. At the back of the room there would be a nondescript jumble of blankets, sleeping bags and fur where everyone slept. Various things would be strewn about, for want of any better place for them, a rusty rifle on the floor perhaps, where everyone could trip on it, perhaps a bag of flour or sugar in a corner, with some of the contents spilling out of a hole in the side onto the ground below, perhaps a piece of meat or liver in a black old aluminum pot, all bashed in and lying on the stones. Outside, there would be sealskins hanging on lines, or stretched on racks before being taken to the trading post. And all around, those hairy, massive, great huskies, all looking thoroughly ferocious, yet seeming to live at peace with their human owners, handsome animals always waiting and searching for the next piece of seal.

To a newcomer, every part of Arctic Bay, every home and every person, every open door, every dog, even the stones on the beach, gave out an aura of seal, an unmistakable, unforgettable, unavoidable aroma, sharp, pungent and rancid. Seals were the very bread of life itself, the answer to a multitude of human needs, just as the coconut tree is to an atoll-dwelling Polynesian.

Aibilie was the name of the young man who was working for the time being as the school janitor. He lived in the same house as Atoat. School still hadn't started but Aibilie worked on through the summer anyway, mostly with the mechanic who was supposed to be keeping things running in the little settlement, particularly the tractor and the diesel generating plant.

Arctic Bay, like practically every place in the Arctic, depended on honey bags and one of the janitor's duties at the school was to tie up those black plastic bags in the toilets at the end of each day, knot them at the top, remove them from the galvanized pails under the toilet seats and take them outside for removal. He then had to stick a new, clean bag into each pail for the next day, top folded over the edge, and put a dollop of nice-smelling disinfectant in before closing the lid in disgust.

For some reason Aibilie considered the honey bag in our house also to be his responsibility, and I was told that he might be upset if I insisted on changing it myself each day. He really didn't mind doing it in the least, and he might have felt unwanted, or felt that I was attempting to usurp his authority! We shouldn't have been using him as a personal domestic, but in the meantime I let him go to it. I was too preoccupied in those first days to bother changing his routines at the outset.

Down there in Ottawa they went on and on about municipal services. We had to organize a proper sewage and garbage service, including the establishment of a land site as a dump, not just for the school, for the whole community. There had to be a regular supply of water to every house. Electricity. Routine maintenance. The works. And in between teaching 30 kids I was responsible for seeing to it that this all came about. Who, *me*?

These were fine sentiments down there so close to the seats of power, but on the actual ground in Arctic Bay they seemed at first to be nearly impossible. Services like this had never existed and still didn't. Aibilie's daily visit to collect our honey bag provided us with a sampling of how things had always been and gave us a sort of base line for change. Here was Aibilie's traditional system for disposing of that great, disgusting, bloated

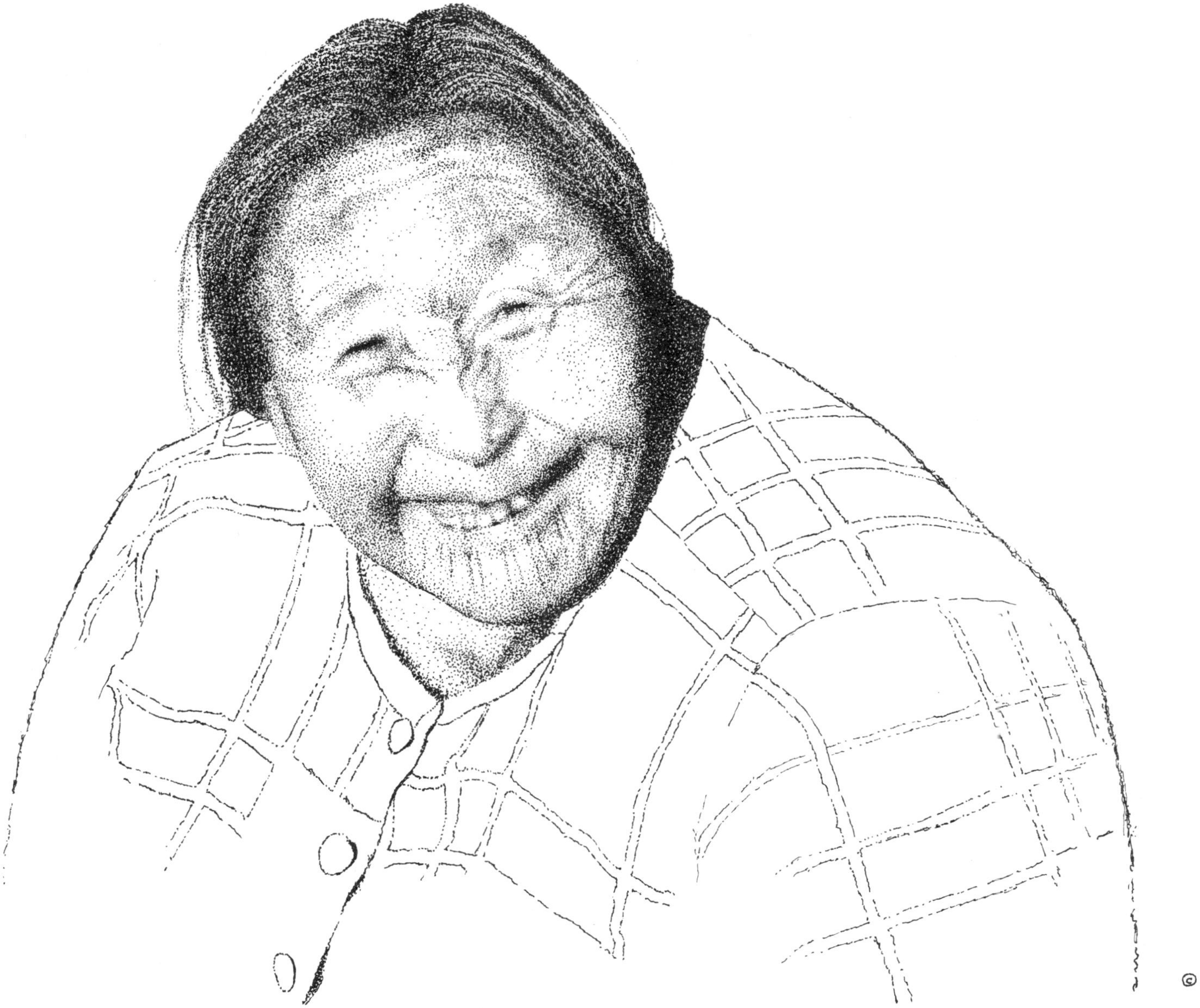

Atoat.

black bladder that he removed each morning from our toilet pail: he came in with his usual genial grin every morning, strode manfully into the bathroom whether somebody was in there or not, and knotted the plastic bag firmly at the top. He then took that heavy, bulging bag out the door and marched straight down the gravel slope to the water's edge. Then, with his right arm, he began swinging it in a great circle, forwards, up and over his head, round and over again, faster and faster, round and round, and finally he let the awful thing fly off, upwards and away out, ker-splash! into the waters of the bay. Surely he must have understood that the bag could have split from all that centrifugal force? Or snag a sharp stone at the bottom of the swing? It would only have had to happen once.... I think Aibilie was just about the bravest man I ever met. But this was what happened to all honey bags, not just ours — everybody's, and general garbage too. It all went into the bay!

One evening, walking along the beach shortly after we arrived, Katie and I saw a seal come to the surface and splash around a lot, rather oddly. Foolhardy behaviour so close to the settlement as any seal ought to have known. Down it went. Back up again, splashing, down and up, several times, thrashing around. Eventually as we came closer we saw what the problem was: it had an old tin can jammed over its nose. Something had to be done about municipal services.

But the mechanic said that municipal services would just have to wait because the tractor was broken down halfway up the hill, one of its tracks having broken off. I wandered up over the mountain slopes soon after this. There was a wonderful view from up there, overlooking the entire bay and the adjacent fiord, and the distant mountains to the south. But I hadn't gone up for the view. I wanted to see that tractor for myself, and give it a kick, and to look into the interesting set-up which had prompted the driver to take it away up on that mountain slope in the first place.

Mostly the settlement was backed by precipitous rocky bluffs with scree slopes at their foot. Low Arctic vegetation grew on the lower edges of those slopes close to the waters of the bay. It would have been difficult reaching the plateau lands behind those precipices, except that there were a couple of saddles which gave easy access for hiking, and just beyond the ridge of one of those saddles was a nice little lake, a perfect source of clear, sweet water for the settlement. What the mechanic and his driver had done was to drag an enormous, long, black plastic hose over the saddle to the edge of the lake. With one end in the lake, and the rest of it trailing over the saddle and down a mile or so to the settlement, they created the possibility of a siphon. They got it started with a water pump, forcing lake water into the pipe, over the saddle and down the hill. Soon the thing would run itself so then they could quickly switch the end of the hose from the pump directly into the lake itself, and, hey presto, unlimited, clean, fresh water was flowing out onto the ground at the settlement.

Well, not quite. The system would work okay for an hour or so and then quit. Somewhere up there, on one side or the other of the saddle, and above the level of the lake, there must have been a pinhole leak letting air into the loop, and that would kill the flow. But no one could find the pinhole. However, quite apart from that, it was then late August, already freezing hard in those rapidly increasing nights, and we had no answer whatever to the question of where the water would come from in the winter.

True, there was a nice little iceberg grounded on a ledge out at the centre of the bay. If only it would stay there until freeze-up... but there were still some big spring tides ahead of us, and, combined with a northerly wind, the tides could release it and let it escape from the bay.

Before school was due to start, and before the chaos of sealift descended on us, Aibilie took Katie and me by canoe out to the wider waters of Adams Sound for a brief seal hunt. There was a wonderfully stunning line of high vertical cliffs along the northern shore of Adams Sound not far from the entrance into Arctic Bay, and I was more interested in seeing those majestic cliffs, admiring their overwhelming grandeur, and painting them, than in actually knocking off seals, which just shows how far removed my interests were from Aibilie's. Quite understandably, he couldn't have cared less about the cliffs. He just wanted to take some meat home for his family.

We landed on a small scree slope at the foot of the cliffs and Aibilie scrambled up as high as possible to survey the wide, dark waters of the fiord through an old brass telescope. There were several 19th-century nautical telescopes in the settlement, all old family heirlooms; they were all obtained in trade several generations earlier from the Scottish and American whaling ships that once frequented Baffin Bay during the brief summers in search of the "right" or bowhead whales, which now of course as a direct result are still almost hopelessly decimated.

Aibilie cut a fine, romantic figure standing up there searching for seals, rather like the officer of the watch on some Hollywood poop deck scanning the horizon for pirates, or the Spanish enemy. He did spot a seal a quarter of a mile out, and we raced over to the spot, stopped the motor and lay there a long time, waiting silently.

A light wind blew into the fiord from Admiralty Inlet, and the canoe slewed around to lie beam on to a gentle swell, rocking us back and forth, back and forth, until we began to feel just a little queasy. A few years earlier, a Hudson's Bay Company trader had been out with a group of Eskimo hunters in exactly these conditions and had become quite seasick until finally he had to throw up. The trouble was that the trader had false teeth, and his native companions were amazed quite beyond belief to witness this White man actually losing not only his breakfast, but the very teeth that had *chewed* his breakfast, *all* his teeth, top and bottom, all still attached to their gums, as he vomited over the side. Once they got over their dazed astonishment at seeing those teeth actually coming out of his mouth and then sinking down through the water, the native hunters roared with incredulous laughter that such a thing could possibly be. The trader had to wait a full year before he could get his dentures replaced and in the meantime, while the native people were certainly not without sympathy, the whole matter was an enormous joke to them all, as well as being a very great wonder, prompting a little ribald speculation about what other parts of a White man might, under stress, come away like that.

We waited and waited for our seal, and occasionally Aibilie rubbed his paddle along the gunwale of the canoe three or four times. Seals were curious enough to want to investigate an odd noise like that, and sometimes that was their undoing. But not this one and finally we went home empty-handed. It wasn't as easy as it used to be to get seals close to the settlement, he explained. Too many people.

Early in September the time came for school to start up, and it did start, but only just. Twenty children of all ages showed up, all keen as mustard. But there was no school to put them in. A construction crew had arrived just ahead of us in August and had been quartered in the building then used as a school, and they refused to move out. Interesting. Theoretically, I was supposed to be the boss around there, the Area Administrator, which sounded impressive, at least to me, and so in that capacity I told the foreman that he had to get himself and his French cook and his assorted tradesmen out of the school before the school year began. But the foreman declared in no uncertain terms that it couldn't be done, and he wouldn't The only other place, an abandoned, old wartime meteorological station at the west end of the beach, had no running water and he would have to put his men to work fixing it up for themselves first, instead of getting on with the erection of the new three-bedroom rental prefabs for the native people, which was one of the reasons, and the most important one, for the construction crew being there. They were nice and comfortable in the only decent building available and it came down to one against eight. I lost. So for the time being I took over an old rectangular welfare house, a "biscuit box," as a temporary school. It was rather awful, but the kids were wonderful. They seemed to thrive on crowding, discomfort, inconvenience and deprivation. Two to a desk, six on the floor, an old space heater with a leaky carburetor, one 60-watt light bulb, one honey bucket, no water. There wasn't room to swing a cat, but the kids thought it was great fun.

Concurrently, the ships came in and life changed. They anchored in the middle of the bay, a big red icebreaker and a general cargo freighter which, rather like a mother loon, soon unburdened and surrounded itself with a clutch of little ones, landing barges which, at sea, were carried on deck. And what those barges then brought ashore that year onto the beaches at Arctic Bay changed that little place, not immediately perhaps, but profoundly, irrevocably and forever.

Until that year, all across the Arctic, the people made do as best they could, just as they had always done, in providing some sort of shelter for themselves and their families — snow igloos, skin or canvas tents, turf and stone homes half underground, or shacks that spoke eloquently of the absence of available building materials and the general poverty of their inhabitants. True, small modest houses (those same biscuit boxes) were located here and there for people on welfare, families with TB and the like, and the Port Harrison emigrants of the High Arctic had had small heated homes provided to them for a number of years. Now, modern homes were to become available to everyone in all settlements, not perhaps all in the first year but at least soon thereafter. They would pay rent according to their means, and they would get copious unmetered electricity and heat, furniture, water deliveries, garbage and sewage removals, periodic painting and routine maintenance, the works, all included!

Arctic Bay was due to have 12 houses that first year as well as a new, two-classroom school, a 15-bed students' hostel and a new, much larger, diesel electric generator.

So, soon after the arrival of the ships, busy little forklifts from the landing barges dumped onto the beach above the high-water mark not just the annual school supplies, the rations and the endless steel barrels of heating fuel, but an ever-growing mountain of building materials. I was supposed to check and sign for all this, and I rushed around frantically for two days with a clipboard in my hand, but it all came ashore and piled up faster than I could check it off and I finally gave up.

The ships departed for other settlements, and for a time all the men who wanted it had employment; the work was interrupted only by the arrival of Sundays or narwhals. Large pods of the beautiful, long-tusked creatures invaded our bay, departed, returned again, and each time the hunters went frantic, downed tools, rushed for their outboard-powered freighter canoes and sped away in hot pursuit. The people had a craze for the outer skin, the vitamin-rich *mattaq*, or muktuk. Generally, the dogs got the carcasses and the Hudson's Bay Company got the tusk.

The snows of September fell and covered the land, and the bitter north wind hurtled down off the mountain slopes and piled it high in drifts while the first of the new rental houses were erected on their gravel pads. With October, the ice froze right across the bay and the skies cleared. The nights were then very long and very cold, too cold for there to be any more snow, and the sky was mostly as clear as crystal. For several nights there were spectacular displays of aurora. This surprised me a little for at Arctic Bay we were rather close to the magnetic North Pole. The most spectacular displays were reckoned to be seen at a radius of about a thousand miles from the magnetic pole, more or less where we had lived in the bush. Sometimes Katie and I went outside at night and stood there gazing in delight at those magic curtains of light swirling and spiralling about against the distant black velvet of star-studded space. There are no words to describe the Northern Lights. They have to be seen. Much of their beauty and magic derives from their movement, their silent, celestial ballet, something that cannot be captured in a picture any more than can the awful grandeur of great, storm-driven waves be captured on a painted ocean.

It seemed that most Northern adults were quite blasé about all that beauty. Having been raised and lived all their lives under the spell of those displays, they seemed rarely to raise their eyes. But the kids noticed them, and all through the settlement when the sky-wide performance began its crescendo, we could hear the children whistling outside their tents and little shacks, trying to call the lights to spin and dance faster, or to come down lower and (in their imaginations) to touch the tops of the surrounding mountains.

And still that cursed tractor lingered up there on the slopes of the mountain, all forlorn and covered in snow. And still the construction crew lingered on too, warm and comfortable in the school, and then complained to me of the dire shortage of water, for that was my fault. But patience has its rewards. An official from the engineering office came in, fixed the tractor, fired the mechanic and kicked his construction crew out of the school and into the first rental house they had built. Meanwhile, the ice of the bay had thickened nicely in the great cold, and best of all, our beautiful iceberg was now held securely captive for the duration. This then was the answer to our water crisis.

The ice of the bay would still not support the tractor, but we had received on the sealift a new, yellow-painted steel farm wagon on rubber tires, a thing intended to be used with the tractor for removing garbage and honey bags. But it was still brand new. I asked some of the hunters if their dogs could be used to tow this big thing across the bay to the iceberg and they were most agreeable. So we hitched up three teams, a total of 31 dogs, in a large fan hitch attached to the shaft, each dog on its own trace, and off we trundled across the bay, the men watching over their own

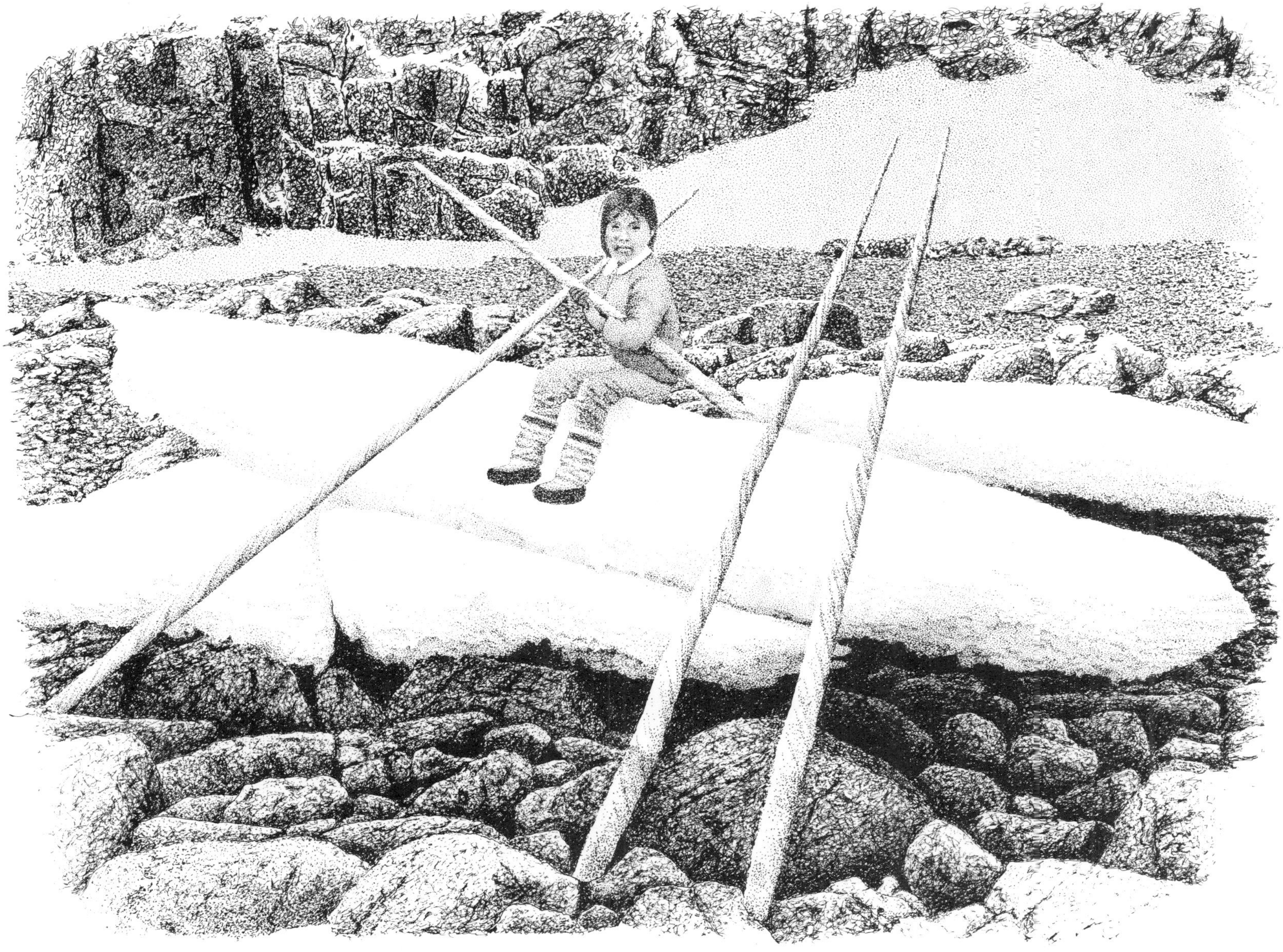

Child of a narwhal hunter.

teams and riding along in the wagon with their long dog whips trailing behind. The men thought this a wonderful lark, and the dogs were happy to be up and about. We all attacked that huge iceberg and filled the wagon with broken chunks which went partly to the school and partly to the people in the old houses. Then next day another load for the rest of the houses.

I always liked it when those big chunks of glacial ice were brought into our warm house from 35 or 40 below, and dumped bodily into the big aluminum water tank in the furnace room. As soon as that intensely cold ice hit the warmish water inside the tank, there immediately followed a long series of loud, shattering explosions as the sudden tension inside the ice produced fractures in every direction throughout the block. This could go on for several minutes before some sort of temperature equilibrium was reached. The sudden sharp reports could be heard all through the house.

You would think that the ice now lying in that tank of carefully conserved water would then proceed to melt. But if there was only a little water in the tank (which was typical) and then a great deal of very cold ice, it was the water that froze rather than the ice that melted, and then for a day or two we were actually worse off than before. In that case, the only recourse was to chip ice out of the tank into pots and kettles and melt it on the stove. Or better still, chip it into chunks two inches thick, add them to a glass of rum and sit back at the end of a long day and watch those effervescent lumps release the prehistoric air that was trapped inside them when it was all just compressed snow on the great Greenland icecap ten or twenty thousand years ago.

Gradually, all those new homes got erected, one by one, filled with furniture, their stoves lit, connected to the power lines, and at long last the people gradually moved, family by family, out of their tiny, cold, age-old encampments, dwellings honoured only by time, and into modern homes. Their great heavy *kudliks*, filled and refilled for generations with seal fat, burned for the last time and were abandoned on the greasy stones where the people had once lived. A new day dawned.

I had an enrolment usually of about 26 children of all ages. That swelled to about 40 or so when all the camp families came in, but equally it could drop away to 16 or less when other local families went hunting. Still, it was a lot of kids.

Apart from the endless complications of age and grade levels, I had not one but two children, a boy and a girl, who were deaf, one totally, and the other seemingly a little less so. I felt so humble and inadequate. They looked at me, those two little ones, with what seemed to me to be love and yearning in their eyes, and I looked back deeply into theirs with the same. But in between all the rest, I could find only a few scattered minutes for these ones. The fact was I had no training and no time. How awful it seemed. And yet they were so intelligent and so endearing, those two little kids, so happy when they understood what I wanted of them, and I felt like a fraud.

The only good thing to be said was that they were happily accepted and absorbed into the social groups by all the others. It was, after all, in their own settlement where they would have to spend their lives, and I felt it was far better for them to grow up there with the other local kids, to let their lives intertwine where they belonged, than to have them sent south for the attentions of educational specialists, even if it meant that they had to be content with the exceedingly little that I, or the likes of me, could do for them. I often felt like enfolding them in my arms, and telling them — somehow — that everything would be all right. But would it?

All the children were happy, well adjusted, high spirited and great fun, and I enjoyed my work with them, although the profound language problem continually challenged both me and the kids themselves. The trouble was that they had not the slightest occasion to use this alien English in their own community except with me for the 25 hours each week that they spent in the classroom. Also, I found it very challenging to come up with programs and materials suitable for the likes of Kaunerk who came in to live in the settlement from one of the camps. He was 15 years old, almost 16. He had never been to school before and could speak almost no English. Yet he was already a skilled hunter and provider for his family. He went out often with his father's dog team, and apparently he had already killed his first polar bear. So what was I supposed to do? Put this capable young hunter in with the younger beginners and teach him all about those two tiresome nitwits Dick and Jane, their younger sister Sally and their little black decorative dog Spot? Above all, I didn't want to insinuate alien cultural values in my teaching if I could avoid it, even if it was age-appropriate, and the hard thing was I had to invent programs as I went along, day by day. Not just for Kaunerk. For everyone. I was sick of the official readers and I made up my own material, each day for the next day, right through the year. Good riddance Dick. Run Dick, run. Look. See Jane go. Go go Jane. Go Sally. Go Dick. Out, damned Spot.

At the beginning of November, we saw the last of the sun for the year, the last of the scheduled plane flights ("scheds" to people in the North) and the last of the construction crew. They had still not built the new school, but all the houses for that year were completed, and we had some fine bonfires on the beach as the old dwellings were destroyed. How happy the people were to move into those new houses!

With the dark period then upon us, we knew there could be no more "scheds" until after the return of the sun in February. Sometimes there could be long gaps of as much as five months between mails, and, years before that, the mail came just once a year on the ships of the Eastern Arctic Patrol. So to help overcome this very long isolation and to bring a little Christmas cheer to the people scattered in tiny settlements across the vast tracts of the Arctic, the air force and the post office had put their heads together, and instituted an annual Christmas mail drop by parachute for each of the most northerly settlements beyond the Arctic Circle.

For some months all our mail was directed to Edmonton and held in an air force hangar, and the date of its delivery was scheduled to coincide with the last full moon before Christmas so that there would be maximum visibility in an otherwise dark, frozen world.

Coming in out of the crackling ionosphere on the Hudson's Bay Company's transmitter, a radio message advised us of the approximate timing of the flyover when the big Hercules aircraft would loom out of the darkness, flying low over the edge of the hills, and deliver the goodies, so we prepared for it well beforehand. We advised them that we would light up a large square in the centre of the bay for their use as a visual target. We then unearthed a number of flarepots that were stashed in the warehouse, filled their reservoirs with diesel fuel and took them out onto the sea ice. Panipuk took four of them and placed them at the corners of the square and then spaced four more equidistant on the side. That wasn't much of a show. There should have been more flarepots but no one knew where they were. Maybe they melted down through the ice last spring. So we took a case of school toilet paper from the warehouse, soaked each roll in a bucket of diesel fuel and set these also around the perimeter. We arranged that old Jim, the Hudson's Bay manager, would stay on the radio and give us a final ETA well before the actual arrival of the plane. We stood out there, excited and freezing. No postman was ever awaited with such eager anticipation.

Jim sent a runner out to tell us that the plane was due overhead at 5:10 P.M. so at around five o'clock we lit up all those toilet rolls and waited. Most of the Inuit gathered inside the four long, bright, smoky lines to watch all the action. Sure enough, a few minutes before the ETA, we heard the distant drone of a large plane approaching from south of east, coming towards us from Pond Inlet. It came in high, far overhead, lights flashing, banked around far away to the south almost out of sight, and then turned back towards us, losing altitude gradually and coming straight in towards our target.

As the plane passed with a heavy roar overhead, something momentarily lit by lights inside the hatch shot out from behind. A parachute opened and a great wicker basket filled with mail bags was borne slowly down onto the ice over to one side of the square. The kids all rushed over to retrieve the whole thing, basket, bags and parachute. The plane then gained elevation, circled wide to the west and approached us again from the south. Again a parachute and basket were sent hurtling out the rear hatch to come drifting down onto the centre of the square. Far more mail than we had expected. The plane banked and went off again to the west and south, probably we thought, on its way to Igloolik. But, no, it was coming in again. Surely not yet more mail?

Again the great, gorgeous roar of this flying behemoth from the distant Outside, thrilling us again in the depths of our winter blues. And this time something quite small came tumbling out, barely visible in the moonlight, but down, down it fell, this time with no parachute to support it, and it landed with a soft flump a little way over to the west of our burning square. Katie was the first to reach it. It was a six-foot Christmas tree, a nice thoughtful touch of kindness from the boys in Alberta. The trouble was, of course, that in crashing from that height onto the ice the tree had lost practically every green needle it had ever had. A dark circle of pine needles lay splayed out over the snow all around.

But no matter, it was a Christmas tree, it smelled like a Christmas tree and we picked it up, this poor, lonely, naked skeleton so far from its own kind, and bore it off in happy triumph to the school.

Christmas to the people of Arctic Bay was not the intimate family affair that it was to White people. There were no stockings, no ostentatious decorating or extravagant spending. Santa Claus was just a rather odd, harmless little fancy of the qadlunaat. Christmas was celebrated rather as a communal occasion, a time when everyone came together to feast and dance, as much perhaps a celebration of the solstice as a religious festival, just as it was for early Europeans. We had a party at the school for the kids, and a great communal feast there on the 25th, a blow-out of caribou, seal, char, muktuk, and a great stew made up from unused rations in the warehouse that were supposed to supply the non-existent hostel. And they danced there all through the long night. And the next, and the next.

Many times back in the summer Katie and I had gone hiking up on the hills or walked far around the shores of Adams Sound near the settlement, and we were intrigued at the many little signs of ancient habitation in the area. On one of those walks, I was surprised to find a human jawbone lying amongst the stones above the beach. Just that, nothing more. The teeth were perfect. I looked around and noticed a big pile of rocks not far away, and by lifting one of the rocks from the top, I was able to see some human skeletons inside. One skull was jawless, and sure enough, this jaw fitted perfectly, the teeth fitting exactly together like long-lost friends so I was happy to return it to its rightful owner. Walking on from the gravesite we came upon a number of circular depressions in the ground where several families at a time had camped in much earlier years. These old *qarmar* or ancient house sites are scattered in countless strategic places along the Arctic coast. Generally, they are just circular depressions in the ground, walled with heavy rocks, dug out down to a floor level of two feet or more below the surrounding ground, and located at some short distance back from the water's edge. In some of these there are the remains of great bowhead whale jawbones, or ribs, that were once used to support a roof of skins. The bones were banked around with an insulating wall of sod, where sod existed, or simply walled in wintertime with snowblocks. They were probably much more permanent places, these semi-subterranean homes, than that brilliant invention of the Thule culture people, the snow igloo of classic form, and I wondered to myself many times, staring at those ruins, just how it would have felt to be inside those ancient houses when they were warmed and lit by burning blubber oil, reeking of grease, fish and old skins, and alive with cheerful people.

Well, we were not long in discovering this for ourselves because there still were such homes in use out there at the two closest camps, Abvartok and Qiqertaq. Old Kongasereetook and his wife and their 12-year-old foster daughter Apitak seemed entirely happy in their dark little Hobbit hole in the ground, and we visited them for long hours at a time whenever we travelled to Qiqertaq. From the outside, Kongasereetook's home looked just like any regular igloo with an untidy dark mound of skins and other junk directly behind it. But the round snow igloo was just the entrance porch, and this led down to a lower level, the home itself, the apparent mound of junk. And what a cosy cave it was if you could regard as "cosy" a room that would remain both gloomy and freezing all winter. But this was all relative. It did seem cosy and the old couple appeared entirely content sitting there over the seal-oil lamp, the *kudlik*, with its ten-inch-long yellow flame burning along one side at the edge of the pool of melting blubber. In their own humble way, they seemed to want for nothing. Frozen char lay scattered about, half a seal carcass, warm down sleeping bags on the platform on top of caribou skins, a tin of tobacco, an old gas stove and a few utensils, boxes of store food....

Kongasereetook asked me about my father, and when I explained that my father had died, years before, the old troglodyte declared that in that case he was going to adopt me as his own son. This was no idle pleasantry. Kongasereetook intended to be my new father, and he was going to teach me all that he knew so that I might be able to live in his land and become an Inuk like himself. The declaration having been made in all seriousness, the deed of adoption was then considered done. Apitak, my adoptive sister, had come into the old couple's lives in just such a way with no more formality than that. Luckily, he did appreciate that Katie and I would have to return to Arctic Bay since I had to work there, but that made no difference. So thereafter, Katie and I always had to spend long hours visiting these good people whenever we travelled to Qiqertaq but Kongasereetook never succeeded in bringing about my metamorphosis and, I hope, never quite appreciated how inept his pupil or how ludicrously hopeless was the task he had set himself.

Nevertheless, we stayed in touch with the old folk on and off for years, long after leaving Arctic Bay, sending them news of our lives and our travels, and photos and little presents from the other corners of the Earth, a vase from Greece, an ornate but wicked-looking knife from Ethiopia.... And periodically we received in reply the most endearing and delightful little letters from Apitak, my sister.

Atagutsiak and his wife lived in another such traditional old house at Abvartok, the other camp, an affair of sod, stone, snow and skins. They could have received a little prefab cabin from the government if they had wanted it, but they seemed quite content in their happy hollow. Again, there was the surprise coming in to such a home in having to step unexpectedly down well below ground level, first through one door three feet high, along a bit, and then through another. Atagutsiak was a much more modern man than Kongasereetook. He spoke limited English with some confidence and had plastered the inside of his sod walls with pages from newspapers and magazines (not that he knew how to read them). He loved to regale us with tales of his earlier years, travelling in distant areas along with his dogs, times when he felt truly free, a complete man, dependent on no one but himself, the only human within the vast, frozen horizon.

But he must have been a little dependent on the outside world even then. Kongasereetook had demonstrated to me his prowess in striking sparks from a flint and coaxing a smouldering glow of paper (something I found impossible). But Atagutsiak the Modern depended on matches, and he once described a time when he almost ran out of matches many days' travel from other people, potentially a disastrous thing. He had the old-fashioned type of match with white stems of wax and thread, and, to spin the last of them out, he split each match lengthways, including the head, and ended up with four new matches from each original one. He also told of the hardship of being without tobacco for his pipe. He always carried his tobacco loose in his trouser pockets, and on one long journey when there was no more left, he cut up and smoked the bottom hems of the pockets themselves.

Atagutsiak was a true leader of men, a laughing optimist, a man whose home was always replete with seals, fish and caribou, as well as the things he and his wife needed from the alien outside world. He was employed every year by small groups of *qadlunaat* who scratched around in the hills near Arctic Bay every summer, looking for a mine. The rumour was that there was plenty of lead and zinc in them thar hills, and so it proved of course, for, not so many years later, a mine did indeed open close by Arctic Bay at Nanasivik.

Being a camp leader, Atagutsiak had wanted to extend his skills so that he could understand motors better, and make repairs to the new machines that people were buying and using, outboard motors and the like. He had the first and only snowmobile in the whole area. (The end of all our dogs, I wondered?) So he had been sent south a year earlier to Nova Scotia, together with a number of other Baffin Islanders, on a motor-maintenance course run by the Canadian navy in Halifax. I would have thought that this remarkable man, still living largely in the ancient ways, would have been greatly impressed with Halifax and the wondrous technologies of the teeming, civilized South. But no, not at all. He sniffed, and looked a little sour and disgusted when I asked him about his visit down there.

"No woman," was all he said.

From the time when the sea was first frozen, all through the long winter and on even into July, Katie accompanied me on all my journeys out to the camps. I thought she might have backed out during the dark period, when it fell to 40 below with a breeze from the north, but no, she persevered as long as I did, so that we were always able to relish those wonderful but extremely cold journeys together. Katie of course wasn't a teacher, and there was no more chance of work for her in Arctic Bay than there had been at Split Lake, so there wasn't much for her to do

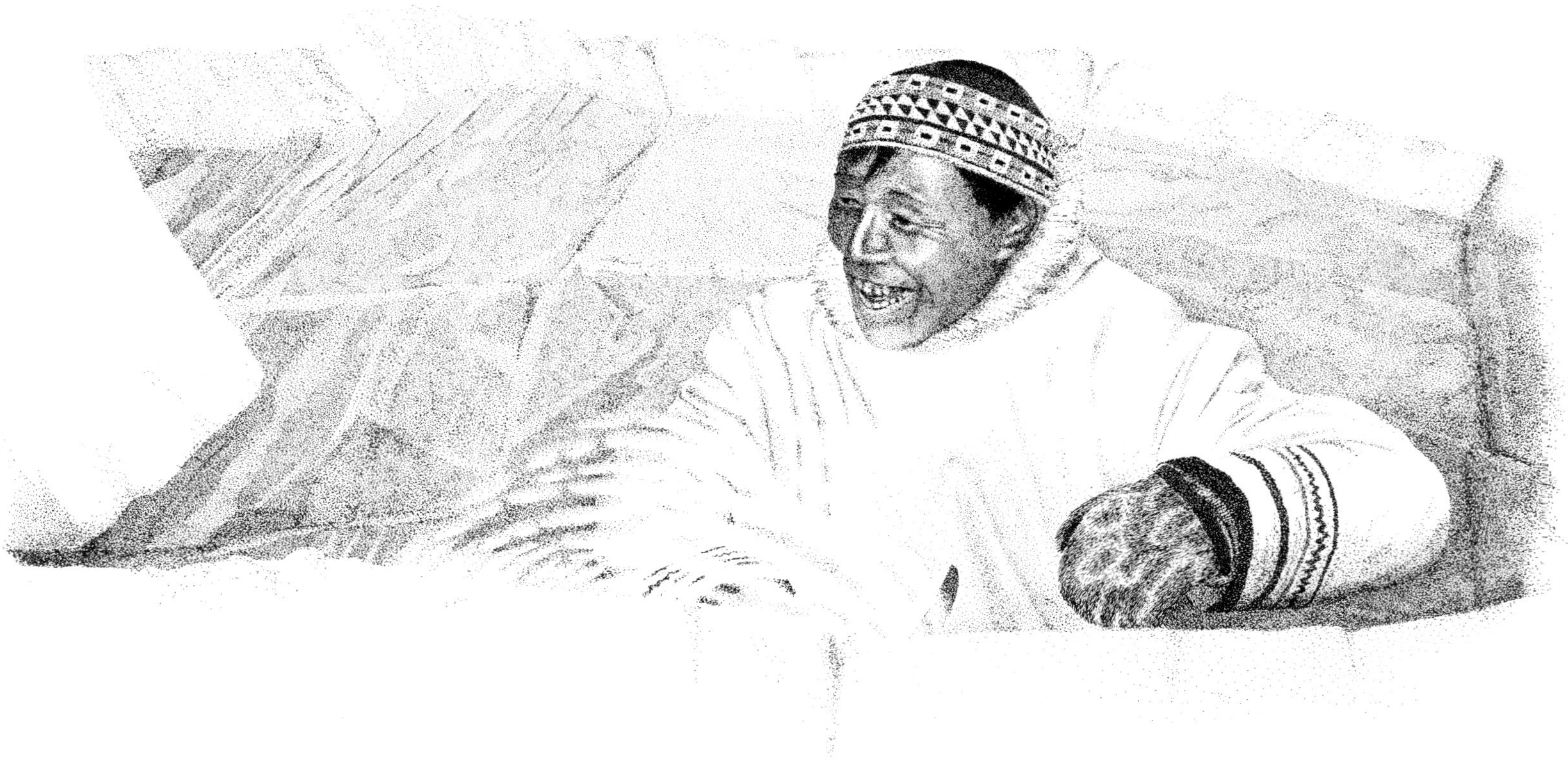

Atagutsiak.

outside of home. This might have driven a lesser woman mad, but Katie managed always to keep busy and cheerful. Some of the local women got into the habit of dropping by at our house to visit, and despite the profound language barrier Katie became well known to them and formed a few fast friendships. At the end of every school day, an assortment of people, men and women, drifted into our house clutching bundles of rags to their bosoms. Katie and I then cleared the table, got out a booklet of government forms, and prepared for the daily intake of soapstone carvings. We had some very talented artists in Arctic Bay, two or three quite outstanding, and one of my many extra jobs was to buy carvings on behalf of the government. This was an extremely interesting little sideline, but it was a lot of extra work too and I fretted constantly that while I didn't want to pay excessively, I wanted to be really sure that each carving, slowly unwrapped and revealed with such modesty and shyness from its wrapping of rags, was, at all events, very well paid for. In that regard Katie was always at my side to help me with a second opinion on the value of each piece, and gradually through the winter our prices tended to creep higher and higher, so impressed were we by the beauty and skill shown in every piece of sculpture.

They came, too, with items of clothing, hoping that the new teacher and his wife would be in need of a pair of sealskin *kamiks* (boots), or mitts, or a woollen toque with "Arctic Bay" spelled in letters around the rim, or something else. This became a problem because after the first few weeks we already *had* all those things, extra parkas, scarves, skin boots and every garment that could be thought of. The clothing was beautifully made, but there were not enough *qadlunaat* to buy it all.

Old Elisapee, wife of Alooloo who was one of the best carvers, was always dropping by to visit Katie and eat another five of her cookies. She was invariably good natured and well disposed towards the two of us. Elisapee had made our *kamiks* in the fall, and for some months we wore them nearly all the time, indoors and out. When we first went to her house to be measured for these skin boots, there was great merriment at the sheer size of my feet, and in the midst of all that, Alooloo made as if to go off hunting for the extra seal that such feet would call for. Still, Elisapee got it right and, when she brought them to us, they fitted perfectly. After a few weeks, the smelly *kamiks* got rather hard, black and stiff, the smell of sweaty feet competing with the rancid reek of seal fat which accompanied all *kamiks*. So Katie tried scrubbing them, without seeming really to get them back to their nice new condition. The *kamiks* were hanging to dry in the hallway one day when Elisapee came in to visit and when she saw their condition she took them down and showed Katie what had to be done to get them right. She folded a large part of the sole, stuck it into her mouth and began to masticate the thing. Like so many others', Elisapee's teeth were all worn down to a straight line and we then understood why. Elisapee soon perceived that this *qadluna* woman would never learn how to do a job like that properly, so she took the *kamiks* away and brought them back next day as soft and supple as they had been when new. I felt very humble about my *kamiks* after that, wearing them only on special occasions, hanging them up carefully, keeping them scrupulously clean, and treating them with a certain new reverence and respect.

Gradually, the people of the little settlement accustomed themselves to their dramatically improved circumstances, learned how to handle electricity, conserve heat, cook in an oven, use a vacuum cleaner, guard against accidents, and generally, in a thousand ways, how to manage a modern home. Including paying the rent. The sudden appearance of all these wonderful amenities in the settlement had the inevitable result that before the winter was through, most of the people in the camps began to wonder (aloud sometimes) what they were sitting out there for, and many of them expressed an interest in abandoning their quiet, simple, hunting lives out along the coast for the relative glitter of the settlement. The new, three-bedroom houses, of course, were the big drawing card but the camp people must also have envied the other amenities of the settlement — the food store, the excitement of plane scheds, the school, medical and social services and plenty of neighbours to gossip with. This meant that the already very high enrolment at the school would get higher again the next year, far too many for one teacher (as indeed there already were). But there was still only one teacher's residence, so Katie and I decided to ask for a transfer out so that a teaching couple could be posted there instead. We applied for the northernmost of all schools, Grise Fiord, and we got it.

Still, the superintendent asked me to stay on for part of the summer to lay the groundwork for these changes and to give camp children a chance to gain a little more English. This seemed an impractical idea to me, but it offered the possibility of more travel to the camps, which we enjoyed, plus a bit more money in our cruising fund, so I happily agreed.

As it turned out, the intended benefits of my remaining through the summer were pretty elusive. Many of the families remained scattered at various temporary localities along the coast, and, at the settlement itself, quite in defiance of the superintendent's intentions, they came and went so unpredictably, and slept at such inconvenient hours, right through the day sometimes, that there was not a great deal I could do, no clear program that could be followed. The best that could be done was to be out and about with the kids, those who happened to be awake and interested, doing fun things with them, hiking, hunting, drawing, singing, playing, making little cane baskets as cages for lemmings.... They absorbed more English that way in any case than in the stuffy, structured, classroom approach so dear to the hearts of all superintendents of schools.

In early August, Dick, one of the pilots flying for Wheldy Phipps out of Resolute, came to see me. It was such a drag in the summer having to meet each plane away across on the other side of the bay. Without a road of any kind to the swampy old landing site over there, and no vehicles in any case, we had to use dog teams and komatiks, struggling over the rotten ice, leaping from floe to floe, rescuing the mail bags from a dunking in the open leads and sometimes getting a bootful of frigid seawater in our gumboots, or, instead of all that, staying on the land and dragging the komatik over the dry, rocky shore. It took ages, and the pilots got annoyed if we were late meeting them.

Dick pointed out a bit of flat beach over on the western shore near the settlement. "Why don't you just smooth that off?" he asked. "We could land on it and it would be far more convenient. Wheldy reckons it would be fine. Push the rocks out of the way into the water. Extend it a little with the tractor. It would be okay."

I was a bit horrified, but he was the expert and if he thought it would be all right why should I argue? We had been given a fund for "road repairs" so I used that fund to hire Levi the tractor driver. He put in a couple of days pushing and raking and smoothing it out with the blade on the Payloader. I was still a bit aghast at the thought of a plane actually using that new strip. It seemed so short. There was a long mountain slope rising up at one end, and the other end dropped straight off into the waters of the bay. No room for error. We told Wheldy that his new strip was ready, but to use maximum discretion before committing to it.

Late in August, it was time to tie up all our loose ends, pack our bags and fly north over the waters of Lancaster Sound and the icecaps of Devon Island to our new home on Ellesmere Island.

In the chaos of final departure from our home at Arctic Bay, Katie's cat, Nellie, disappeared. Nellie had been a great curiosity to the people of Arctic Bay, the first cat that most of them had ever seen. When we had first arrived at Arctic Bay, little clusters of children would gather outside our house, waiting at a window in hopes of glimpsing this very remarkable animal. Then, if Katie lifted Nellie up to the window they would go into an absolute state of ecstasy, jumping up and down and laughing. Before long, adults too came along to wait at the window and see for themselves if what the kids said they saw was actually true. Many times, when adults came to visit us and sat down on the sofa, Nellie would jump up to settle on their laps, and they would respond by leaping back onto their feet in alarm, wide-eyed with astonishment and uncertainty.

While Katie was outside calling "Nellie! Nellie! Where are you Nellie?" all along the road, looking underneath all the new houses for her lost cat, I took a final honey bag out of its pail in the bathroom, knotted it and bore it forth to be deposited in the steel drum outside. But there was a wooden packing case in the hallway, almost ready to go, except that the top had still not been hammered down. A nail sticking out from the case snagged the honey bag as I hurried past and the awful thing gushed its horrible contents onto the hallway floor. Horrors! Luckily, Aibilie was not around to appreciate my idiocy, and luckily too I had most of the mess cleaned up before Katie returned.

There was still no cat and the plane was already in the air out of Resolute, when finally by following the faint sounds of rustling paper and the occasional muffled "mew," we found her. She had been shut into the half-empty bottom drawer of my steel filing cabinet.

Our departure from Arctic Bay was the first-ever take-off from Levi's new airstrip at the edge of the settlement, a nerve-wracking experience (at least for us if not for the pilot), and when we landed at Grise Fiord ours was the first plane to use the new landing strip there. We were sorry indeed to leave such a happy little community as Arctic Bay, but on the other hand, we were overwhelmed by the stunning beauty of our new surroundings on the shores of faraway Ellesmere. Two years there, we decided, and we would get that boat, buy a sextant, and sail away.

A Dog's Life

Throughout the North in earlier times, wherever there were people who lived off the land, there were dogs. They were chained in long lines along the banks of the rivers, staked individually at the edge of streams and lakes, penned inside wire compounds, tied to trees at the Indian encampments of the western mountains, marooned loose on small islands through the long Mackenzie summers, or left to roam loose as bear-guards around the far scattered camps of the Arctic coast. They came in various sizes, from medium to huge, and in all colours. They were housed in little log-cabin kennels, or small dog-igloos of snow, or (mostly) never at all, and when used they were hitched one behind the other in single file, decked out with saddle bags, or tied individually ahead of great heavy sleds in an Arctic fan hitch. They were incredibly tough, as they had to be, and as draught animals, well- or ill-treated, fed or not, they served their human masters well. The advent of the noisy gasoline snowmobile resulted in the rapid disappearance everywhere of the family dog team, and for those who admired and felt affectionately for those dogs, there was a feeling of great sorrow and regret that their days were numbered, but at the same time a relief, too, that the hard abuse, neglect, starvation and suffering of so many of those animals would now no longer have to be.

My first experience with a dog team was at Fort Norman in the fifties. The Mounties there had a large compound of Samoyed dogs from Siberia, and were breeding them to supply

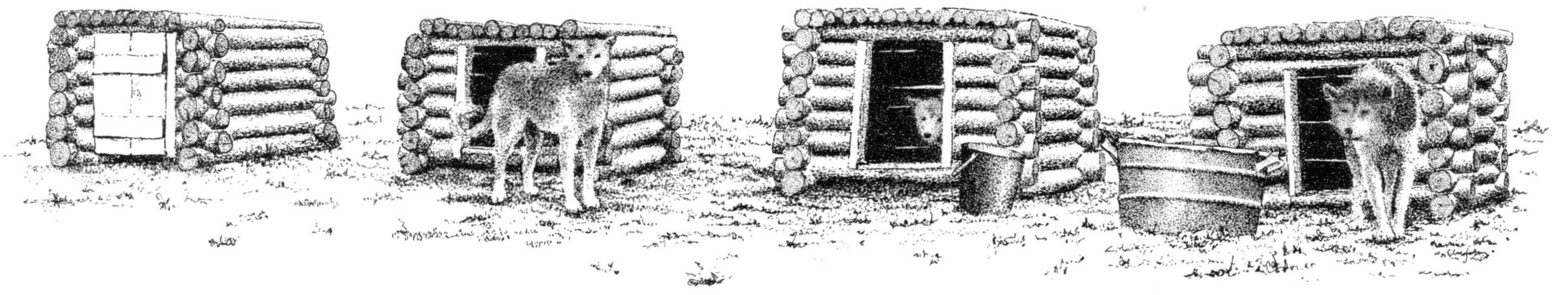

Dog kennels of the Cree.

police teams all across the Arctic. These dogs had to be exercised and I volunteered to do it, taking my first team of six down the river bank and out onto the ice, bound for Willow Lake, some hours away on the trail. I had to cross the ice of the Bear River which had piled high into ridges at freeze-up time. I was quite unaccustomed to the speed and motion, and in riding the jolting toboggan over those high, hard, chaotic ice-ranges, I was thrown off into the snow. The cheechako having been unseated, the Samoyeds, still fresh and peppery, took off in wild abandon and it was long over an hour before I finally caught up with them in the bush.

When I found them, they had their lateral harnesses snagged around a stump, and looked at me as if to say, "Where have you been all the while?" I released the leather harness from its hook, hauled the leader back onto the trail and we were soon on our way again, tinkly sleigh bells ringing rhythmically with every step. I should have trailed a long line behind the toboggan as an emergency brake, and thereafter I made sure I always did.

Despite an inauspicious start, I enjoyed the excitement and pleasure of the trail and went out many times again, not just at Fort Norman but at other settlements too, both in the bush and on the Arctic coast. But it was at Arctic Bay most especially that our dog mileages mounted up to something respectable. Katie and I had never seen as many dogs before as we saw at Arctic Bay. Every hunter there had a huge team, and they were staked out in long lines of chain all along the empty gravel slope above the high-water mark. And what dogs! They were all quite amazingly massive, much bigger than the wolves from which they were at least partially (and perhaps not so distantly) descended, and while stories abounded in the bush of the Indian dogs staked around the camps being killed by wolves, there were no such tales on the Arctic coast, nor, looking at those massive huskies, any likelihood either. Those Eskimo dogs could each have taken on three scrawny malamutes of the forest and had them for supper. Their paws left a print as large as the palm of my hand. They were all huge, heavily furred, active and completely unabashed at the presence of humans.

They didn't seem to regard mankind as other dogs do. We were not their worshipful masters, and I hate to think what a pack of such dogs could have done to an unfamiliar solitary person if they were all prowling on the loose, for they could then display the boldness and aggressive confidence that is part of the psychology of the pack (exactly the same assertive, collectively reinforced boldness that can sometimes be observed in a similar "pack" of humans). Once, at the end of a long day of travel out of Arctic Bay, Katie and I watched while the dogs' owner decided to feed his hungry team of 15. He had just the one seal to feed them. Commercially, the skin was not worth worrying about and he was too tired to bother dividing the seal into 15 equal portions. So he dumped the carcass out on the ice near our camp, and released the entire team all at once by casting off the toggle that held all their traces to the komatik; there was an instant snarling maelstrom of fury and dog fur where the carcass had been, and in an incredibly short time there was nothing left whatever except blood on the snow. God help a vulnerable person attacked by such a team.

The existence of dogs in such numbers at Arctic Bay, and their sheer size, were testimony to the rich hunting that could be had around the North Baffin coast most of the time. When Katie and I first arrived in Arctic Bay in the summer of 1966, fresh from years amongst the Cree, we were astonished at the dog population. The whales had still not come in and the dogs mostly were having to get by on the occasional seal.

There was an animal welfare organization in Ontario at the time which seemed to have had its attention drawn to the neglect and starvation suffered by so many dogs in the North, and they had shipped large quantities of dry dog food for distribution to hunters when times were thin. This had arrived on the beach off the supply ship at the end of August. I told the local men that it was intended to be held for use in times of bad hunting and dire shortage, but the hunters couldn't have cared less who sent it or why, and worrying about what may never happen wasn't their style. They wanted the food right now, so they got it and it was gone in an afternoon.

After the summer, as the first snows covered the land, the dogs still had a fair period of idleness and enchainment to go before their working season would begin. That would come with the freezing of the sea, the highway and lifeblood of the Eskimo people. Except for the odd mother with pups, and a few young half-grown dogs running loose, they were all kept in those dog-

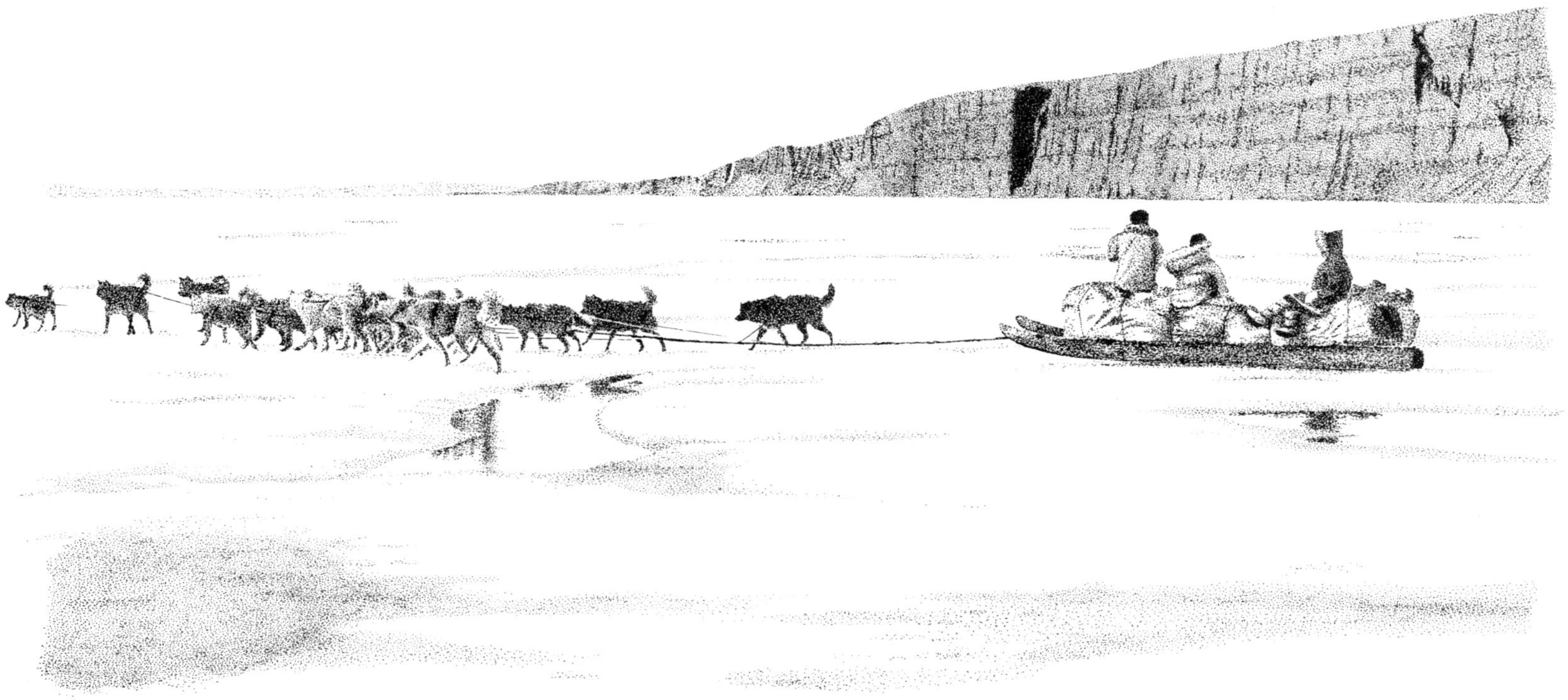

Dog team from Arctic Bay.

lines above the gravel beach. Once the narwhals started coming in, the dogs fared a lot better, for the people took from the narwhal carcasses only the outer muktuk for themselves and the rest went to the ever-hungry huskies.

Just as wolves never bark, neither did those Eskimo dogs. For myself, given the enormous numbers of dogs at Arctic Bay, it was a sort of sweet relief not to have to listen to the kind of unstoppable neurotic yelping that distinguishes so many ordinary domestic dogs. Instead, the huskies made their own highly distinctive noise, and it was a sound that seemed to us just as beautiful, evocative, wild and haunting, as the house mutt's bark is harsh and irritating. It was like the sweet sound of the loon on a quiet evening when one might have had to endure the maddening noise of a chainsaw.

This sound would start usually when our increasingly frozen little world was stilled and darkened. No wind, no longer people walking around outside doing things. No disturbances. The ration of whale meat would have been long gone and long digested, and the next frozen lump would be long in coming. The rattling of chains would have stopped, and there would be nothing of interest, nothing to do except to settle for another endless night inside the hard, well-trodden, pissed-upon perimeters of snow that the chains allowed. There is wonderful insulation in snow, but there was none whatever in those hard icy dog-circles.

One solitary dog would sit up, raise its muzzle high towards the aurora-lit sky and give full vent to a sad howl, long-held and heart-felt, rising high and then falling away slowly to a softer, lower note, and stopping. Again, two or three times with long silences between, the same plaintive crying soliloquy. The other dogs would now all be listening, and one other would decide to make it a duet, and these two would go at it for a short while, imitating, answering, harmonizing. A third would then take up the cry, and then a fourth, transforming the yearning duet into a chorus, and before very long half a hundred dogs would have sat up and joined in.

What a hauntingly magic-sounding thing was this canine cantata. It seemed a little like the preliminary tuning of an orchestra, each working away on a different note. But it was much sadder and more drawn-out than that. It could be heard far and wide throughout the settlement, ringing across the sea ice and up on the dark, star-silhouetted heights above. It would go on and on for 15 or 20 minutes, seeming to evoke the very essence of wilderness and melancholy. And then it would fade finally as the choristers gave up one by one and settled down. One last sad solitary cry of the heart, and then the silence would descend again over them all.

True, it was a dog's life on those chains, but is that really what they were all going on about? I can only assume that this wonderful song, so often repeated through the winter and ringing clearly yet in my memory, must have sprung from some innate dog-emotion, some canine religion, something deeper than mere complaint over their hard enchainment. Perhaps after all it wasn't out of melancholy at all. Wolves howl, too.

Back at sealift time in early September we had received all the building materials for the construction of a student hostel. At that time the Arctic Bay population was scattered around the coast in various localities. About half of their number had moved permanently into the settlement itself, but the rest were still living more or less year-round at three camps at locations to the north and south of Arctic Bay along the shores of Admiralty Inlet. The government of course was fretting that all those camp children were missing out on their education, so the idea had been to set up a small hostel at the settlement to accommodate those kids right there where the school was.

Nice idea, but the boss of the construction crew came to see me one day in early October. Forget the hostel, he said. It wasn't going to be built. His crew had been sent in after sealift to build 12 three-bedroom prefab homes for the local people then living in the settlement, getting them out of those hovels, and in doing so they had had to cannibalize building materials intended for the new hostel. Half the hostel had gone! Typical Northern snafu, I thought to myself. I eventually realized that in fact it would never be built, and for a very good reason. The hostel was needed only because families were living on the land a long way from the settlement. But because all those nice, new, three-bedroom homes, heated, watered, electrified, furnished and serviced, were being provided to the people right where there was a school, store and medical facilities, the camps were doomed anyway. In the face of all these new facilities, nobody would want to continue staying out there, and it was increasingly obvious that before much longer, the families at those far locations would all be moving into the settlement, lock, stock and barrel.

Not yet though, and in the meantime I had to resume what had become standard practice in the past. Each weekend through the winter I would have to travel out to one or another of those three camps, deliver a certain amount of materials and do a bit of on-the-spot teaching with the children who lived there.

There was only one way to get there, and that was by dog team, going along with one or another of the local hunters whenever that was possible, and staying overnight with the local camp people, or in our own igloo. So Katie and I piled up the dog mileages that winter. We outfitted ourselves with full caribou-skin suits, parkas and pants, to go over everything else, just as the local people wore on their long journeys. I closed the settlement school at midday on Friday and the two of us lashed our grub box, sleeping bags and school books onto a komatik (the Eskimo sled or *qamotiq*) and took off, crashing wildly over the tidal ridges at the shoreline and out onto the smoother surface of the bay, south to Qiqertaq, the island camp, or even occasionally to Iqalulik, the fishing place 50 miles distant, or north to Abvartok on the north side of Strathcona Sound. The camp children were happy to have books, pencils and crayons in their hands for a few hours every other Saturday or so, and they did learn a little English, but I didn't deceive myself that I was making any big difference. Still, they seemed to enjoy it, and so did we, although the long, bitterly cold hours on the trail took some getting used to. The cold itself I can hardly even begin to describe.

In the settlement, you basically just went, most of the time, from one heated building to another, and on the way, well-dressed though you may have been against it, you would think to yourself, "Damn me, but this has to be the coldest day yet!" The children would pile in on top of each other after recess, a swarm of flailing parkas and swirling vapour at the entrance porch, each child crying out "*Eekay!*" ("cold!") as they poured in to the warmth. So they felt it too, although far less than I did. But in the settlement it didn't matter very much. You would soon be through another porch and into another warm room, and when you slammed the door behind you, the stunning Arctic cold was left outside where it belonged.

It was only when we left the settlement that we had to face reality, and live with it. Through the worst of the winter Katie and I wore our caribou-skin parkas and pants, sheepskin boots over sealskin boots, heavy, sealskin-and-duffel mitts over woollen gloves, thick longjohns, sweaters, knitted toques and so much insulative junk it seemed sometimes we could hardly move. But on the trail, we still got cold, and had to jump off the komatik periodically to run alongside and keep the circulation working.

Running alongside, though, had its own problems. Not only were we hampered by the sheer bulk of our own clothing, but as soon as we jumped off, the dogs immediately sensed the sudden lightening of their load and they would speed up and leave us well behind, flailing and panting. Also, at first, whenever Katie jumped off she couldn't seem to allow for the fact that the ice surface that she was leaping down onto was already receding rapidly under her, and on our first journey she kept falling flat on her face as she jumped from the komatik. It must have amused Tarktoo, and Akitirk, and Aeyout and Eenoogoo and the other hunters who took us out on those journeys, but though they laughed at almost everything, still they were much too polite to laugh at us. We never observed any native adult jumping off and running, the way Katie and I did, though children sometimes would. The native people managed to stay warm no matter what. They just seemed to have been better constructed.

It was Tarktoo, mostly, who took us to the camp at Abvartok. His elderly parents still lived there so he was always very willing to make the journey. He worked for a time as my janitor at the school and we liked him a lot. He was a quiet, congenial man, proud father of a young and growing family, with a ready smile and an unusually dark complexion which was what his name meant: "dark."

The first time we went with Tarktoo to Abvartok, it was well into the winter and the brief daylight at midday was already fading before we even got away, so most of the journey was made in the starry darkness, like many subsequent journeys in the dark period.

The most exciting part of the journey from the settlement to the Abvartok camp was the crossing of the mountain pass. Most of the distance was over the sea ice of the next fiord to the north, but to reach that we had to cross an isthmus, going up over a steep saddle that rises up from Arctic Bay itself and then down to the sea ice on the other side. In either direction it was a wild, dramatic, exciting experience that was not for the faint of heart. The climb was slow and easy, the dogs having to put their full weight into their harnesses, and we trudged slowly behind, happy to have the chance of exercise without burning our lungs in a minus 35° sprint. At the summit, Tarktoo laid the long whip lightly, gently, over the backs of the dogs as a command to lie down, and then he prepared for the descent.

The dog whip was an invariable part of a man's equipment. This had a short handle onto which was bound a supple, thin, 30- or 40-foot length of sealskin tapering gradually and delicately to the end. To the dogs, the whip was both the symbol and the instrument of a man's authority, and as any laggard with a slack trace would learn before long, a practised driver sitting on the komatik could land a perfect, effortless crack right onto (or alongside) the ear of any recalcitrant slacker almost every time. The boys at school loved practising with their own smaller whips, flicking ptarmigan feathers and gum wrappers off the snowbanks at recess time.

Tarktoo gave the dogs a breather at the top of the pass for they would need all their energy on the way down the other side. Once we were launched into the long downward run, there would be no stopping, no slowing down, and everything would be more or less out of control, so we had to be well seated and we had to hang on like hell. Tarktoo went to a great deal of trouble to prepare for the long downhill run, and his caution was well founded, for a little earlier in that season, while hurtling down this same hill on his own, he had managed to impale himself on his own harpoon. He rooted around on the komatik and hauled out a heavy polypropylene cargo sling, ends spliced together, which had been liberated at sealift time from the equipment on board the supply ship. He looped this loosely over the forward projection of one of the two sled runners. That was to be our brake, giving us, when it was released, the only friction we could hope for on the way down.

Tarktoo called to the dogs, stirring them to their feet, and then we were off, easily at first. The dogs seemed to know what they were in for and hurried ahead, but kept glancing back over their shoulders. The slope increased and the komatik picked up speed. So did the dogs, and in no time at all we were plunging pell-mell down that dangerous trail, the heavily laden komatik catapulting from one side to the other, bouncing off rocks, leaping over snowbanks and out across the empty void beyond to another bone-juddering crash, hurtling ever onwards in a frenzy of flying snow and frantic dogs. Tarktoo released the polypropylene brake and at the point where the heavy rope looped under the komatik runner, the snow flew up in a white geyser, but nothing whatever could stop that komatik and the brake seemed hardly to have any effect.

The dogs were racing for their lives, but one allowed his trace to fall slack for a moment. The loop in his trace was overtaken by one of the komatik runners. The dog was jerked to a sudden stop while the komatik surged on over the trace, and then he was being dragged backwards behind us, feet in the air, a yelping bundle of flying fur in a cloudy wake of flying snow. Then another dog was caught in the same way, and another, and this time the heavy komatik rode directly over both of them. I felt the slight thud of their bodies through the sled. The unambiguous sounds of dog-agony behind us kept the others in front flailing desperately on and on. But eventually, we levelled out and reached the bottom, and the komatik slewed a little sideways on its brake and came to a stop. Tarktoo, Katie and I all looked at each other for a moment and then together we laughed. Amazingly, the two dogs that were run over seemed to be quite uninjured. How could that be? They ought to have been mangled into mincemeat.

We stopped there on the shoreline to make tea, an ever-recurring necessity to the travelling hunters. There was a long way to go yet, and the dogs deserved a rest. While the snow was melting in the pot on his little camp stove, Tarktoo heaved the komatik upside down, and swept the whalebone runners with a segment of polar bear skin, the white fur still attached. He then took successive mouthfuls of water from the pot, brought his face close down over the runner, and spurted the water from his mouth in a stream all along the bare whalebone surface, following immediately behind with his polar bear brush to smooth and spread the water evenly all along as an instant film of ice. I knew that this wasn't as easy as it looked, but he did it in a way that made it seem quite effortless, and the end result was perfect. The going would now be easier for the dogs.

This was all done, like everything else, in the dim, shadowy light of the stars alone, and a slight aurora. I was amazed at the skills of those people.

Usually, after a couple of such tea-breaks as this along the trail, Tarktoo (or the other driver) and I would feel the need to have a leak before resuming, and would do so. And so of course would Katie. But in her case Tarktoo would gallantly position himself between her and the dogs, with his long whip at the ready, flipping it back and forth over the snow as a reminder to his team, because the dogs were ever hopeful that Katie's (or anyone else's) needs might prove to have been greater than they actually were, and that the first one to get there might be rewarded with a warm lunch right there on the snow. This too was the frequent complaint of our Australian friend, Judy Wilson, who also travelled a lot along the coasts of Baffin to teach at those camps in earlier times. Such was the hunger of those dogs, and such were the hazards of the trail!

Tarktoo had 12 dogs in his team and they were really good steady pullers. He only had to use the whip a few times, and even then the whip hardly touched its target, although of course the dog at the receiving end of that long whip, touched or not, always let out a shriek as if it was being murdered, a reaction that served as a helpful reminder to all the rest not to lose their enthusiasm for the journey.

We travelled many times back to Abvartok, and to Qiqertaq also, places where we greatly enjoyed the company of warm, happy people and delightful children, and where we struggled mightily to overcome what at first seemed an almost insurmountable language barrier, while we (literally enough) chewed the fat with them, or the frozen caribou, or char, or boiled spare ribs of seal, and shared with them our porridge, baked beans and pork and Katie's homemade bread. Sometimes we camped in the home of one of the families, sleeping on the floor. Sometimes we slept in our own igloo. The first time we tried this, we had arrived at the camp with the hunter Kanayu who offered us the hospitality of his home. But we sensed that Kanayu's wife might have been a little self-conscious at the state of her home with all that seal blood and dirt and litter all around and then to have a couple of *qadlunaat* on her doorstep. ... So we asked Kanayu if he could help us build a snowhouse and he very readily agreed with some amusement. I helped him cut the blocks, in between taking pictures and setting the camera back on upturned blocks so that the still-famished dogs would not tear ravenously at the camera straps as they had done on other occasions.

The igloo was finished in about 30 minutes, and a nice, snug little home it was. I spent some time worriedly chinking in between all the snow blocks with loose snow, but I needn't have bothered as it was as cosy as could be. When we finally decided to go to bed, and started up the little gasoline stove that Kanayu had lent to us, we found that all that heat was rather unnecessary. The doorway was plugged with its own block of snow. Katie had to have a pre-bed leak on the igloo floor in preference to baring her soul to the prowling dogs outside, though she did hide the meagre evidence with a handful of snow, and so to bed.

Ventilation is an important consideration in an igloo, so it was necessary to have a small hole at the top of the dome when the doorway was plugged. This worked well. We turned in at midnight and it was fully ten o'clock next morning before Atagutsiak scrambled up the outside of the igloo and looked down at us through the little ventilation hole and asked if I was going to do any teaching or was I going to sleep there all day?

Although we avoided it in midwinter, we found that igloo living was at least as much fun as any other form of camping. We had to make sure that any lamp or stove was not melting the inside surface of the igloo, and so long as we kept the temperature reasonably below zero, but not too far below, the igloo made a delightful home. We always carried the best sleeping bags available on loan from the government for these camp trips, and with several caribou and polar bear skins underneath, we were always warm and dry.

On one of our trips to Abvartok, we found that all the men were off hunting when we got there, only the women and kids at home. At first, we were rather puzzled at all the three-legged dogs that were hopping around and we couldn't figure out how they had all managed to hurt themselves like that until we saw,

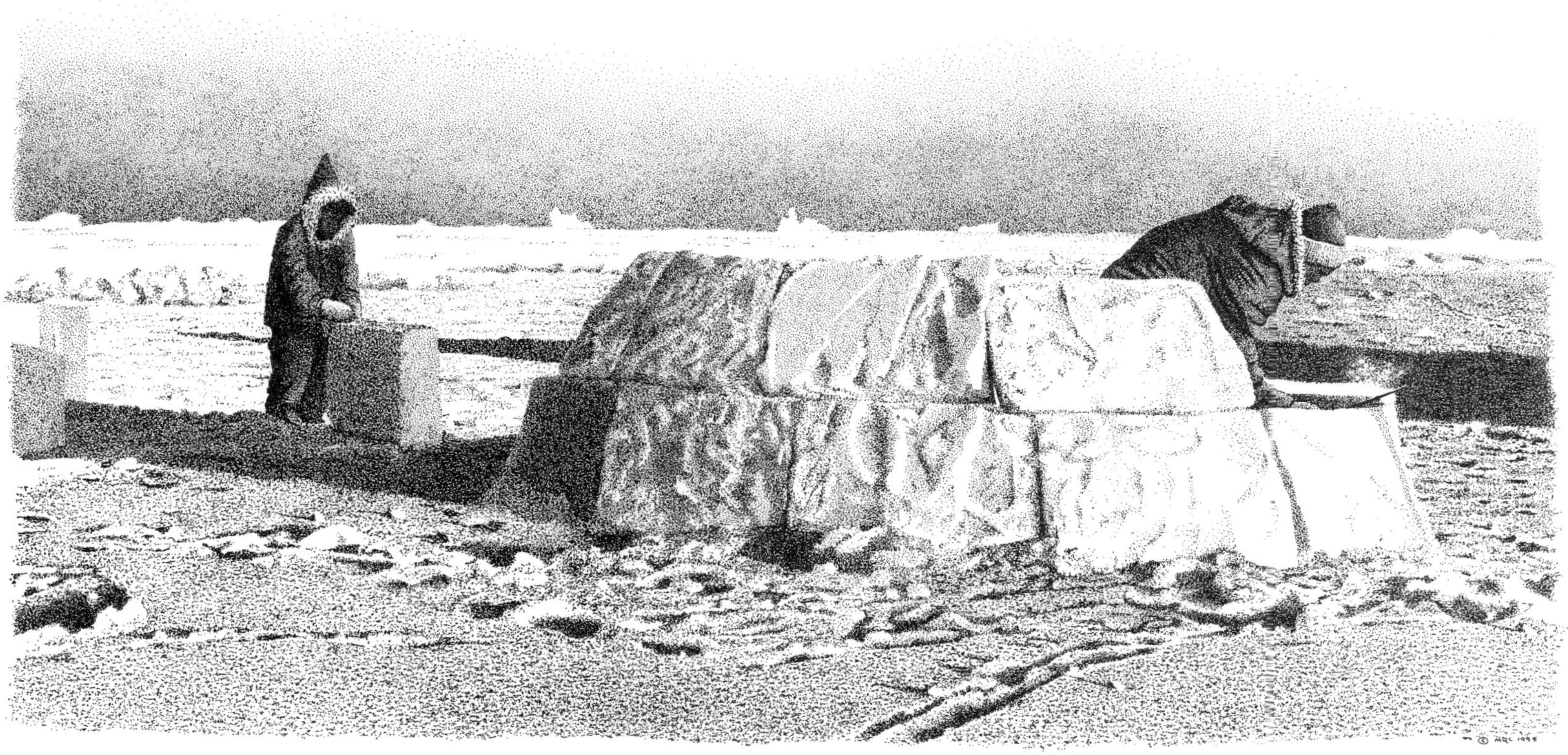

Shelter for the night.

on closer inspection, that they were all hobbled, with one foot tied under their chin to stop them from straying too far. It didn't seem to inconvenience them greatly for they still hopped around at a fair old pace on their other three.

It was Tarktoo also who took us on our very first visit to Qiqertaq, though more commonly we travelled to that camp with Akitirk or Ishuhangituk or one of the other men. After leaving the smooth surface of the bay, we had to cross an area of extremely rough, jumbled ice on Adams Sound. Those komatiks had to be strong, for they took tremendous punishment when riding over rough ice. And so did we. Even so, Tarktoo's 12 dogs got us to Qiqertaq in a record two-and-a-half bitterly cold hours.

We stayed at the home of the camp leader, Kakasheak. There at Qiqertaq, the people had the same deal as those at Abvartok. All had once lived in traditional homes of turf and snow blocks, but three small prefab homes had been provided for them, so some of the families (though not all) now lived in relative luxury, and Kakasheak was one.

Kakasheak was the most considerate host we have ever known, Arctic or otherwise, a cheerful, kind man, endlessly attentive and always anticipating our every need. He wasn't in when we first arrived, just his wife and children were home, so we drank our soup with Tarktoo and ate a sandwich, made a quick tour of the houses to introduce ourselves and I started teaching at three P.M. There were seven school-age kids at Qiqertaq, six girls and one boy, the exact opposite of Abvartok which had one girl and five boys. They were delightful children and very eager to have this little school session on the floor of Kakasheak's home. Halfway through school, the door opened and a frozen white fox body came hurtling through the air, followed a little while later by Kakasheak. This flying fox was put in a corner to thaw a bit prior to being skinned. Kakasheak and his wife took a great interest in all that was going on, and soon after 5:30 P.M. I called it a day.

Kakasheak then skinned the fox and when that was done he produced a huge frozen Arctic char for the family and his visitors. He offered to heat our portions over the stove but we felt that clinging to our own set ways would be a bit decadent and that we needed to do as the Romans, so we ate it raw. We shared bannock around and then black tea. Kakasheak got a bowl of warm water for the family to wash their fishy hands in, and then he brought another bowl of clean water for Katie and me, and a clean towel too. Only, I think, amongst the Arabs of the Sahara did Katie and I ever experience such equally fastidious attention, such immaculate courtesy and attentiveness as we received on each occasion from Kakasheak.

The return journey with Tarktoo from Qiqertaq to Arctic Bay was colder, and was made much slower by the disappearance in the night of three of Tarktoo's dogs, they having taken absence without leave and gone back on their own to the settlement. We were almost up to the entrance of Adams Sound when we came upon one of the camp men, Angnayoomayook, alone away out on the ice, in that classic pose of the Arctic hunter with his nose nearly touching the ice and his bottom sticking up in the air, rifle ready, harpoon on the snow, completely clothed in caribou skins, waiting and waiting, silent and motionless over an almost invisible *aglu*, with a soft ptarmigan feather lying over the tiny hole to betray the rush of air that would precede a surfacing seal. What patience and endurance there is in hunting a seal! Just so much as wiggle your toes and it will be gone.

We kept well clear of Angnayoomayook, not to disturb his hunting, and stopped to make tea, but he gave up his long cold vigil and joined us for a cup, before going back to it.

Getting to the far distant camp at Iqalulik was for us more of a problem, because the hunters preferred to cover the much greater distance with an overnight camp somewhere along the way. The distance could be covered, at a pinch, in one very long day, but that was bad economics and bad management, for it demanded a great deal of the dogs and at the same time offered no opportunity to do any hunting. How do you drive dogs without feeding them? Rather than carry dog food with them, which White people would want to do, the people always hunted along the way, and what was the hurry to get there anyway? In life it was the journey that mattered, not the arrival. (It was the same for Katie and me when we went voyaging.) So since none of this could be reconciled with our alien notion of inflexible weekends, we had to put Iqalulik off until the springtime when dear old Eenoogoo and his smiling, gracious wife took us there, camping together all four of us and a horde of dogs, on a desolate beach away beyond Qiqertaq. Every now

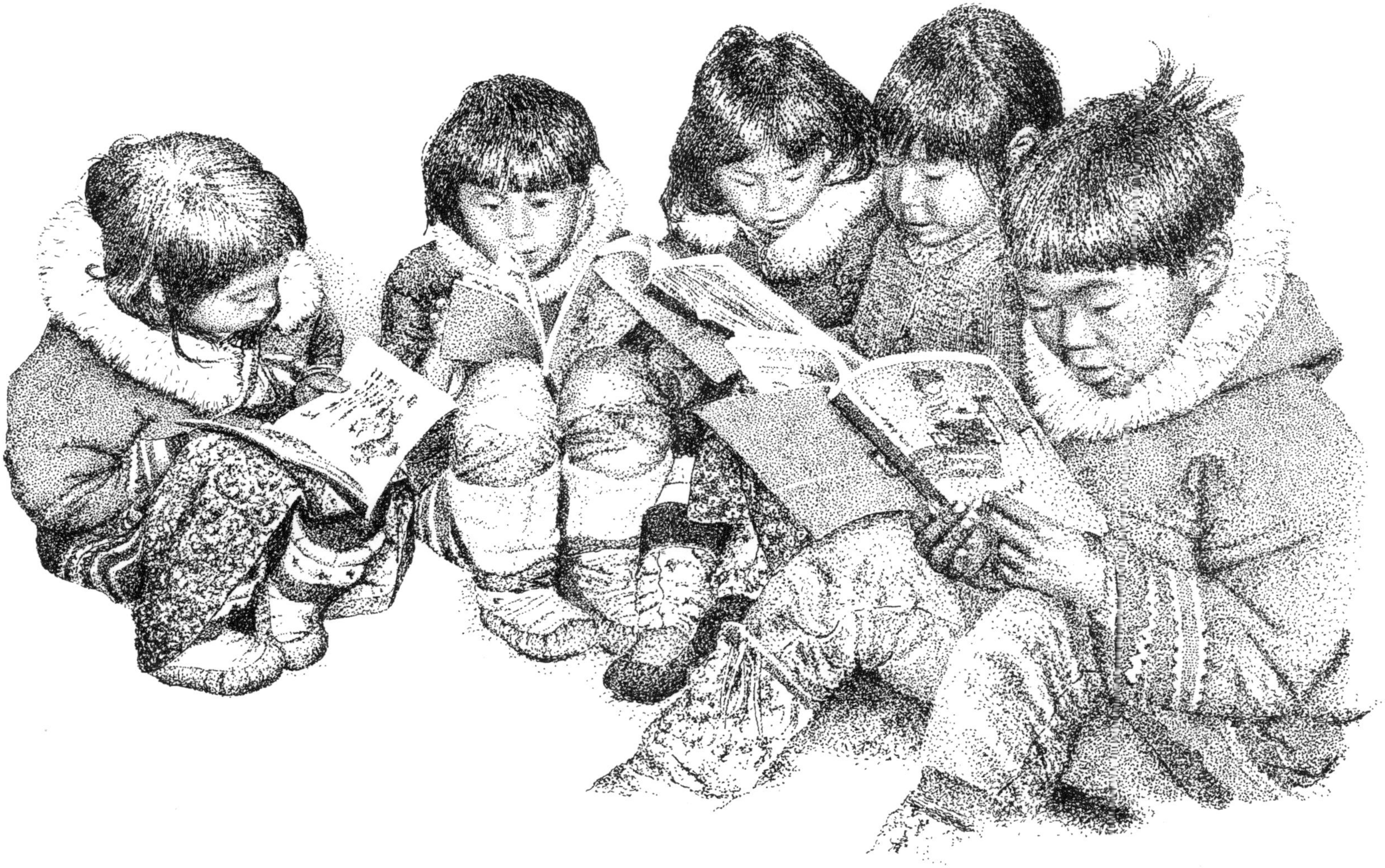

Reading class at the camp.

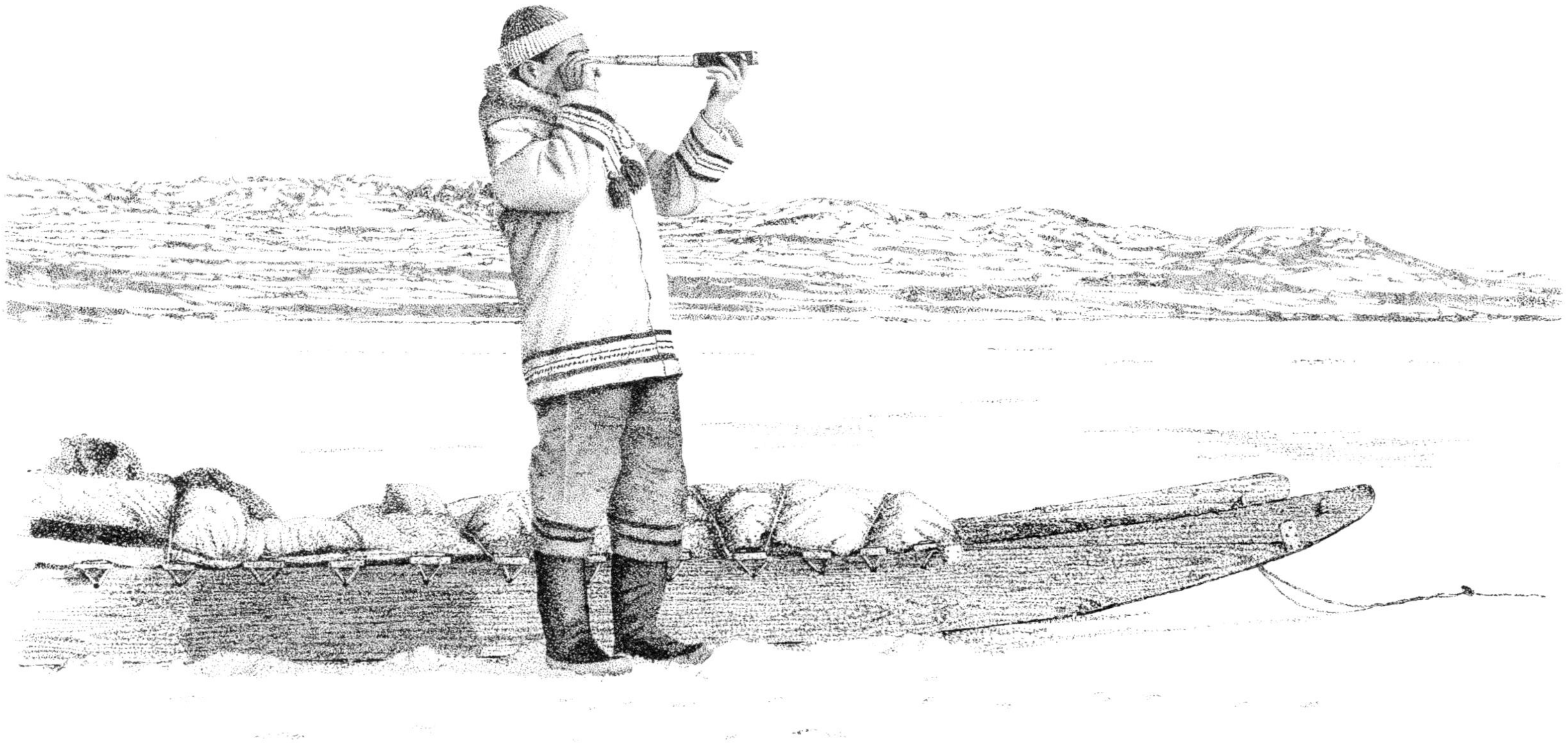

Seal hunter.

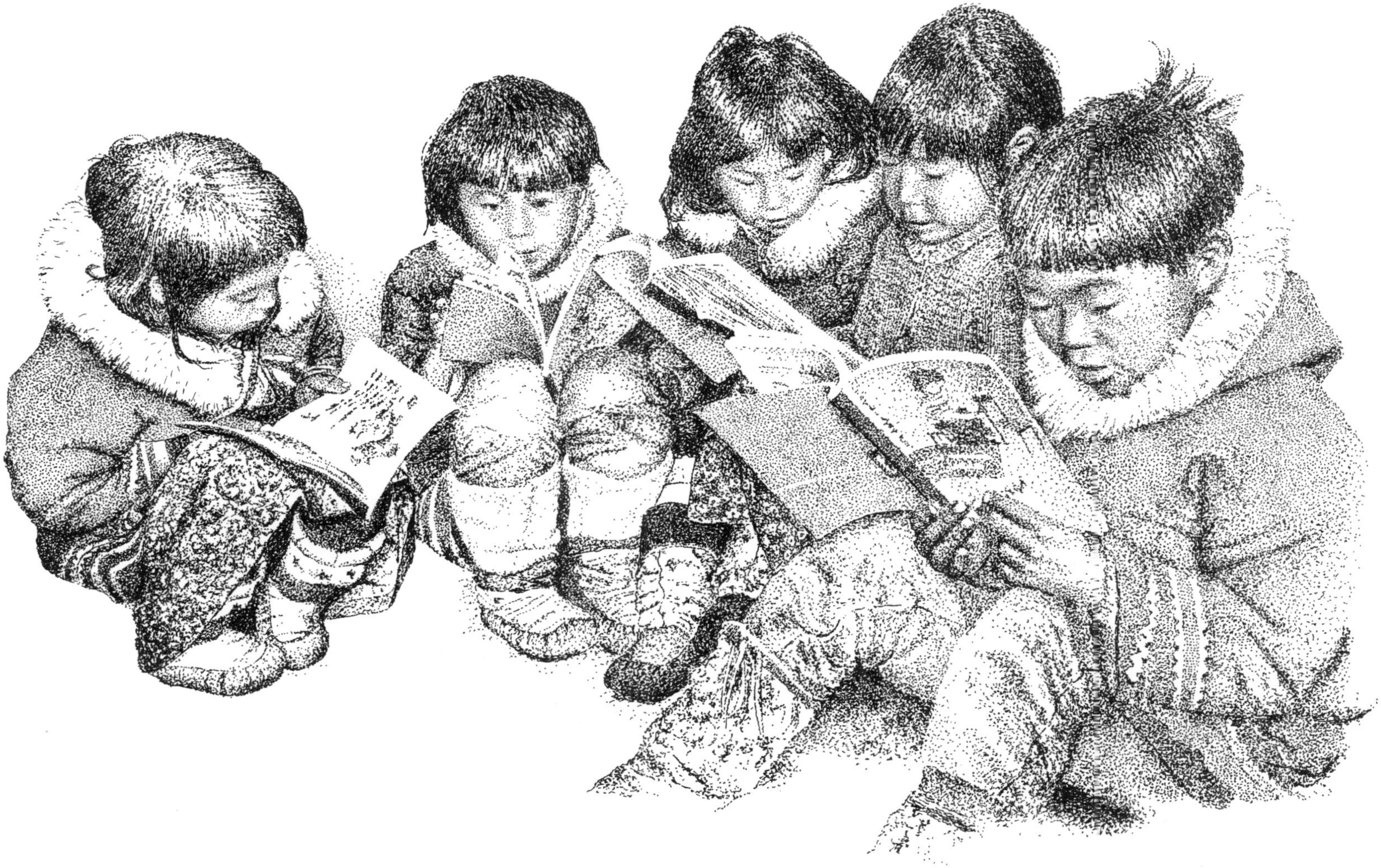

Reading class at the camp.

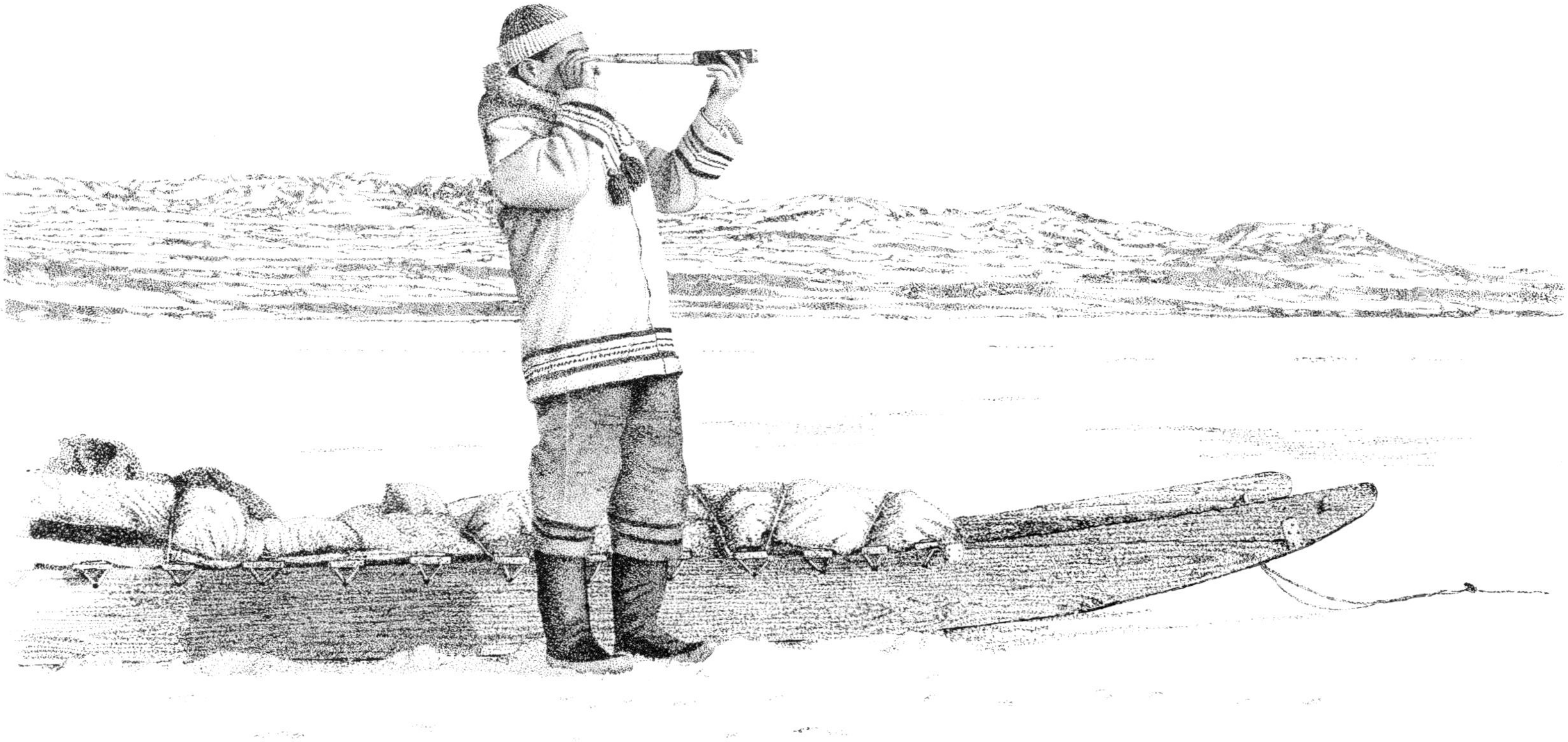

Seal hunter.

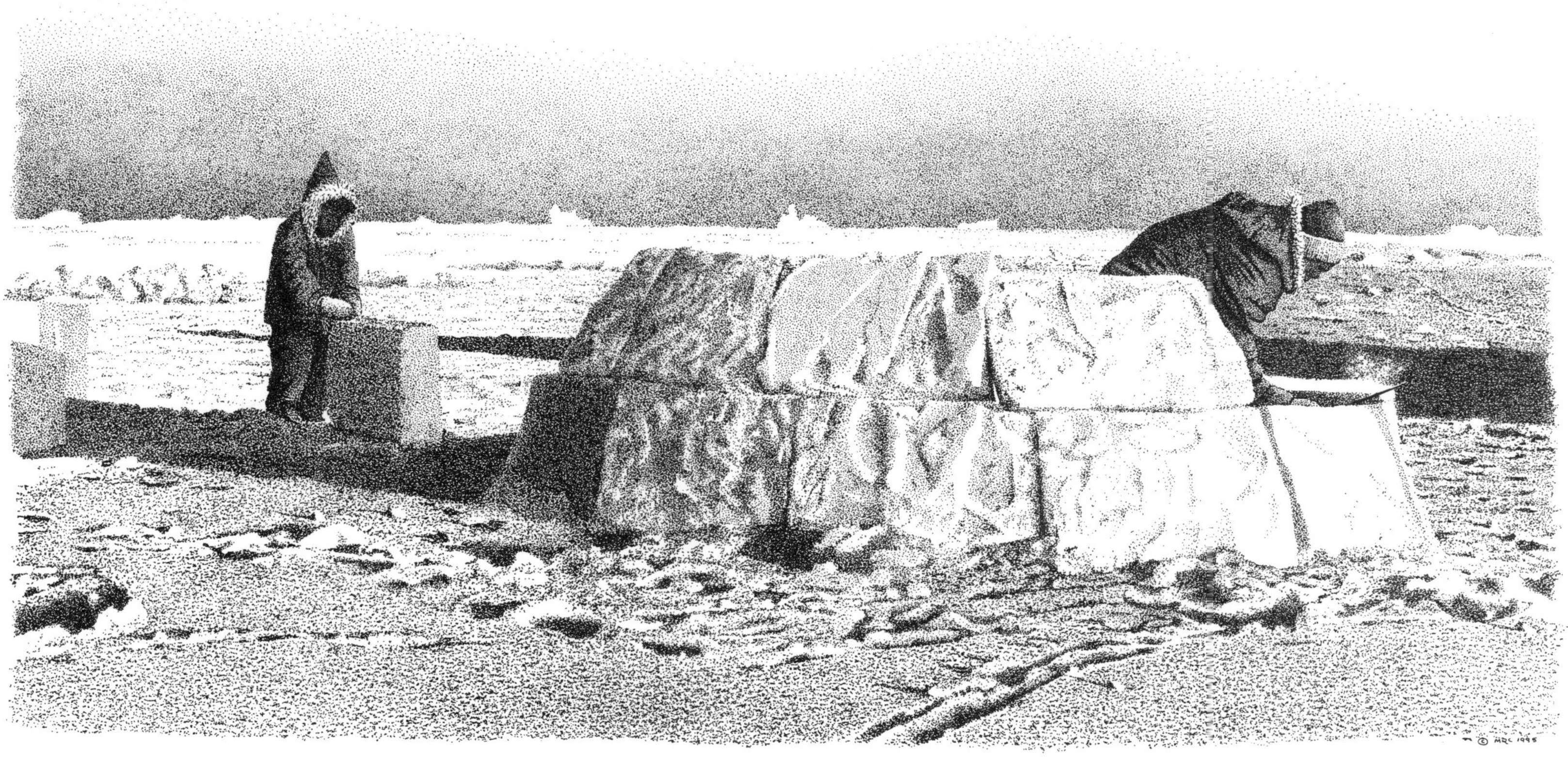

Shelter for the night.

on closer inspection, that they were all hobbled, with one foot tied under their chin to stop them from straying too far. It didn't seem to inconvenience them greatly for they still hopped around at a fair old pace on their other three.

It was Tarktoo also who took us on our very first visit to Qiqertaq, though more commonly we travelled to that camp with Akitirk or Ishuhangituk or one of the other men. After leaving the smooth surface of the bay, we had to cross an area of extremely rough, jumbled ice on Adams Sound. Those komatiks had to be strong, for they took tremendous punishment when riding over rough ice. And so did we. Even so, Tarktoo's 12 dogs got us to Qiqertaq in a record two-and-a-half bitterly cold hours.

We stayed at the home of the camp leader, Kakasheak. There at Qiqertaq, the people had the same deal as those at Abvartok. All had once lived in traditional homes of turf and snow blocks, but three small prefab homes had been provided for them, so some of the families (though not all) now lived in relative luxury, and Kakasheak was one.

Kakasheak was the most considerate host we have ever known, Arctic or otherwise, a cheerful, kind man, endlessly attentive and always anticipating our every need. He wasn't in when we first arrived, just his wife and children were home, so we drank our soup with Tarktoo and ate a sandwich, made a quick tour of the houses to introduce ourselves and I started teaching at three P.M. There were seven school-age kids at Qiqertaq, six girls and one boy, the exact opposite of Abvartok which had one girl and five boys. They were delightful children and very eager to have this little school session on the floor of Kakasheak's home. Halfway through school, the door opened and a frozen white fox body came hurtling through the air, followed a little while later by Kakasheak. This flying fox was put in a corner to thaw a bit prior to being skinned. Kakasheak and his wife took a great interest in all that was going on, and soon after 5:30 P.M. I called it a day.

Kakasheak then skinned the fox and when that was done he produced a huge frozen Arctic char for the family and his visitors. He offered to heat our portions over the stove but we felt that clinging to our own set ways would be a bit decadent and that we needed to do as the Romans, so we ate it raw. We shared bannock around and then black tea. Kakasheak got a bowl of warm water for the family to wash their fishy hands in, and then he brought another bowl of clean water for Katie and me, and a clean towel too. Only, I think, amongst the Arabs of the Sahara did Katie and I ever experience such equally fastidious attention, such immaculate courtesy and attentiveness as we received on each occasion from Kakasheak.

The return journey with Tarktoo from Qiqertaq to Arctic Bay was colder, and was made much slower by the disappearance in the night of three of Tarktoo's dogs, they having taken absence without leave and gone back on their own to the settlement. We were almost up to the entrance of Adams Sound when we came upon one of the camp men, Angnayoomayook, alone away out on the ice, in that classic pose of the Arctic hunter with his nose nearly touching the ice and his bottom sticking up in the air, rifle ready, harpoon on the snow, completely clothed in caribou skins, waiting and waiting, silent and motionless over an almost invisible *aglu*, with a soft ptarmigan feather lying over the tiny hole to betray the rush of air that would precede a surfacing seal. What patience and endurance there is in hunting a seal! Just so much as wiggle your toes and it will be gone.

We kept well clear of Angnayoomayook, not to disturb his hunting, and stopped to make tea, but he gave up his long cold vigil and joined us for a cup, before going back to it.

Getting to the far distant camp at Iqalulik was for us more of a problem, because the hunters preferred to cover the much greater distance with an overnight camp somewhere along the way. The distance could be covered, at a pinch, in one very long day, but that was bad economics and bad management, for it demanded a great deal of the dogs and at the same time offered no opportunity to do any hunting. How do you drive dogs without feeding them? Rather than carry dog food with them, which White people would want to do, the people always hunted along the way, and what was the hurry to get there anyway? In life it was the journey that mattered, not the arrival. (It was the same for Katie and me when we went voyaging.) So since none of this could be reconciled with our alien notion of inflexible weekends, we had to put Iqalulik off until the springtime when dear old Eenoogoo and his smiling, gracious wife took us there, camping together all four of us and a horde of dogs, on a desolate beach away beyond Qiqertaq. Every now

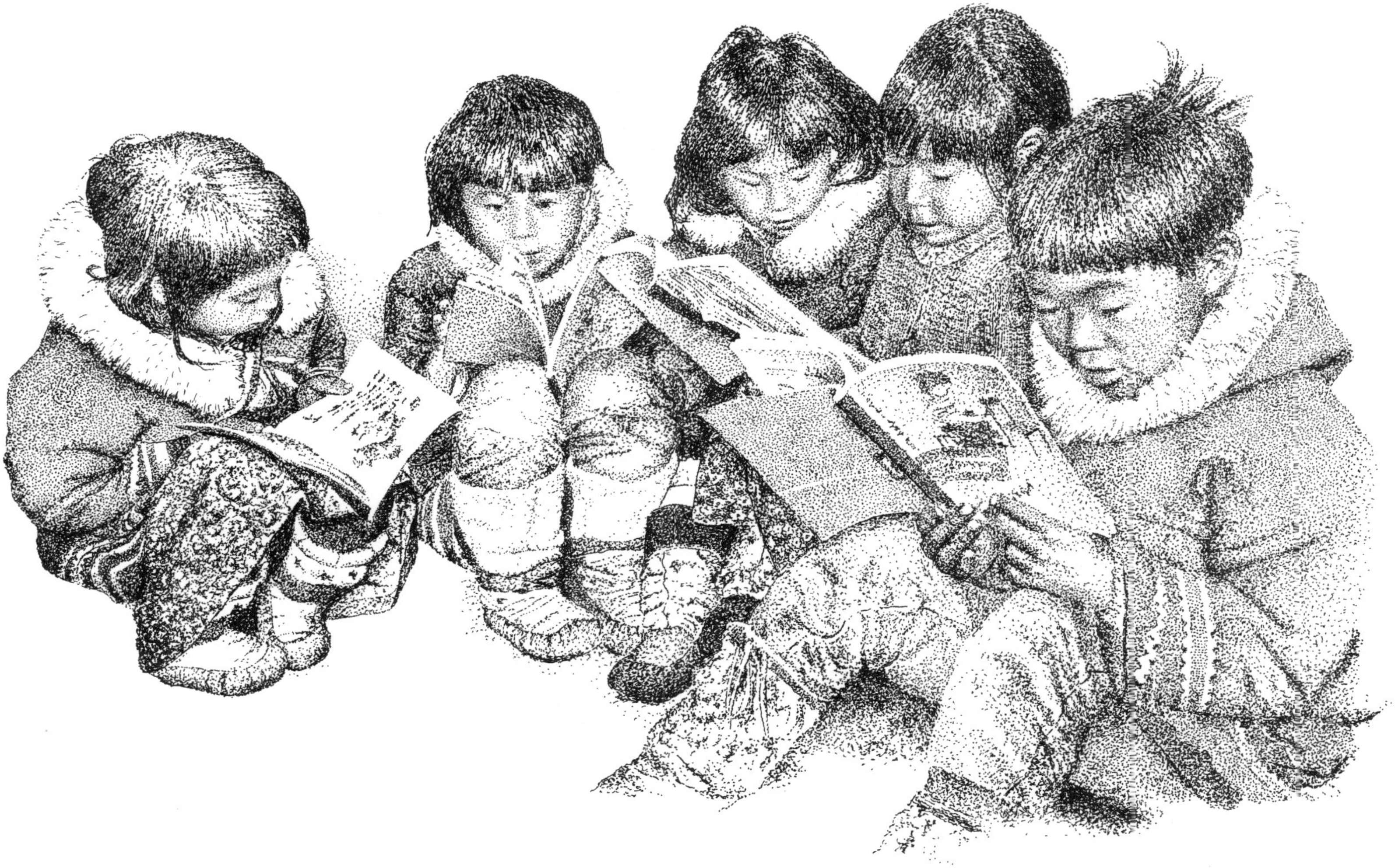

Reading class at the camp.

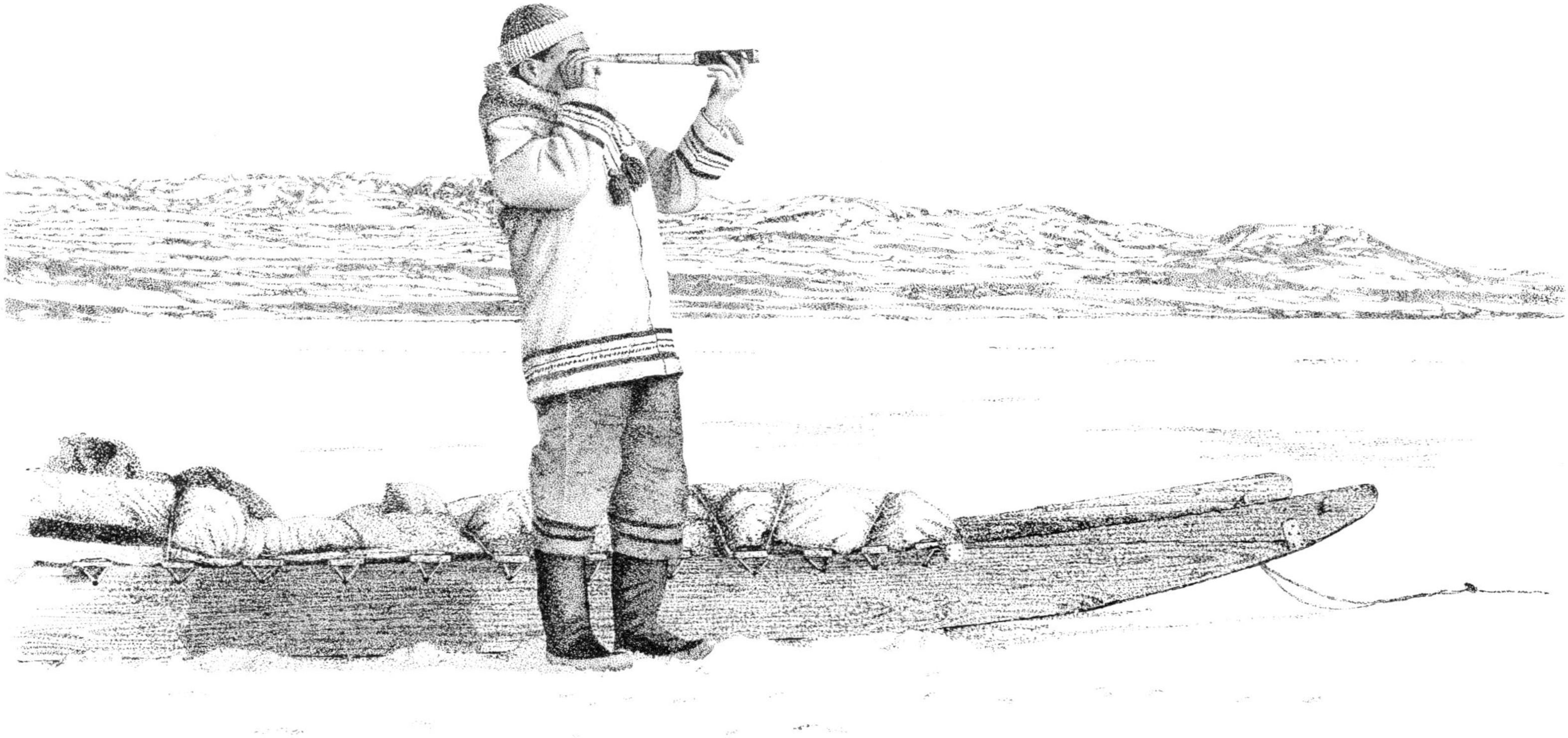

Seal hunter.

and then Eenoogoo stopped, leaving his trail-worn team to take their rest while he searched everywhere with his old brass telescope for seals, for at that season they were all out of the water more than in, basking on the ice in the nearly continuous sunshine, beside breathing holes or at the edge of the long leads criss-crossing the great inlet. Eenoogoo stalked the wily creatures behind a large white cloth blind, like a kite with a small peep-hole cut from the centre. His patience appeared to be without end. The seals seemed to me impossibly cautious and wary and many slipped away on his approach, but not all, and he did feed his dogs.

Usually on all these journeys we passed other families travelling with other teams and we nearly always stopped to rest and drink tea with them and to sort out the tangled traces of the dogs while the outriders played with the harnessed dogs, teasing them for their captivity. You almost never saw a team without two or three outriders, camp followers, dogs belonging to the team but running loose, grown pups perhaps, pregnant females, or some dog with an injury or other excuse.

We returned to Iqalulik three weeks later, this time with our friends Leah and Aeyout. Iqalulik meant "place of fish." A river disgorged there into Admiralty Inlet, flowing down from the far mountains through a nearby lake, and, the river at that time being in full spate, and the fish on the move, several families were camped there, living on char and hanging them on drying racks. We had brought our own tent along with us this time and Katie used an old soapstone *kudlik* and a big chunk of seal blubber to cook on in the ancient way, balancing the pot on stones over the long, yellow flame burning all along the edge of the soapstone dish. But it was a slow, tedious business, like cooking over candles. No wonder people ate their food raw.

Leah and Aeyout had a wonderful team of ten strong dogs but they were a pretty hungry lot by the end of the journey because Aeyout managed to get just one small seal along the way, and the dogs got none of it. Unless they were killed outright with a bullet through the brain, the seals dived quickly into their *aglu*, and were lost. It had been a hard journey from the settlement, and during our overnight camp it had come on to rain and blow strongly, so Aeyout let all his dogs off their harnesses and left them to look for their own shelter. But he was careful to bring all the precious *ujuk* (bearded seal) skin traces in with him to the tent so the ravenous dogs wouldn't eat them in the night.

During the night one of the females had a litter of pups. Before resuming our journey Aeyout took these little things away from their mother, plonked them quite unceremoniously into a flour bag which he then tied to the komatik and hitched up the mother with the rest of the dogs. It required quite a few stones and kicks to turn her attention from the crying pups on top of the komatik.

The school year being then over, Katie and I stayed on at Iqalulik for several sunny days while the winter snows melted down off the hills, and into the gushing streams. The sudden warm spell resulted in extensive flooding of the winter ice all over Admiralty Inlet. I went out with Aeyout seal hunting and it was very tough going in those conditions. The melt water was lying on top of the surfaces in myriad vast, interconnected pools with less than a third of the total ice surface standing dry and clear above the flood. At times the dogs had water well up over their bellies, swimming almost, and at the deepest places Aeyout and I had to stand on the komatik as the water washed over the deck and around our gumboots.

With the snow all gone, there was just ice for the dogs to run on. It was sharp and crystalline by that time, and there were little patches of blood left behind in the tracks of most of the dogs. Back on Great Bear Lake many years earlier, we had tied little moosehide boots onto the feet of the dogs when the ice of the lake was exposed and sharpened into crystals by the sun, but the salt ice of the Arctic was perhaps a little easier, less cutting than the harder ice of the lakes, and dog boots were never used. Poor creatures, apart from sore feet, they were ravenously hungry, and hard to control. And because they could not be kept back at a distance we got no seals. So we brought the dogs back to the camp, left them there, and Aeyout and I went back out on the ice on our own. Aeyout killed another small seal. But when we returned to the camp we found that the famished dogs had chewed up all their own traces, so they all got a thorough thrashing from Aeyout. Poor Aeyout! Poor dogs!

The water flooding the sea ice drained away within two days, down through the cracks and *aglus*, leaving the huge expanse of the enormous inlet once again high and dry. But access from the

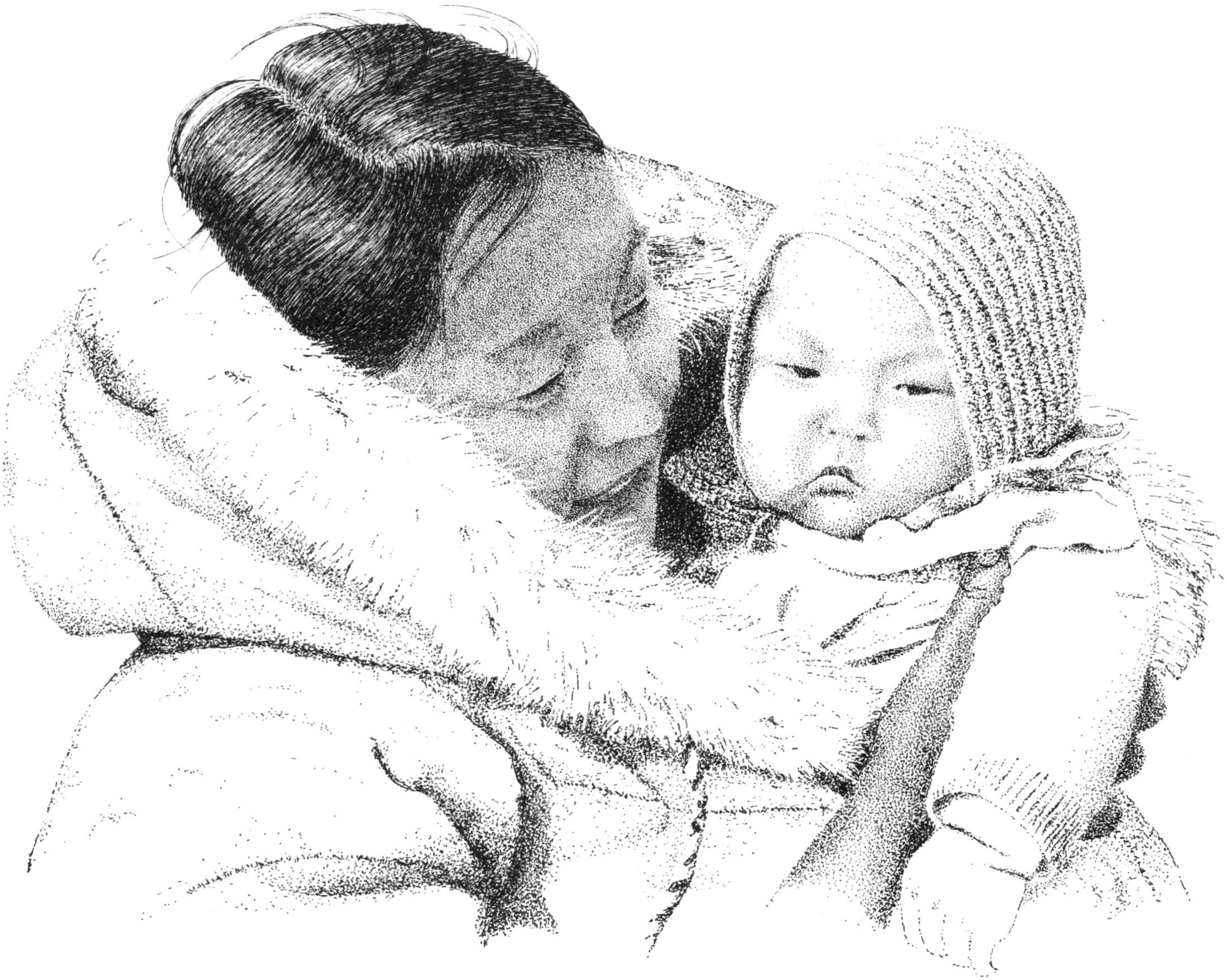

Katie's friend, Leah.

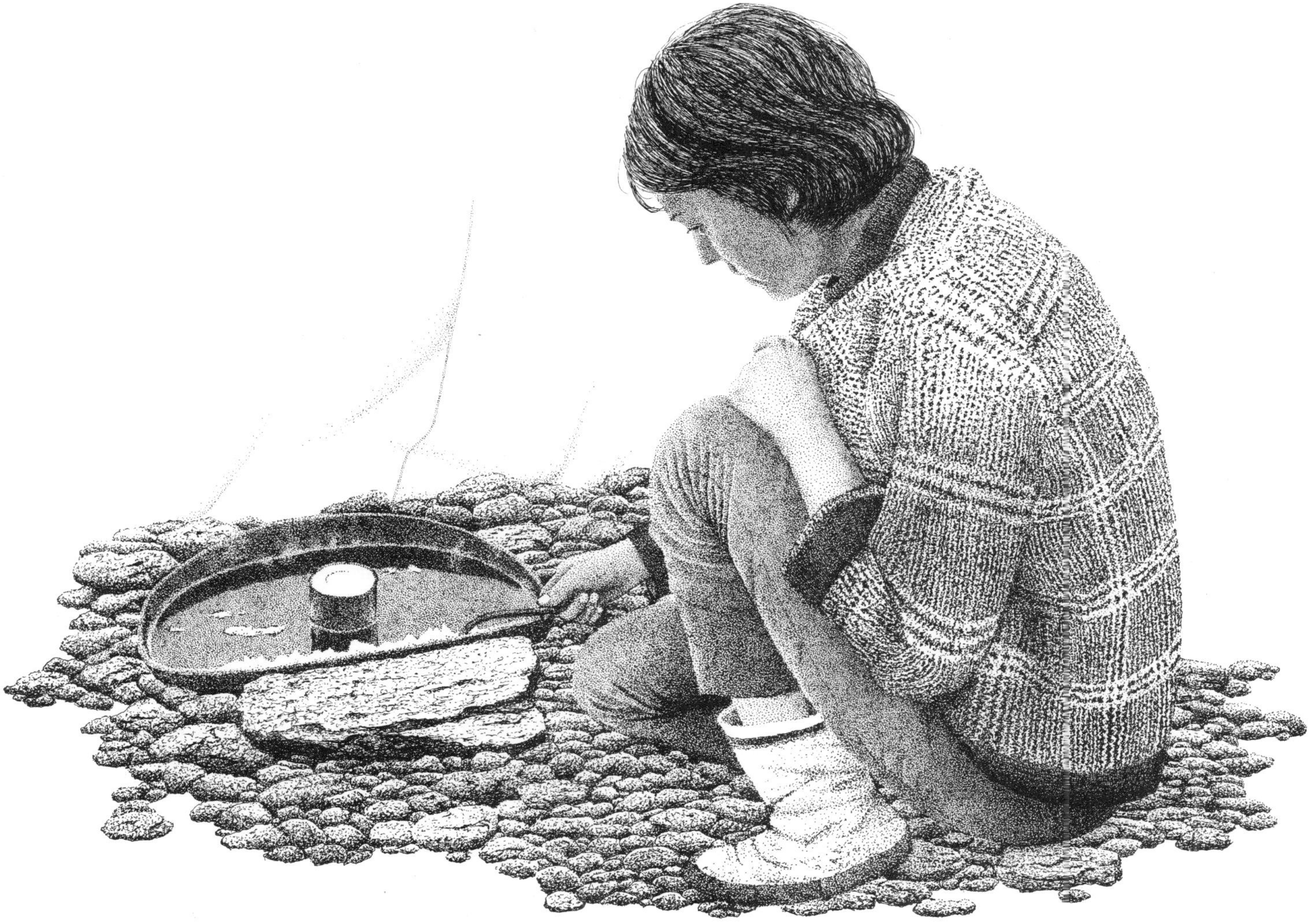

Katie prepares to make dinner over a KUDLIK.

shore was difficult as the ice rotted and disintegrated all along the edges. With Leah and Aeyout, we returned to the settlement in two stages, travelling at "night" when the sun was low to the north and the temperatures were cool enough for the dogs. Their long work season was by then about done.

I think the greatest dog congress that Katie and I ever witnessed in the North was at Arctic Bay, though we did have big gatherings of teams for races and other special events elsewhere, especially at the Indian settlements in the bush. Easter was the big festive event of the year at Arctic Bay, coinciding as it did with the happy season of late winter, bringing long daylight and warmer temperatures, the favourite season of the native people.

Most of the families came in from the camps for Easter, and it seemed there were dogs and people everywhere. We had a sports day out on the sea ice. It was organized entirely by the local people and there were all sorts of events that you wouldn't find on the program anywhere else. Dog races, juggling contests, demonstrations of dog-whip accuracy, seal races.... Well, not *actual* seal races. The men were expert at mimicking the movements of seals, a skill that a hunter might need, when stalking seals on the top of the ice in the spring. They lay stomach down, and with spasmodic jerks they hefted themselves bodily forward. Atagutsiak and his partner won the igloo-building contest for biggest, best and fastest.

But the event that drew the most appreciative crowd was the one at the end of the day, the White man's dog race. They lined up three equal teams, each hitched to a komatik, and assigned each to one of the three *qadlunaat*: the Hudson's Bay trader, the mechanic and the teacher. They gave each of us a long whip, and we had to race our teams south across the bay, around the iceberg and back again. There was no escape, and everyone had a big grin on their faces, except the three qadlunaat.

I knew this was ludicrous. The dogs would know perfectly well that they were in the hands of a trio of bozos and anything could happen. Or not happen. Anyway, we all got off to a good start, if only because just about everyone in the crowd behind us yelled at those dogs with all the appropriate noises, and cracked their whips, and the dogs knew better than to muck about, so off we went trotting along happily for a brief few minutes more or less in the direction of the iceberg. What a farce! I thought to myself. This is hardly a race. I soon noticed, smugly, that the trader's dogs were falling back a bit, losing interest, and the mechanic's team was beginning to wander off a little to the west, he yelling at them all the time. Did he know how to call them back to the left? I rather fancied that I had the commands well memorized. Katie and I had travelled about 800 miles during the winter with local hunters, so I regarded myself as the expert. My team was a bit lethargic, but not doing anything totally stupid, and on the principle of "Don't fix it if it isn't broken," I just let them trot along. Three of my eight dogs though had slack traces, and I knew I ought to land a crack of the whip on the ears of one of them, the way their owners did, and they would all smarten up. Easier said than done.

The mechanic got his team turned at last, but a bit too far the other way and they all came racing across in front of my own team, and I thought we would have a fight on our hands. But the yelling of the mechanic seemed to discourage my lot and they turned off and went in a new direction, a bit faster, no slack traces. I tried the trilling cry that meant "turn left" but as I rather expected the dogs took no notice. There was a light breeze from the southwest and my team seemed to have picked up the scent of an *aglu*, because they were running straight upwind. These things can be almost invisible, even when you're standing right over them, roofed over as they normally are with snow, but the dogs smell them. "Damn! I'll never stop them now," I grumbled.

Some way ahead they came to a faint little raised circle of snow that might once have covered an old *aglu*, but the dogs, after sniffing around for a while, decided that they weren't all that interested after all. I gave them the "let's-get-moving" cry, and then the "turn left," and they resumed their desultory wandering.

The trader's dogs had now caught up with the mechanic's dogs which had stopped to investigate a pile of garbage, and a bit of a fight ensued. I could hear the mechanic's furious bellowing far behind me, and distant laughter from the settlement.

My team wasn't interested in any iceberg and kept going until they were away beyond it, and I only got them turned back by yelling with the turn-left sound, and brandishing my whip at those on the right, and reluctantly they came around in a wide half circle. Now round that iceberg and home.

The trader's dogs had stopped for a rest over by the shore near that garbage and I couldn't see the mechanic's team for the iceberg, until it suddenly appeared ahead of me coming the wrong way round. My team speeded up and sure enough we had a fight on our hands. Curses, kicks, the maniac screaming of the mechanic, a few ineffectual cracks of the whip, and eventually the two teams lost interest in hating each other and decided to carry on going their separate ways.

"You came the wrong way round," I yelled at the disappearing mechanic.

"Who gives a shit?" I heard him answer angrily from the other side of the iceberg.

I thought I was in fine shape then to win the race as my dogs settled in for the run home. The mechanic was now far behind me and away off course, heading off at right angles for the western shore; the trader's team was still taking a rest. The trader himself was walking back over his tracks to retrieve his lost whip. Halfway back, my dogs took a sudden interest in the pile of garbage, and did a switch to the right. I tried to outflank them by running to the right and brandishing my whip, but as soon as I got off the komatik the dogs responded to the lighter load by putting on a sprint, and they left me far behind, running and cursing. I let them go. Again I could hear the appreciative hooting of the crowd back at the settlement. I slowed to a walk and watched developments. The trader's team decided at that point to get up and go off on their own without the trader. The mechanic was so far west that nobody could hear him any more. My team stopped at the garbage dump. There were now two teams on their own without a driver and one going the wrong way. I could almost feel the deep sense of happy satisfaction on the settlement shore that the organizers had been so wise as to include this wonderful race as the culminating event of the day.

The trader's team skirted the shoreline and trotted home, leaving their driver to mope along far behind, dragging his whip behind him. The mechanic's dogs had stopped for a rest. Another *aglu* perhaps. I reached my dogs at the dump, landed a couple of hard kicks on two of them, and since they had found nothing to eat there anyway we were soon on our way again, more or less homeward, four traces slack, though it was more their decision than mine. I shouted to the distant trader offering him a lift home, but he removed one of his mitts and gave me what I took to be not the hitchhiker's thumb, but the finger.

The mechanic's dogs decided to sprint home, tired of all that yelling maybe, and reached the settlement shore just ahead of my own team, which came last. My dogs might have beaten the mechanic's except that about eight of the kids in my class came out to meet me and all piled onto the komatik for the ride back.

At school a few days later I talked to the kids about helicopters, how and why they worked, and I showed them how they could make their own toy *qulimaguli*, as they called it, making it fly upwards off the classroom floor. This impressed the kids, and apropos of this, one little girl commented casually, in English, "My momma, she say White peoples can do anything."

Well, not quite, Little One. Did your momma not watch the Easter dog races?

Mr. Bumble's Ass

From time to time, after my arrival in the North in 1957 as a fresh young foreigner from the other side of the world, I found myself struggling to understand one aspect or another of Canadian law as it applied to people in the Arctic. Are those people allowed to vote? Can this guy drink? Are those two married or not? Are these kids Indians, Eskimos or Others? Whose kids are they anyway? All simple enough questions, but sometimes they could have surprising answers.

Back in the sixties, when we were living on Baffin Island, a matter that raised a few eyebrows, including mine, was a decision by the Supreme Court of Canada declaring that old, traditional-style custom marriages, still common then throughout the Arctic, especially amongst people who had lived far beyond the long reach of missionaries, had no basis in Canadian law. They were not in fact legal marriages. Dear oh dear, did this mean that old Shapa and old Atoat had been just "living together" these past 40 years? "Shacked up?" "Living in sin?" (to use that nice judgmental expression of so many people whose religion deplores the casting of stones). And Pilapusie and Anna? And old Alooloo and Elisapee? And *almost* everyone else?

Well, of course, I'm sure all those Supreme Court judges never meant to cast any such unfavourable reflection on custom marriages as such; they just couldn't figure a way to grant any legal status to them. What would seem like simple common sense to the person on the street became an impossibility if you had studied as much Latin and law as those guys had.

I pondered this odd dilemma at some length. I was not sure what the stumbling block was. Perhaps the absence of a formalizing ceremony in the old traditional arrangements? How about jumping into bed together, I thought to myself, could that not be construed as a formalizing ceremony? (And a darned fine one, too!) Of course not, stupid, I reflected, then almost everybody might end up being married to half a dozen others. Hmmm. Well, the arrival of the first baby could be a great formalizing ceremony couldn't it? That doesn't work for us, why would it be okay for them? Maybe signatures on a piece of paper are what the judges need? That might be getting closer.... No paper of course in the old days. Incisions on soapstone? Reverse-appliqued syllabic signatures on sealskin? Now you're getting stupid again.

Well, I gave up trying to figure that one out. I could never be a lawyer in a thousand years. It really didn't matter much at all to me except that at about that time there was a young woman whose status was in some doubt and I couldn't decide if she was married or not, and I had to make up my mind before the plane came in. What an odd situation!

In the dear old simpler times, of course, a man took a woman to be his (or she him, or both each other), and as long as it was agreeable to all, including their families, that was that. Indeed, the families, the parents, might themselves already have arranged the matter years before the young people even thought about it. (I knew some children who had been vaguely promised to each other, though there seemed nothing binding about those old parental understandings. The young people would make their own decisions in their own time.) Either way, it was just a matter of deciding when the time was ripe and that was it. She was his, he was hers for as long as they wanted to stay together, which was usually for good. (And how much happier and more stable all those unformalized relationships were than are the general run of relationships formalized by marriage in our own Western societies!)

Anyway, this young woman was about 18, and she arrived in the settlement from a distant camp where she had lived on and off most of her life with her family. This attractive young woman — let me call her Susanna, though that wasn't her name at all — had been bugging me for some time for permission to travel down to Frobisher Bay (as Iqaluit was then called) on a returning charter flight. She knew one was due at the settlement in a few days' time, and she knew too that she could have a free seat if I just gave the word. She said she wanted to get herself a job in Frobisher.

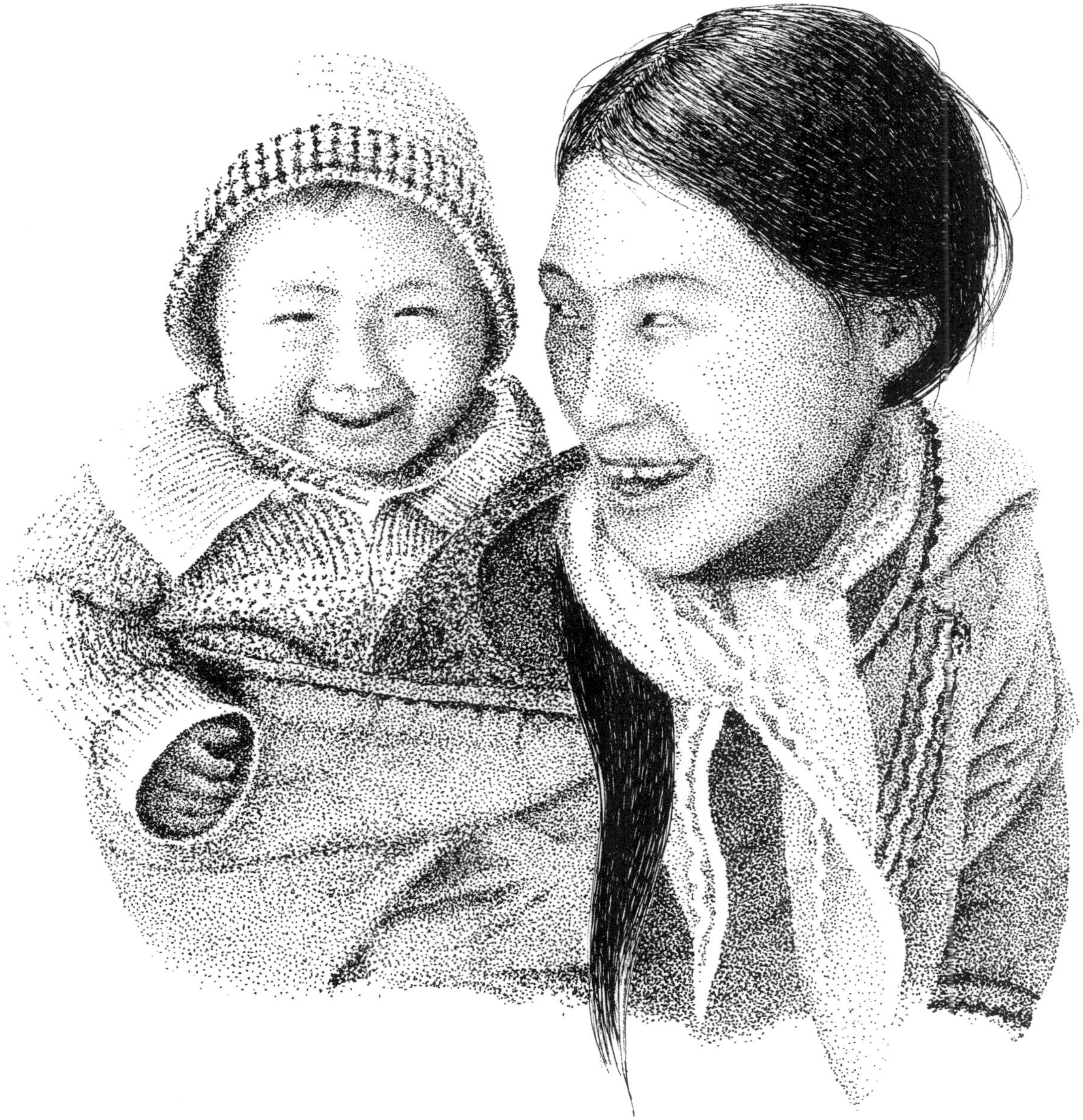

Madonna and child.

Now it happened that this same Susanna had been medevacked out to Frobisher Bay in the spring for observation and treatment after apparently being bitten at the camp by what was thought to have been a rabid fox. No problems developed and she was eventually returned back to her home several weeks later. It later transpired that during her stay in Frobisher she had met up with a handsome young fellow from that community and in the natural course of things a passionate affair developed so that in a sense she became smitten by a different, infinitely nicer malady after having been bitten by a different fox. Apparently she took some persuading to return home.

I learned all this when I called the social worker down there to get the nod for Susanna to travel on the charter flight. The social worker was quite agreeable about letting her catch the plane, but pointed out that she was sure Susanna had a much more powerful motive for wanting to return south than merely getting a job, and she explained the whole story.

"Well actually," I replied, "she is sort of married already to one of the guys at the camp. It was one of those arranged marriages and it hasn't worked out very well. Susanna has walked out on the guy."

Silence at the other end. "Oh well, this is different...." More silence. "Has the minister married them yet?"

"No, and he won't be back in here till next winter."

"Well, if it's one of those arranged marriages we don't want to be seen to be contributing to breaking it up. It would be different if they'd just been living together casually of their own choice. But a situation arranged by their families, that looks more like a genuine custom marriage to me."

"So what'll I do?"

"You'd better find out what their present status is and use your own judgment based on that. If you're not sure you'd better not let her come."

Damn! I would have preferred either to let her go or to leave the decision with Susanna's parents but they were not around. Actually, my sympathies were very much with Susanna. She was a big girl and surely she could be allowed to run her own life. I far preferred the imperatives of love to those of law.

Nevertheless....

I talked to one of the older people from that camp but my language problem made it difficult to reach any conclusion. Yes, they had been married, but now they weren't really married quite so much. Yes, we'd like them to be married. Maybe they will be again....

There was a problem here with words.

The young man himself (I'll call him David) came in shortly after this from the camp. He was a good hunter, but a quiet, unassuming, grey sort of chap. David was about as bilingual as I was, which at that time was almost not at all, and we made little progress except to establish that, no, he didn't want Susanna to go "looking for a job" in Frobisher Bay.

Finally I said to him, "Is Susanna really your wife, or just your girlfriend?" a question that suddenly seemed, and sounded, indelicate and intrusive, and which I instantly regretted asking. But David just thought for a moment, and then broke into a smile and answered, "Yes."

Oh well, I thought to myself, I really don't know. I suppose I'd better play it safe and not send her, and with some regret I went along to her house and said to her, "I'm sorry Susanna, but you can't go on the plane."

I felt I had murdered something.

Time went on and the matter of poor Susanna's foiled ambitions slipped completely from my mind. The daylight was fading fast and we expected only one more plane before the onset of the long dark period, our time of total isolation.

One day after school at about that time, a couple of women came to see me, one acting as interpreter for the other who had had a very odd, inconvenient little accident. There she had been, poor woman, working at home, stitching together some sealskin boots, *kamiks*. She'd had all her sewing things strewn haphazardly about the area where she was working. She had got up to make some tea, and when she sat down again she came down on a long needle which had penetrated, not her rear end, but the side of her right thigh. One might have expected that such a painful piece of bad luck could easily have been undone by grabbing the eye end of the needle and dragging it out again, but, no, it had buried itself completely beneath the skin. Unfortunately, too, it just happened to be a needle with no thread in it, which might otherwise have allowed it to be withdrawn. What bad luck! Even worse, the eye end of the needle was not *just* under the skin as anyone would expect it to be, but was well buried. Otherwise, I might have been tempted to go and boil an X-Acto knife from the school's craft supplies and have a go at it.

Well, the victim of this quite extraordinary accident was none other than Susanna whose escape to Frobisher Bay and away from David I had foiled so reluctantly back in September.

I asked if I might at least see where the needle went in. Sure enough, there was a firm, slightly raised, red mark at the top of her thigh a little way back from the side. Was there *really* a needle there? I looked in the school science kit for a magnetic compass, but there was none. Of course; I remembered I had thrown it out in disgust after a failed science experiment. Such things are useless so close to the magnetic North Pole, but at least one might have indicated a piece of steel inside that thigh. Actually, I hardly doubted that the needle was there all right; my doubts were only for how it got there.

Okay Susanna, I thought to myself, you win this one I guess.

When I called Frobisher Bay by radio for instructions, the guy at the other end, after listening to all the details, groaned.

"This young lady really wants to get down here to Frobisher, right?"

"Right, she does."

"And she's right-handed. Right?"

"Right."

"Okay, well, let her sit on it for a while and hope it hurts, but I guess you'll have to give her a travel warrant before the last plane leaves."

So, with a neat little trick, Susanna had now obligated the government to fly her at great expense to Resolute on the Twin Otter, accommodate and feed her there, fly her south to Frobisher on the jet, put her up somewhere in Frobe, and pay the doctors to remove that needle.

Although I greatly regretted not letting her go as she had wanted on the earlier charter flight, at no cost to anyone, I still felt slightly annoyed at Susanna. People in the North can be incredibly indifferent to the huge burdens they place so thoughtlessly at times on the poor old taxpayer. (Though I suppose in that respect they are hardly any different from all the rest of the feckless population. The government has always been seen, quite wrongly of course, as a bottomless pit.) It might have required a full year's federal taxes from some backwoods roadworker down in Nova Scotia just to pay for this one medevac. Still, at least Susanna was unlikely to claim the return portion of her warrant, and I must admit it was hard to blame her for employing such a cleverly executed little ruse. If her motive was ulterior it was also the greatest one of all, pure and universal. Love triumphs in the end, and as a matter of fact I was glad of it.

Two cheers for Susanna!

Actually, the visiting minister had attended to a number of church weddings during his last visit, but Susanna and David had stayed at their camp at that time. Those church weddings were almost never the starting point of a new relationship, but rather the formalizing of one that had existed for long enough to be considered stable and permanent. I suppose because of that latest Supreme Court ruling, the minister on this last occasion had also married a number of the settlement's older couples, and Etook and one or two others, grandparents all, had been dropping by at our house to laugh about it, and show us their new gold rings.

I had a total of 31 kids in sort of regular attendance in the little one-room school. They were high spirited, happy and enormous fun to teach. I was late back to the school after lunch one day, shortly after the minister's visit, having been delayed by some of the adults visiting from the camps. They wanted to see me about home improvements, and to bring in some soapstone carvings for sale through the government marketing system. Some of the kids were playing outside when I got back to school, but ten or so of the middle group were in the classroom, all gathered around in a corner giggling and playing at something that I didn't bother to take any interest in. They looked a little sheepish, their mirth subsided, and their little game broke up as I prepared to call all the rest inside.

Only later did I realize what they'd been doing. Young Jimmy, the 11-year-old son of the lay preacher, had had one towel draped over each shoulder and these had been joined together fore and aft. Church vestments! He'd had a black-covered library book in his hand. Apparently Jimmy had already married off two pairs of nine year olds (they later confided gleefully) and was about to start on a third when I'd interrupted the ceremony.

Kids love to mimic the adult world. All that afternoon, I noticed, Julie and Alice each had on the fingers of their left hands little coloured rings of twisted pipe cleaners.

If the actual timing of an official marriage ceremony was a matter of no importance whatever to the people of Baffin Island, it did sometimes have some rather interesting consequences for the Dene Indian people back there on the banks of the Mackenzie River. There was one particular case in Fort Norman when I was there which seemed to me to confirm perfectly Mr. Bumble's declared opinion that "the law is a ass." In those times, back in the mid-fifties, the people who had Treaty Indian status had certain constraints and certain benefits and privileges applied to them simply by reason of their being "Treaty." Those with "Non-Treaty" status were regarded as being on the same footing legally as Whites, all lumped together as "Others" in the school register. (Everyone in the Northwest Territories was Indian, Eskimo or Other.) These Other people were no concern of the Indian Agent's, any more than I was. They might have been as indigenous as the forest itself but they did not belong to the Band. They were not "Treaty." It was possible to be a full-blood native with Non-Treaty (or Other) status, and it was also possible to be a full-blood White with the status of a Treaty Indian. This confusing business came about partly because any woman of either race automatically took the status of her husband upon marrying him, and so did the children born to them after the marriage.

It happened, back in those times, that Treaty Indians were not legally allowed to buy alcohol, which explained of course why they so commonly resorted instead to brewing their own under the bed. All the Others on the other hand regularly jumped into their canoes (in season) and went down the river to Norman Wells for their beverages, there being a legal liquor outlet there. I suppose for the Treaty Indian people this must have rankled a bit, and possibly for that reason one or two of them had gone to the trouble of having themselves legally enfranchised as Others, abandoning their Treaty status and whatever rights that status carried with it. This change then automatically applied also to the man's whole family, Mum and all the kids.

Martha was the teen-age daughter of one of these newly enfranchised Non-Treaty men, and she of course had thereupon lost her status. But she had a Treaty Indian boyfriend, Charlie, and once married to Charlie, Martha had the prospect of regaining her lost status as a Treaty Indian. In the natural course of things, Martha became pregnant and the two were a bit slow about organizing a wedding, so that their little boy, Tommy, was born before the parents got around to marrying. But they did marry and subsequently went on to have several other children (small "o") and no doubt all lived happily ever after, Mum, Dad and kids, all Treaty Indians, except for their firstborn Tommy, who was just another Other.

Those discriminatory drinking laws of course eventually became a huge embarrassment to the government, and the time came at last when the Territorial Council saw fit not only to legalize the sale of booze to all comers, whatever their racial status, but also to legalize the brewing of one's own beer. At the time there was great opposition to this. It seemed to many a radical, hideously dangerous move. There would be an explosion of drinking. All hell would break loose. The cops would never be able to cope.... But in fact there was no increase in brewing, and all that happened was that all those people who had previously been breaking the law suddenly weren't. At least that was progress.

Quite naively, I once contributed to a badly tangled legal situation involving one of those Non-Treaty families who had arrived in the settlement just before I was asked to assume my duties there. The mother (I'll call her Emily) had brought her five school-age children with her from another settlement after leaving an abusive husband. They had nowhere to stay and ended up camped for the time being in a grungy old shed, a trapper's warehouse with one tiny window, until something better came along.

The husband had been Non-Treaty, so the welfare of the family was not the Indian Agent's responsibility, but the Mounties'. The corporal at the detachment came along to see me about the situation. He'd already had to issue relief to the poor woman, but he was damned if he wanted to see all those kids living in those conditions all winter, and him always having to be responsible. How about arranging to have them all sent down to the new residential school at Inuvik? The school year was about to begin.

Emily had been quite agreeable to this possibility, (otherwise I would have opposed the idea for, on principle, I disliked that monster institution down on the Delta). But upon carefully reading our directives, I found that the kids were not eligible. I explained to the corporal that I could send kids to Inuvik only if they had reached a certain age, or a certain grade level, or they lived too far away to commute daily to the local school, or they were wards of the state. None of these things applied to these five children.

I was just 24 at that time, and didn't have any idea what was meant by the term "wards of the state."

"The only way we could get Emily's kids into that school," I explained to the corporal, "is if they could be made wards of the state. I wonder how we would go about doing that?"

The Mountie explained that it just required a formal hearing when the magistrate came around, which he was due to do. He would then sign the papers and the kids would be free to go.

Oh well, if it's that easy....

The magistrate did fly in a week later, and after he'd finished hearing all the drinking and home-brewing cases, the three of us sat around the desk at the RCMP detachment, the corporal going on about what a terrible situation those children were in, abandoned by their father, left homeless with a mother who had no hope of coping, and me adding my bit by confirming everything the Mountie had said and going on about how a bad situation now would be far worse in winter, and so on. So the magistrate signed the papers and I soon had the kids shipped off to Inuvik. She may not have had a house, but at least Emily wouldn't have them to worry about until next year.

Actually, of course, what we had done, what the magistrate in particular had done, was to ensure that Emily would *never* have to worry about those kids again. She no longer had any legal claim on them whatever! They were not hers. They were now held for safekeeping by the government to be disposed of at the discretion of the superintendent of social services.

Well, down there in Fort Smith (our capital in those times) the superintendent of social services was aghast when he learned what had happened, stunned at the ease and audacity of the whole thing and amazed that the magistrate could have done such a thing on the basis of a casual chat around a desk with a couple of local bozos. Fortunately, he had a fine sense of humour and the sense to realize that the whole mess had been innocently enough conceived; we had just wanted to get those kids into that residential school.

He now had two problems on his hands: getting Emily out of that dirty, black old shed and into something else more or less decent, and much more problematical, finding a suitable permanent foster family to take over Emily's kids. The first he had to solve right away but at least he had all winter to think about the second. It was always easy enough finding a good home for one child, or maybe two. But he didn't like to see the children separated from each other, and finding a home for all five might be a major problem. A small, rentable cabin was eventually found for Emily, not wonderful but adequate, paid for by social services, and she was very happy to have her own place at last, free of that husband.

The following June, the five children were released from the residential school and taken under the wing of the superintendent of social services. He, meanwhile, had been successful in locating a more or less ideal foster home for all five of them. So they were flown back to the settlement and boarded out on a sort of permanent basis with their new foster mother. Looking after just one foster child for that department was a nicely paid little business. Looking after five was a goldmine. So the new foster mother was very handsomely paid to fulfill her responsibilities to the five waifs. It was, of course, Emily.

Northernmost Everything

I suppose by anyone's measure, Grise Fiord must be considered a very special, unique place but it has been especially so for Katie and me ever since the late sixties, when for a time we made that wonderful little place our home.

At 76° North, the people of Grise Fiord are the most northerly population in Canada, and so in all the Americas. There are various camps farther north in the Canadian High Arctic, but these are places where scientific or military personnel are posted for a season, or a year or so at a time, before being flown back home to the South. These remote bases are not "home" to anybody, just as Antarctica, with its ever-burgeoning hordes of scientists and visitors from everywhere, is home to no human, (and it is fervently to be hoped that it will stay that way). Of course, in these present times the hordes are coming also into the Arctic, and amongst these jet-borne New Age adventurers it is a nice little piece of one-upmanship to be able to say that you have been to Grise Fiord. But in the first two decades of its existence, the fifties and sixties, Grise Fiord was an unimaginably distant, inacccessible place, rarely visited apart from the annual supply ship, and a byword for remoteness and sheer unreachability.

The little settlement, then of 95 people, was located on the south coast of Ellesmere Island, close to the mouth of the fiord that gave the place its name. (*Grise* is the Norwegian word for "pig," and the fiord was so named by the explorer Otto Sverdrup for the gruntings of walrus herds in the area.) All the little homes stretched in a line along the shore under a stunning backdrop of mountain walls that seemed to wrap themselves half around the little community. Visible far away across Jones Sound to the south were the icecaps of Devon Island. At the northeast end of the settlement were the larger buildings of the two-man RCMP detachment and, beside a pretty little tarn back from the beach, the little one-room school itself, with a teacherage attached. We transferred there in 1967 from Arctic Bay on northern Baffin, and I took over for two years as teacher/administrator.

Long centuries ago, Ellesmere Island supported large numbers of the Thule culture people who had migrated and settled from the south and west, and the shores of Ellesmere are now a rich field for any archaeologist brave enough to risk having polar bears coming by for dinner, or moving into the tent in the middle of the night-that-isn't-night. Grise Fiord had its own little crop of *qarmar* sites where the ancient people had dwelt, but there are much greater and richer concentrations on the east coast. Marine life flourished there in the vicinity of the great polynia, the area of permanently open water known to the whalers as the North Water, so it was a land ideal for the hunter, and the excavations in that area by Canadian scientists in recent years have added greatly to our understanding of those earlier peoples. Dr. Peter Schledermann of the Arctic Institute in Calgary has even uncovered Viking artifacts in the old Thule house sites in this region, scraps of woollen cloth woven in the style of the Norse settlements of southern Greenland, iron rivets from Viking long ships, and even a scrap of medieval chain mail. These would be astonishing discoveries anywhere, but they are far more so halfway up the east coast of Ellesmere, and they point to the great probability that they were brought into that region by the Norse explorers themselves, rather than having been looted or traded from the very distant Norse farms far to the south.

The ever-nomadic Thule people migrated on from Ellesmere all along the rich shores of Greenland, west and east, eventually populating the lands of the Vikings of southern Greenland, in the final centuries before those Norse people themselves vanished so mysteriously from the face of the Earth.

By the 19th century, although Ellesmere continued to be visited by itinerant hunters from Greenland and from Baffin Island, there was no longer any resident population in the

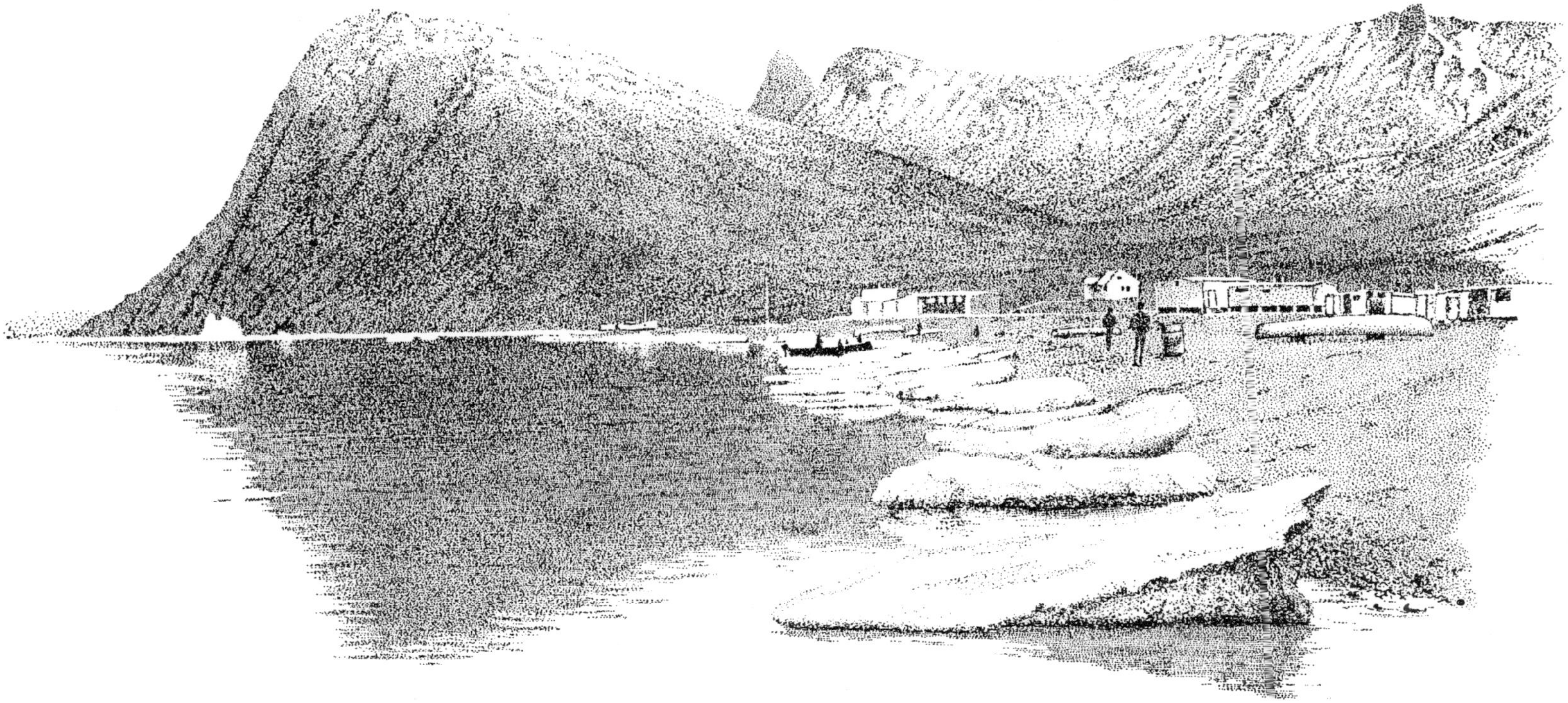

Grise Fiord at the end of summer.

Canadian islands north of the Parry Channel, and in the twenties, to counter any possible claims on those deserted lands by the Norwegians or Americans, Ottawa established a couple of lonely RCMP detachments on the empty but rich coasts of Ellesmere Island.

And that's how the situation might have remained except for a problem down on the shores of Hudson Bay. The Eskimo people of Port Harrison on the Quebec mainland were going through hard times during the early fifties as too many hunters competed for too few resources in too small an area. As a partial solution to that problem, the idea was hatched in Ottawa to offer to a selected group of competent hunters from Port Harrison the chance to be relocated with their families a thousand miles north to start a new life on the relatively far richer coasts of the High Arctic. This would be rather like offering to destitute families in northern Denmark the opportunity to go and live on Spitzbergen. The distances and the differences from one to the other are colossal. Still, it must have seemed an exciting prospect to those with a spark of adventure in their souls, though it also meant a long and possibly permanent exile if they took to their new life.

In the earlier years of the century, with just a few million people grappling to tie together the monstrously large land of Canada into a nation, Ottawa's policies towards the bewilderingly gigantic Northland were characterized more by absent-mindedness and benign neglect than by bold innovation. Whether or not the authorities in Ottawa would actually have gone ahead with this plan is a little doubtful had it not been for the perennial fretting in the capital about Canadian sovereignty out there on the frigid perimeters. On the principle of "Use it or lose it," how better to clinch Canada's claim than to have a permanent, indisputably Canadian population living on the far northern islands? Kill two birds with one stone. (Not that anyone wanted to come right out and put it that way.) And with the Americans setting up bases all along the Arctic coast in those Cold War years, especially at Resolute Bay, well, we'd better give some of the Port Harrison people a chance to go and live there too.

So, for motives both pure and ulterior, the federal authorities made their pitch, and the people willing to embark on the adventure were brought aboard ship at Port Harrison in 1953 with all their worldly goods, their dogs chained along the decks, and transported out through Hudson Strait and up Baffin Bay to the unknown, far-distant lands that they were to make their home. They were put ashore, some families on the southeastern tip of Ellesmere and some on the barren beaches of Resolute Bay, with nothing but their dogs, tents, hunting equipment, their few possessions, their kids, and their native ingenuity. And there under the watchful eye of the Mounties they were left to start life anew.

The people of these new communities called their new land "Qausuituk" meaning "No tomorrow," because they now found themselves in a strange place where daylight and darkness did not automatically alternate with each other every 24 hours as they always had at home in Port Harrison. Here the sun circled the sky, irradiating the land and the sea ice with its blazing, searing brilliance for months on end, or hid itself below the horizon for long, awful, bitter months, so that, except for the in-between times, there was nothing to mark and define the passage of continuous time, no discernible 24-hour "day," no "tomorrow." Qausuituk!

The first years of course were the hard ones, as they are bound to be for pioneers, but they were tough, resilient people, shrugging off their nostalgia, learning and adapting to their new conditions, and they survived. The Ellesmere group, after familiarizing themselves with the whole coast, eventually opted for the site at Grise Fiord for the new settlement. Other native families from north Baffin added to their numbers and, with small heated homes provided for them by the government (this at a time when elsewhere the native people made do with their own home-made shacks) here they all settled down. Five years later, they had a school.

If, in the sixties, Shangri-La could be said to have existed anywhere in the Arctic, then it was to be found, surprisingly, a mere 840 miles from the North Pole. Grise Fiord had the feeling of a secret place, a tiny, self-contained world-away-from-the-world, lost and forgotten, where the problems of the rest of humanity never intruded. It was a happy, contented, co-operative little community, entirely free of the stresses and the growing social problems then beginning to appear in other, larger, settlements. There was absolutely nothing bad to say about Grise Fiord: no drunks, no drugs, no TB, no malcontents, no violence, no homelessness, no crime, no truancy, no hunger, no mosquitoes, no politicians. (Admittedly, there were also no oranges, no pizza takeaways, no bananas, usually no mail, occasionally no water; but this is being picky.) Even the climate, which ought to have been truly awful (as it is for example at Resolute Bay), was by Arctic standards surprisingly tolerable, for it was sheltered by the wrap-around mountains from the worst of the Arctic gales, and the bitter katabatic winds draining south out of the fiord hardly stirred a snowflake in the settlement. Once the autumn snows had settled, and the occasional September storm had blown itself out, and the sea had frozen solid, the skies seemed tranquil and forever blue. Or starry.

The children too were happy, intelligent, well adjusted and a delight to teach. At that time they had not the slightest use in their remote community for the English that I had to teach them, but they gradually absorbed it anyway, conversing happily with me in their fractured, primitive, little sentences and listening with rapt attention to the tribulations of Ali Baba and Dr. Dolittle and Pinocchio and other heroes of other cultures, as well as some of their own.

They called me "Ilisaisi", meaning simply "Teacher." There were still a few stuffy bureaucrats around the department who maintained that in order to preserve a proper level of respect and formality, one had to be known to the kids as Mr. This or Mrs. That, a cultural hang-up that was entirely inappropriate in those little communities. Nobody was ever Mr. or Mrs. anything. Everybody, adults and children alike, were addressed by their given name, and respect had nothing whatever to do with that. I always told the kids my name and let them call me whatever they wanted.

Of course, none of the people had ever had family surnames (let alone alien formalities like "Mister") and at that time they still didn't. One was simply Kudluk or Imaruituk or Kango and that was that. I revelled in all the lovely native names that people had in those Arctic settlements: Seeglook, Panipakuchu, Amarualik, Kongasereetook, Ishuhangituk, Komangapik, Soopee, Kilikti, Akoomalik, Kigutikajuk, Peepeelee, Atagutsiak, Nowya, Ningyu, Akpaleapik, Eenoogoo, Uyukuluk, Mukpalu, Tuqiqi, names rich and euphonious, wonderful names on and on without number, rolling off the tongue as long, mellifluous, multisyllable sounds, and I wished fervently that they would keep them and modernity be damned. Some of the names, though, were a bit unflattering ("No Brains," "Old Woman") and some, ominously, were corruptions of Biblical or other Western names.

The beginning of the end? I wondered. Will not Markusie eventually just become Mark? Pilapusie simply meant Philip. Pijamini was Benjamin. Yosepee was Joseph and Oolootee was Ruth, just as Samuelee was Samuel. However, Samuelee had his name recorded by some past cop as "Sam Willy," because that's how it sounded to him, and the result was that "Sam" was considered uniquely to have a surname, and eventually went on in the official annals to spawn a long line of Willys.

In earlier times it was the Mounties who were charged with the task of maintaining the records of all the Eskimo people along the seemingly endless coastlines of Canada's Arctic, and, the Mounties being thin on the ground and the native families more numerous and mobile, it must have been a difficult task at times to sort them all out. For one thing, people did occasionally change their names. Kaminerk might suddenly become Carmen. Or Mary. For another, if there was one Kidlapik in the district there was bound to be another one or two not far away. Also, when someone died, the name was often transferred to the next-to-be-born, and it didn't matter in the least whether it was boy or girl. Traditional names had no gender.

So to help simplify the task of maintaining accurate records of all the native people, the Mounties developed a system of consigning a special number to every individual. The number began with a code indicating the settlement or district. E7 for example stood for the eastern settlement of Port Harrison, E5 the eastern district of north Baffin. This was then followed by one's personal number. Elijah for example might be E7-1368. Also, to help ensure that no confusion would arise about Elijah's number, he would be issued with a metal disc with his own number stamped upon it. (Nowadays it would be a plastic ID card.) Thereafter the official records of the RCMP, the school register, the medical records and so on would show him as Elijah E7-1368.

In recent times it has become fashionable to denounce this old record-keeping system as disgraceful, demeaning, an insult to the tender sensibilities of the Arctic people, assigning numbers to them like that as if they were criminals or cattle. But all that staged outrage seems overstated and slightly silly. We are all numbered. We are one number to the bank, another number to the medical centre. To VISA we are this number and we are that number to the taxman. We have PINs and we have SINs and in all this our own names hardly matter. But no one's insulted and the world keeps turning.

Of course everyone at Grise Fiord had their disc numbers well memorized, but at the time of our sojourn there, no one had Social Insurance Numbers and since we had been given a grant to employ people locally on physical improvements to the settlement, I had first to apply for a SIN for all the adults. The federal application form insisted on the entry of a surname, so I simply entered the disc number. What else? The plastic cards came back from Ottawa with the new Social Insurance Numbers and the names spelled out in the following fashion: Elijah Esevendashonethreesixeight. Now there's an original surname.

I left it to the local people to decide what project they wanted to undertake with their community-development grant. They decided to build outdoor storage bins for frozen seal and caribou carcasses, and the like, safe from the dogs. It was to this same Elijah that I entrusted the supervision of this project during the summer when Katie and I went off to England to look for our sailboat. I emphasized to Elijah that he would need to write down everyone's hours on the job so they could be paid accordingly. Elijah wrote down the names of all the men, in Eskimo syllabics, on the blank inside of a cigarette packet and recorded all the times with little clocks.

Speaking of names, most Canadians, being such nice, compliant people anyway, have by now bowed to the dictates of that curious phenomenon of our times, political correctness, and learned to use the native term "Inuit" in place of our earlier term "Eskimo." This has come about because Eskimo was perceived, quite mistakenly, to be faintly derogatory. The word came to us from Algonquin via French and in the original Indian language meant "eaters of raw meat." Whether or not the term was intended by its Algonquin inventors to be derogatory or merely factual is not known. But it hardly matters. First of all there is nothing demeaning about eating raw meat. Ask any Arctic hunter if he eats raw meat and he will

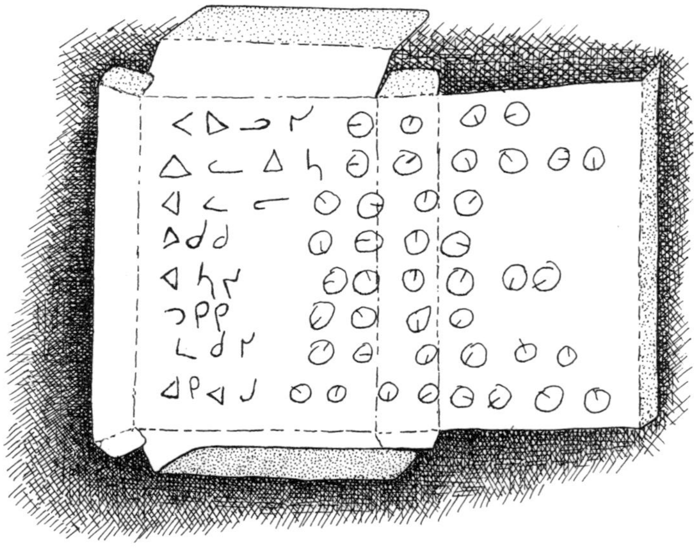

Elijah's time sheet.

reply, "Of course I eat raw meat, stupid!" (Well, he would be too polite to say "stupid," but he would be entitled to think it.) But also, of course, although the original Algonquin term was adopted first into French and later into English, the meaning was never intended or even known in the European languages, and was entirely lost until some researcher went delving.

I must admit I rather grieve the gradual wasting away of this beautiful word. Arising out of my childhood is the still-vivid image of a romantic, incredibly accomplished hero-race of the Arctic, the Eskimos, people on a par for the scope and scale of their travels and triumphs with the early Polynesians, the Vikings and the Elizabethan English. Eskimo was a word that evoked great respect and admiration.

Ironically, the same Northern politicians who have insisted on inserting the native term Inuit into our English language, are now calling themselves John and Andrew and Mary Jane. But still, they have succeeded, and most Canadians have now learned to say Inuit.

The trouble is they haven't learned to say it properly. Inuit is a plural form of the noun; the singular is Inuk. But non-natives generally use Inuit as a singular and Inuits as a plural, and if this grates on my inexpert ears when I hear it, I can't imagine how awful it must sound to anyone whose own language it is. Especially since the word is mostly mispronounced as well, it being generally mangled (mAnglicized?) into INN-you-wit. I know some people who even pronounce the word as I-knew-it! It should really sound, in English, closer to EE-noo-eet.

"Five INN-you-wits have taken part in the games," (I hear someone announce on the radio) "but only one INN-you-wit reached the semi-final."

At least one Baffin Islander I met was sufficiently irritated at all this that he once remarked to one of the teachers, "I liked it better when you people just called us Eskimos. You speak your language and we'll speak ours."

Although it is now entrenched in other European languages, perhaps in time "Eskimo" will fade altogether from English but I sincerely hope not. Actually, if there is one term that does need changing it is "Indian" as applied to a native of the Americas. This endlessly confusing mistake has been passed on down to us still in its original form, perpetuated, in all the European languages of the New World, by bad habit and lethargy, after being coined by that hopelessly lost Italian, Christopher what's-his-name, five hundred years ago. Indians, of course, is exactly what they are not. They might well have been called simply Americans, had not that term been applied instead to the citizens of just one nation on one of the two continents which together comprise America. In some places, most notably Guyana which has both a native population and a huge population of people from the Indian subcontinent, the term "Amerindian" always refers to the aboriginal people. It would be nice if we could get on and adopt the term in North America. I wonder how one goes about making a thing like that politically correct?

Perhaps the last word on the subject belongs to old Rosalie Wetrade of the little Amerindian settlement of Rae Lakes, up beyond Yellowknife. I had said something to her casually about the local Indians, and she replied, rather hotly I thought, "We're not Indians. We're Dogribs."

Quite right, Rosalie.

But to return to Grise Fiord. Our only White neighbours in the settlement were the two Mounties, and a mechanic who maintained the diesel power plant and other equipment. Luckily, these three single men were all great company. The Mounties of course had more or less outlived their original raison d'être as wavers of the Canadian flag in those distant parts, they having helped oversee the founding of the native settlement, and it was in the very nature of the little community, the cops having failed to import any gangsters, bootleggers or drug dealers into it, that they were equally redundant as upholders of law and order. Who needed policemen in a place like that?

So almost all other extraneous, semi-official responsibilities in Grise Fiord were happily shouldered by the guys with the yellow stripes on their pants. They looked after all the medical cases, dispensing medicine as they saw fit. They ran Canada's northernmost post office across their own office desk. They took care of all social services and they operated the little Grise Fiord Eskimo co-operative store.

This store was really just a small, unheated warehouse with a counter. It opened up to the public every Monday morning. If someone happened to need something in the store at any other time, he just went to the Mounties and asked for the key. He then went to the Co-op, helped himself to anything he wanted, returned the key to the cops and told them what he had taken. They wrote this down against his name in a little book and it went onto his account, eventually, some distant day, to be settled. (And it *would* be settled.) No one of course was ever known to abuse this arrangement. Katie wrote to her parents in London in 1967 describing her first visit to the Co-op store as follows: "The Co-op is open just once a week, on Monday mornings, and everyone just goes along and helps himself and then pops down to the Mounties and tells them what he's bought! At the moment though with so much new stuff having arrived off the ship, Dick the corporal goes down to the store Monday mornings just to keep an eye on things and to make sure the families on welfare for instance don't go too wild and buy unsuitable things. It's just a tiny, tiny little room with a loft and attached warehouse and you can imagine what it's like with 91 people all shopping at the same time! I went there last Monday morning and nearly turned back at the door, but then figured it would only be like it on all subsequent Mondays, so I took a deep breath and struggled in — what a scene! The room was fairly seething with people all

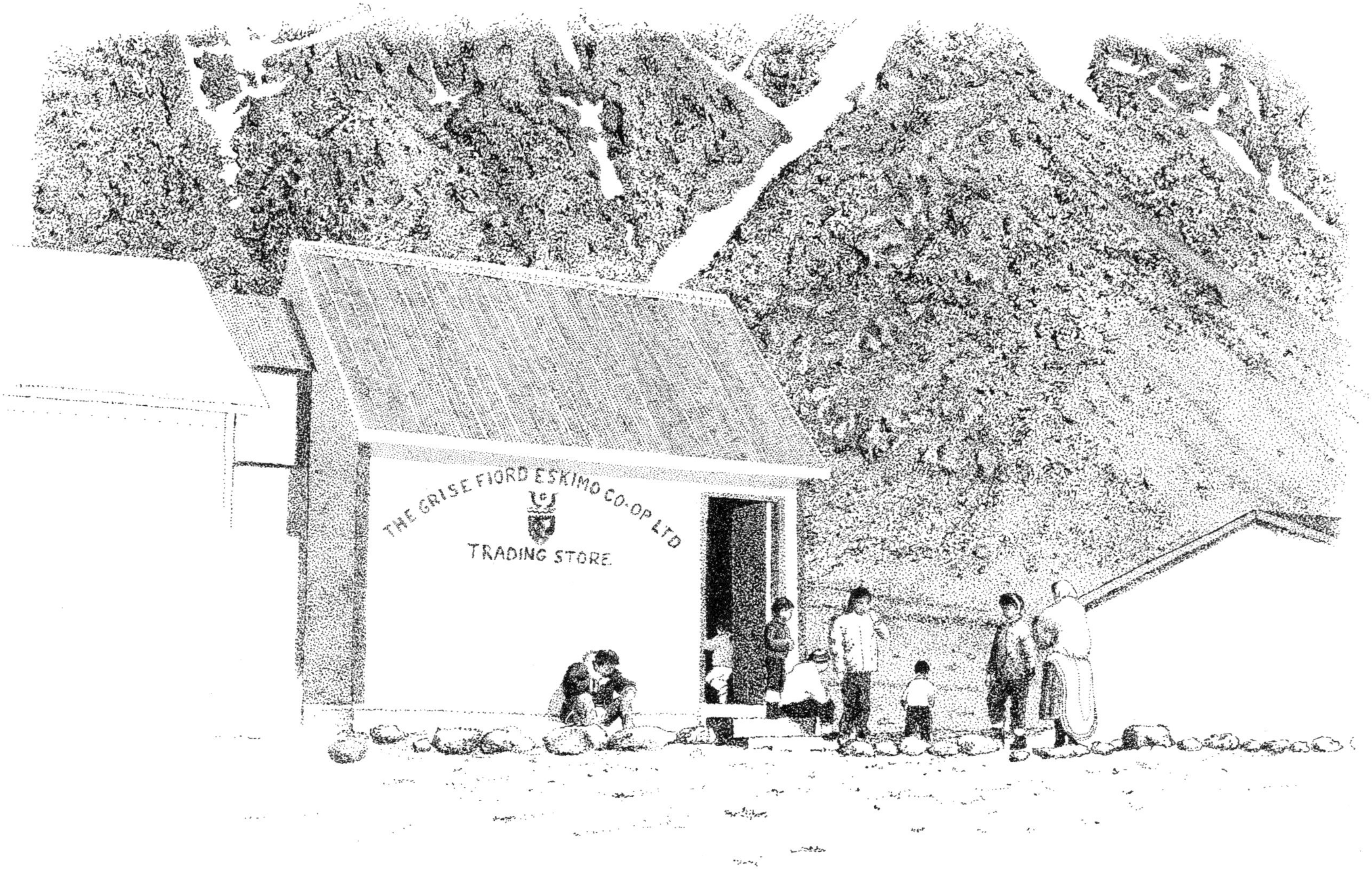

The store at Grise Fiord.

grabbing things off the shelves and scrambling up and down the walls, but not only that, the loft was full of people all throwing things down to their mates, and you'd have to be continually ducking those missiles. Luckily they only store the soft goods like sweaters and materials upstairs, so you're not likely to be injured too much by the falling merchandise."

The men in scarlet and their Eskimo special constables also occupied themselves in a never-ending series of traditional, on-the-land chores that seemed to have a curious kind of circular self-justification. This was endlessly variable, but it went, sort of, in the following fashion:

What did the cops do today?

They took the inboard engine out of their old Peterhead schooner.

Why did they need to do that?

They have to make repairs to it before the summer.

But why do they need that old Peterhead boat?

They use it to go out hunting seals and walrus in the summer.

Why do the cops need to go out hunting seals and walrus?

So they can bring back meat to feed their dogs in the winter.

Why do they need dogs anyway?

So they can go out on the land in the winter.

Why do they have to go out on the land?

Well, for instance, to go looking for muskoxen.

But they're protected. Why do they have to disturb the muskoxen?

Because they have to gather up sacks of muskox turds.

Why do they need to gather muskox turds?

So they can make a kind of muskox-turd porridge for freezing onto the bottom of the sled runners

Why would they do that?

To protect the runners on very long journeys over rocky terrain, and to provide a durable, slick gliding surface for the heavily laden sled.

Couldn't they just use, say, regular oat porridge?

No, it would be less durable, and the dogs would eat it.

Right off the runners?

Yes, right off the runners.

Well, okay, but why do they have to make those long journeys over rocky terrain?

They have to cross the Devon Island isthmus to get to Resolute Bay.

But why do they have to go to Resolute Bay?

To pick up engine parts for the Peterhead boat....

And so on. This sort of thing is what had kept a generation of Mounties from going mad with boredom, ("stark raving bonkers" in Katie's words) from the time of their first establishment on these lonely coasts in the twenties. Force of habit had kept them at it right up to the sixties. But Corporal Dick Vitt's long, six-week odyssey to Resolute Bay with his Eskimo companions in 1968, almost starving on the way west, almost eaten by polar bears on the way back, was the final flicker of a long-burning flame of romantic enterprise in the Arctic that few Canadians know about, or, if they ever did, would give scarcely a moment's thought as they wait through the line-ups at the check-out counter, or wait for the traffic lights to change in their diurnal commute down there in the great cities to the south.

Dick's instructions at the end of his epic-closing journey were to destroy the dogs, the last RCMP team in the Arctic, and the rifle shots echoing off the mountain walls of Grise Fiord in the late spring of that year brought a final, irrevocable end to a long, brave and little-remembered era.

The old Peterhead schooner was destroyed in a sudden, fierce September storm the following autumn, a storm that moved houses, tore the roof off my classroom, smashed power poles and destroyed the half-constructed church (which anyway, as the mechanic pointed out, was being "built on sand").

Grise Fiord was a place of endless superlatives, and most of them had something to do with the word "northernmost." Katie was the northernmost woman in Canada. Indeed, in all the Americas. And but for a small handful of women in Greenland, the world. This was only because our house happened to be situated at the northern end of our settlement.

I could claim no such parallel distinction because the RCMP detachment was located slightly farther north again. I brooded over this a little and felt sure that I ought to be entitled to make some equally stunning claim, and eventually, after fretting over it for a few days, it occurred to me what it was. My own home town lay on the south coast of New Zealand's South Island, and only a few New Zealanders and very small numbers of Chileans and Argentinians, as well as a couple of thousand people on the Falklands, lived beyond that latitude.

"I have it!" I exclaimed one morning to Katie. "No person in the whole world lives farther north from their home town than I do!"

Katie raised just the one eyebrow, not two, and glanced sideways at me, unimpressed. "Hmmm," was all she said.

And yet it seemed to me a remarkable thing. My little one-horse Riverton appeared to my mind far more than another world away and I felt myself enormously remote from the hearth and home that had been mine so long ago. Grise Fiord was hardly a New Zealander's mathematical Antipodes but I felt that I could not possibly have put myself farther from my distant home if we had lived on the moon. I had reached my own personal Pole of Inaccessibility.

But it is a very strange thing how small the world can be. The people of Grise Fiord up until that time had depended just on the annual visit of the icebreaker *CD Howe* for their yearly medical check-ups. However, during our second winter there, for the first time, a medical doctor and a couple of assistants were sent in to carry out midwinter examinations on everyone who needed it.

The doctor came up to our house for a visit, and in the course of the usual social pleasantries, he asked me where I originally came from.

"New Zealand," I replied, thinking that to be a sufficient answer, but he kept narrowing me down with his questions until I had finally named my little home town.

"What was your father's name?" he then asked, and I told him.

"How interesting!" he replied. "I knew your parents well. I was the doctor in Riverton a few years ago, after you left, and I was taking care of your father at the time of his death."

The wide waters of Jones Sound opened up towards the end of August each year, and the Eastern Arctic Patrol icebreaker arrived, bringing supplies and helicoptering everyone aboard to be examined and X-rayed for TB. Our once-a-year food shopping was dumped in a great pile of cardboard boxes on the beach out of the hold of a small freighter, and enormous numbers of fuel barrels and piles of other supplies were barged ashore.

But it wasn't only ships that arrived with open water. Walrus began raking the bottom for clams close along the shores and soon the water ran red as the hunters went in pursuit of them. White beluga whales appeared, and the beautiful, long-tusked narwhals. The cry "*Qilaluga*!" would be called out by some sharp-eyed watcher as soon as the narwhals appeared, and soon all the people were shouting "*Qilaluga*!" and helping the men to pile into their boats with their rifles, harpoons, long coiled lines of *ujuk* (bearded seal) skin, and ten-gallon buoyancy floats. Twenty minutes of mayhem and slaughter ensued while the dark mottled creatures flailed the bloody waters in confusion and panic, piercing the air with their long spiral tusks in their death agonies, and then it was over. Women rushed to the shores with their *ulus* as the men towed the great bodies into the shallows, and then one of the great annual epicurean delights of the people began. The *mattaq* or thick rubbery outer skin of the whale was cut in big rectangular slabs from the beached carcasses and eaten raw. (I could never understand what the people saw in the tough, tasteless stuff.) And when the spring tides of September were low enough, the women went digging along the exposed flats for clams. The sea was so much richer than the land.

In that respect the people probably missed their own lands along the margin of Hudson Bay, where they might have found more berries, more fish, more ducks and caribou than they ever could on brutally stark Ellesmere. Here the muskoxen were totally protected at that time, and the diminutive little Peary caribou were never available in any adequate numbers, when they could be found at all. Even the families from northern Baffin complained that they missed the plentiful char and the caribou of their own native lands.

No sooner had the seas opened up than the snows returned, and the school bell began calling again. Night now alternated with day, and the seas, lashed by bitter autumn gales, glazed the rocks with ice. A few more weeks and the whole sound was solid again all the way to Devon Island. We hoped that the whales had escaped eastwards in time to the safety of the North Water.

The sun at Grise Fiord showed itself briefly for the last time, a mere glowing edge on the distant Devon Island icecap, on Hallowe'en, the last day of October, and that was the sunset of the year. Sunless daylight would return briefly the next day at noon, and the next and the next, but each day it faded more until it was a mere momentary twilight, interrupting the nearly continuous starry dark. And then even the twilight was gone altogether. The kids came to school under the stars, they played outside at recess under the stars and by starlight they went home and returned again at lunchtime. We had nothing but clocks and old habits to determine when the working day would begin, and had it not been for the routine of the school, the Eskimo families would have had no reason to begin their "day" at any particular time at all. We were immersed in the long Arctic night. No today, no tomorrow.

This was the traditional period of long and total isolation in the High Arctic, but at last all that was about to change. Aviation's old pioneer of the Arctic skies, Wheldy Phipps over in Resolute Bay, got himself the very first of the new generation of twin-engine de Havilland Otter aircraft, and this made it possible to fly during the dark period. Christmas mail! A case of fresh vegetables maybe — and hang the cost! Certainly a few bottles of rye whisky to help celebrate the passing of another year. We sent our orders out by radio to the distant South, and timing it for the last full moon before Christmas, we co-ordinated everything by radio with Wheldy. He would come in and land on the sea ice in the dark. This was an unheard-of thing. Olaf, the mechanic, fussed over the airstrip, raking it up and down long after it was already perfect. And half an hour before Wheldy was due to arrive, we lit the double line of oil-burning flarepots.

Alas, after many weeks of clear skies, a bank of heavy cloud slipped in just then around the tops of the mountains, and the moon and all the stars disappeared. We listened to the faraway engines. They came and went, and came back again as Wheldy tried to find us. And then the sound was gone, and so was Wheldy. In extreme exasperation, Dick, the Mountie, went home, broached the reserves of pure ethyl alcohol in the medical cupboard and, this fiery stuff being adequately tamed with tinned juice and effervescent iceberg ice, we gathered at the detachment to celebrate our sorrows. But a few days later, Wheldy did make it in, and those earlier times of total isolation were a thing of the past.

Even so, three and a half months of that darkness was quite enough. Every year the sun returned to Grise Fiord on the 10th or 11th of February, just the merest tip at first, but increasing rapidly each day. And each year the kids in my class were the first to see it.

For two or three days before the sun's return, soft pink sunlight bathed the upper edges of the mountain walls above the settlement, and the older kids, nine and up, badgered me to take them far up the valley to the glacier, and on via the steep glacial surface to the plateau lands far above, where they might gaze on the sun at last. This would have been no mean undertaking at the best of times but at 32 below I wasn't all that keen. It would be a long, tough climb of several miles each way.

So they taunted me. "Ilisaisi, you are not Eskimo. You are Qadluna. You gonna scare." (Derisive hoots.) "Maybe you nose will frozen." And at this all the class laughed with rich glee. So of course we went, hiking far up the boulder-strewn valley in the darkness of mid-morning to the steep frontal surface of the glacier, on and on ever higher up the long glacier in the growing light to the rolling lands beyond, lands that terminate suddenly at the colossal mountain walls of the coast directly behind the settlement. Some of the boys had killed ptarmigan with slingshots on the way up the glacier. We had carried biscuits with us and vacuum flasks of what the kids called "school soup," a supplement provided by the federal department as a daily eye-opener for the notoriously breakfastless native kids. There at the mountains' brink they all warmed their hands on the hot mugs of soup, leaving their thick mitts dangling on shoulder harnesses, while we gazed away off to the south.

Just as the laggards arrived towards noon, there it was, the first dawn of the year. The shouting and horseplay stopped and while Jopee and Kavavow nibbled on their frozen ptarmigan, we all stood there, silently bathing our dark-weary retinas in the cold brightness of the sickle sun slipping sideways along the icecaps of Devon Island far away to the south. Our dark period was over.

The days lengthened so rapidly in those latitudes that within six weeks of that first reappearance of the sun, the nights themselves were no longer completely dark but amounted to nothing more than a few short hours of twilight. Several weeks after that again, the sun swooping low to the north never quite set but brightened the white land with its blinding light for all of the 24 hours, each day edging gradually higher and higher with each 360° circuit of the deep blue Arctic sky.

These were the days that the people loved so much, the 20 below springtime when the men prepared for their long hunting journeys. From this time on I always had plenty of empty desks in the classroom as first the boys and later their sisters joined in the annual polar bear hunt. Until that time, the hunting of bears had been unrestricted and the polar bear population across the Arctic had dwindled seriously as a result. So new regulations had come into effect, limiting the total number of bears to be taken by each Eskimo community. When Grise Fiord's quota of 27 bears was filled, and creamy white polar bear skins hung outside on every clothes line, it was time to travel overland through the mountains to the distant fishing lakes away to the north where Arctic char could be speared through holes in the ice. Then, in May, the seals began to climb out of their winter breathing holes onto the top of the ice to bask in the sunshine, so stalking was then in vogue with the boys.

The younger ones, eight and nine, practised their technique in the playground at recess. They lay prone in the snow in mimicry of the seals themselves, wriggling forward towards their quarry just as they had seen their fathers do. Or they hid behind the camouflage of a white paper kite, if they had one, creeping forward patiently towards a frozen, bloated, black honey bag, pausing motionless for minutes on end while the imaginary seal, the horrible honey bag, lifted its knotted top and scanned the horizon for danger. Then, the dramatic moment of action and triumph; the honey bag, thinking itself safe, would go back to sleep. The hunter's wooden gun would explode from behind the kite, and the hunter would rush forward, harpoon in hand, and plunge the lethal point home just as the wounded honey bag made its last vain plunge back towards the hoped-for safety of its hole.

Each year in May we were visited by groups of Greenlanders who had made the tough, circuitous, six-week journey by dog team from their home settlements. "*Akokeetok! Akokeetok!*" The cry would be shouted through the settlement as soon as the distant parade of dog teams came into view to the southeast. These were the "Polar Eskimos" of Peary fame, and they were usually led by Robert Peary's (unacknowledged) native grandson, Peter Peary, on their enormous journeys, skirting well northward around the North Water, and following the narrow shelf of ice along the east Ellesmere coast, or detouring inland over the mountains wherever the water of the great polynia lapped right up to the Ellesmere cliffs.

These people were supremely competent Arctic travellers and hunters, ranging confidently with their dogs over far more extensive territory than did the snowmobile-culture moderns of Grise Fiord. They had wonderful, well-trained, well-cared-for dogs, strong sleds far lighter than the brutally massive Baffin *qamotiq*, and well-made traditional clothing, including the handsome polar bear skin pants that always distinguished the Greenlanders from their Canadian cousins. (Danish law insisted on polar bears being taken only for subsistence and not in any way for sale.) We raised the Danish flag beside the maple leaf in their honour and invited them around to our homes.

The cops didn't like to act as a wet blanket, but it was plain that these Greenlanders were taking liberties with international borders, and concepts of Canadian law that must have seemed to them, the Greenlanders, arbitrary and without meaning. They readily confessed to having carefully cached a number of polar bear skins on the east Ellesmere coast which, after all, they had plainly frequented ever since they had migrated out of it, long ages before distant alien governments drew political boundaries. The Mounties radioed to HQ in Ottawa, and External Affairs just said to take no action except to tell them not to take any more.

So, "You're not allowed to take any more," it was translated, and Peter Peary and his companions smiled in genial assent. But their thoughts were their own, and who would there be anyway to stop them?

Those superb huskies nibbled away happily on Grise Fiord's remaining whale carcasses during their dog-holiday at the settlement, but plainly Peter and the rest of his party were in need of more dog food for the first part of their long journey home. Walrus could always be had at the open water 50 miles away at Craig Harbour, but with the RCMP looking over everyone's shoulder, it was decided that some of the local men would go along with them and help with the hunting. Katie and I too went along for the ride, enjoying the open spaces, the bitter-crisp

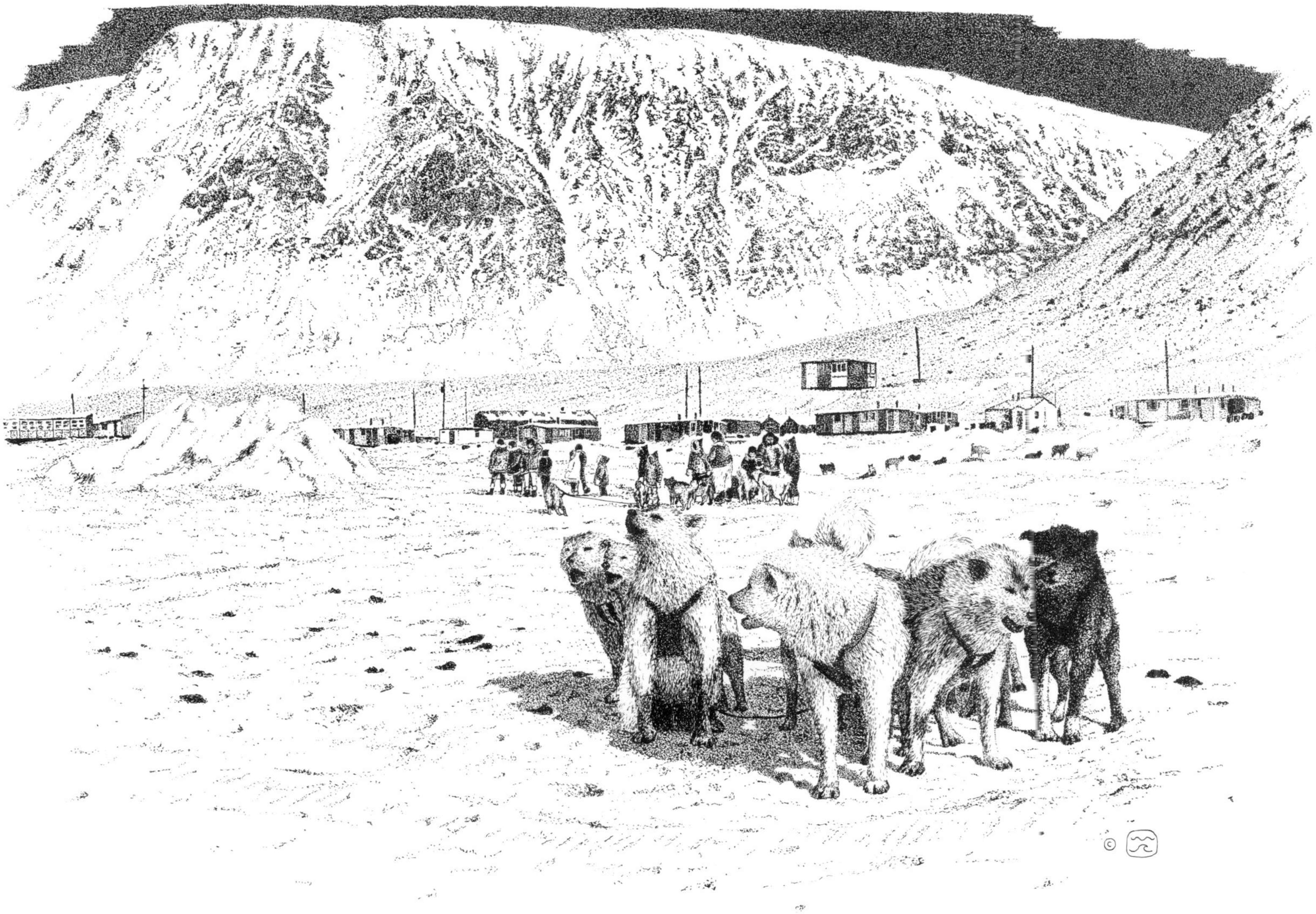

Greenland dog team at Grise Fiord.

Arctic air and the splendour of the great, silent, mountain walls lining the coast all the way to the North Water.

At the end of the gory hunt, one of the men, Markusie, after whittling away at the fatty flesh adhering to a long bone, solemnly presented this bone to Katie as a souvenir of the hunt. It was the *bacculum* or penis bone of the male walrus. It was almost the size and shape of an axe handle, with a nice, natural hand grip at one end and a thickish knob at the other.

Markusie knew we had bought a sailboat in England and he had once seen a movie about pirates.

"Ilisaisi," he said, "the world is full of very bad people. When you go to Elisapeenuna [Elizabeth's Land as the Eskimos called England] and you sail your boat far over the sea where many thieves live, maybe you will need this."

For one-on-one combat, it was certainly a fine weapon, I thought to myself. And no doubt that was exactly how the poor old walrus had regarded it.

"It's strange that the male walruses have those bones," I commented to Markusie. "You and I don't. I wonder why they need them."

Markusie stared at me for a brief moment. "Ilisaisi," he replied patiently, with the air of one instructing the retarded, "don't you understand that the water is very cold? Of course they need those bones. You jump into that water over there, find yourself a woman walrus and see if you can do what they have to do without the help of a bone."

The days of spring could not get any longer, but they could get warmer, and far more brilliant as well, as the sun gradually spiralled upwards, blazing out of the clear blue sky. Again there was no "today," no "tomorrow," and those children who were still in the settlement, or who had returned from their hunting journeys, played outside sometimes all through the sunlit hours of night. Just like everywhere else in the North at that time of year, the people tended to stay awake longer than they should have, then slept longer than they should have, if they were to fit it all into the standard, 24-hour day. Humans operate on an inborn circadian rhythm, and experiments have shown what always seemed quite obvious in the Arctic, that our internal "day" doesn't last 24 hours at all, but more like 25. This is why it is easier for us to lengthen our days than to shorten them, and why we tend to adjust well after a flight westwards across several time zones, which add hours to the day, but not after flying the same distance eastward. I sometimes theorized that if only we could just go along with the pattern and declared, say, a 25-hour day, starting school one hour later each day by the clock, this might be the only way to co-ordinate with the general trend. As it was, we were clearly not co-ordinated when we rang that bell at nine o'clock for kids who had only just stopped playing outside, or who had gone home to sleep at three A.M. So should we not start later each day? Of course we would eventually be calling the kids to school at midnight. But so what? They often seemed a lot more awake then than they were at midday.

But it still wouldn't have worked because while some families slept when the sun was higher in the south, others slept through the "heat" (minus 15°) of the afternoon, or went to bed when the sun was lower in the north. And in some of the houses, one person might be deeply asleep while two others would be sitting talking or carving away at a frozen seal on the floor. There seemed to be no understood general sleeping time, any more than any common mealtime. And if all the adults in a household happened to be fast asleep at the same time there was still no requirement that the children must therefore be sleeping also.

So, just as I had in Arctic Bay and Fort Franklin and Resolute Bay and other places in springtime, I kept a couple of mattresses in a corner of the classroom away from the windows because some of the kids responded to the nine o'clock school bell after having played outside all night long. And when they fell asleep at their desks, sooner rather than later, I deputized a couple of others to shepherd them over to the mattresses and let them sleep it off. It wasn't exactly in the curriculum, but neither were a lot of other things we decided to do.

And when those dark almond eyes that were still awake looked longingly out the wide windows to the great skeins of snow geese flying north against the blue sky, I abandoned chalk and books, in favour of parkas and boots, and with a picnic lunch on our backs and snow goggles on our faces we went climbing our beautiful mountains, up again onto the glaciers, or hunting Arctic hares across the disappearing snowfields in the valleys.

Perhaps one had first to endure the immensely long mega-winters of Ellesmere Island to appreciate the final sweet release,

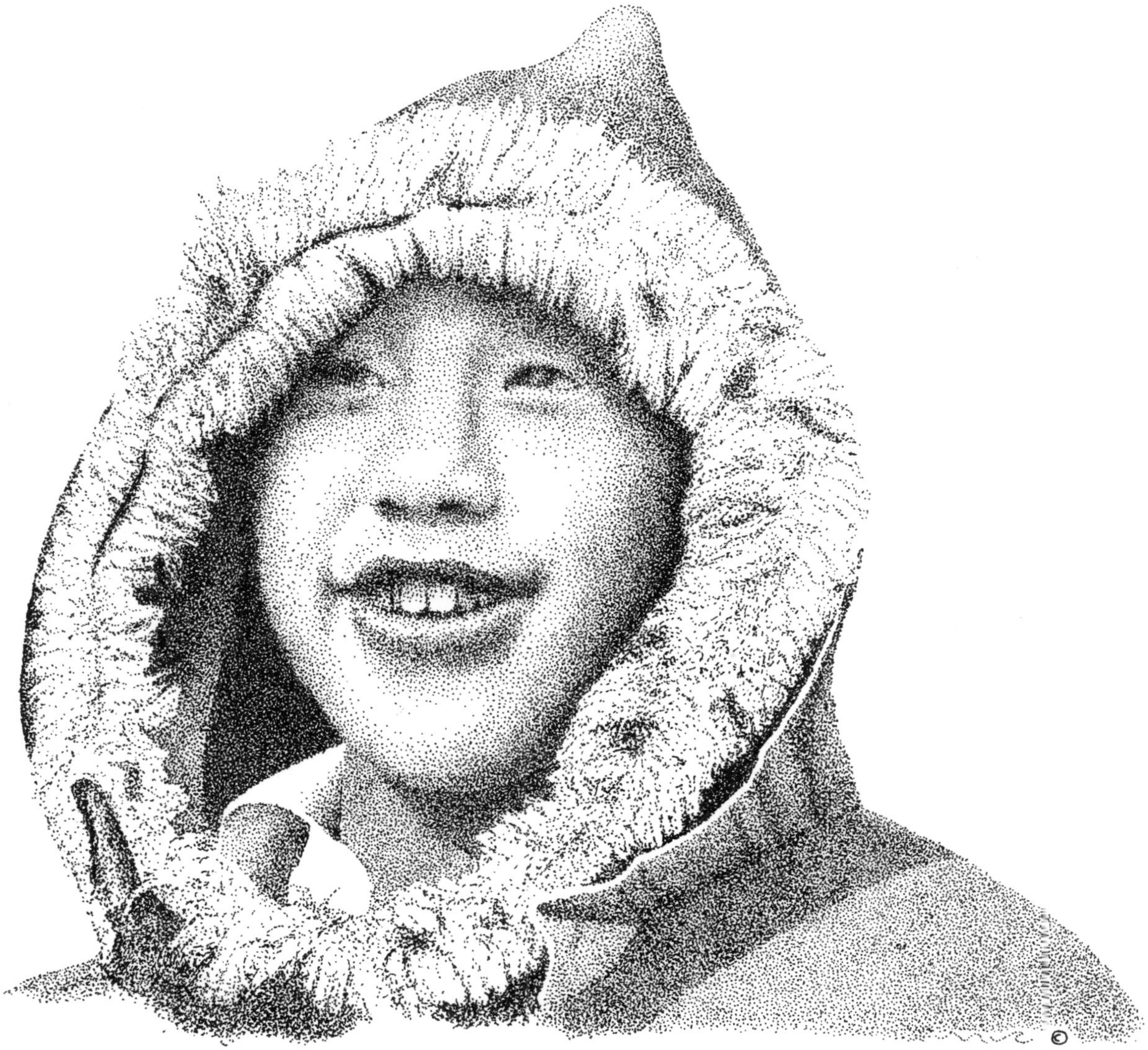

Boy of the Arctic.

but in all our experience nothing could quite compare to this arrival of spring in the high latitudes when winter's solid death-grip was loosened at long last and the streams gushed everywhere over the bright land and out onto the frozen sea. I was overwhelmed by the beauty of that far, secret land.

The people originally from Hudson Bay must have felt (mixed with their nostalgia) the same exhilaration, the same love for their adopted land, the same wonder at the beauty of it all, for most of them stayed on at Grise Fiord and made their lives there, though some did return to Port Harrison (Inukjuak) in Quebec. When it transpired in later years that in moving the people to Grise Fiord the federal government may have had the additional ulterior motive of reinforcing Canada's claim over those lands, there was much grumbling about the need for compensation, and much editorializing in Southern papers about Canada's gulags in the Arctic. No doubt the first years in the High Arctic were hard ones indeed, but it may be fair to say that by the standards of the fifties, and in comparison with native folk elsewhere in the Arctic, the people had been kindly and generously treated by Ottawa, and there was little response to the offer of repatriation south to their homelands; in any case the younger generation had no wish to leave their Shangri-La for the unfamiliar lands of their fathers.

At the end of June of our second year, 1969, it was time to go. Katie and I had bought our sailboat in England the previous year, and we had a date with our dreams. On my final walk out to the winter runway on the sea ice, I picked up a little rounded stone on the exposed beach and put it in my pocket. We said goodbye to all the people gathered around the twin-engine Otter and climbed aboard, the kids calling out, "Bye Bye, Katie! Bye Bye, Ilisaisi!" And then we were gone.

* * *

Having lived in the northernmost community of the Americas, I had always wanted to visit the southernmost. And indeed we did, though it took us fully 24 years after leaving Grise Fiord to get there.

I had always understood Puerto Williams to be the world's southernmost community. It is a town on the northern coast of Navarino Island facing north across Beagle Channel to the Argentine lands of Tierra del Fuego, and it was for this little Chilean port, 70 nautical miles from Cape Horn, that we navigated during our third extended voyage, which had taken us southward from Bering Strait. Late in 1992, we entered the long, tortuous and dramatically beautiful channels of Patagonia, and sailed southwards from the island of Chiloe to the Straits of Magellan, and beyond that, westabout around Tierra del Fuego, to the Beagle Channel. These are wild, gaunt, primeval and bitterly savage regions, exceptionally challenging to a sailor in a small boat, and although they are all gone now, virtually extinct, the aboriginal people who had managed, if not to flourish, at least to survive for many thousands of years in that extremely bitter end of the earth, were often in my thoughts.

I had always considered the Eskimos to be the hardiest people in the world, adapting brilliantly and learning to survive in by far the harshest climate of the inhabited world. But the Amerindians of Tierra del Fuego, and southward from there amongst the final archipelagos near Cape Horn, lived also in a savage, appalling climate, and they, for the most part, were entirely unclothed. Consider this quote of Charles Darwin who visited these shores aboard the *Beagle* (and who had an extremely low opinion of these "savage barbarians"):

"While going one day on shore near Wollaston Island we pulled alongside a canoe with six Fuegians. They were the most abject and miserable creatures I anywhere beheld. [They] were quite naked and even one full-grown woman was absolutely so. It was raining heavily, and the fresh water, together with the spray, trickled down her body. In another harbour not far distant, a woman, who was suckling a recently born child, came one day alongside the vessel, and remained there out of mere curiosity, whilst the sleet fell and thawed on her naked bosom, and on the skin of her naked baby!"

He then went on to mention how the women had to go out at low tide day or night, winter or summer, fossicking for shellfish, or diving deep down for sea urchins in the frigid water. So who was tougher is a moot point. The Fuegian aboriginals, sadly, were not tough enough to survive European diseases or bullets.

Katie and I reached Puerto Williams in January 1993, and when the officers of the Armada, the Chilean navy, came aboard to check us into the port, I explained in my execrable Spanish the interest we had in their southernmost community of the Americas, after our having lived in the northernmost amongst *los Esquimales*.

"Oh, but you are wrong," they said. "The southernmost community in the whole world is a place of about one hundred people round on the east side of Navarino Island. It is called Puerto Toro. You will pass it on your way to Cape Horn."

So of course we sailed on east and south, and we stopped at Puerto Toro, tying *Nanook of the North* up to the little dock, and stepping ashore to the lovely, forest-encircled little human... gathering... I don't know what to call it. A settlement it would be in the Northwest Territories. I want to say a hamlet or a village, but that sounds too much like Fort Simpson or Fort Smith. It was a *poblado* in Spanish, and apart from superficial things like trees, open water and a not-strictly-aboriginal populace, it did have its many resemblances to Grise Fiord. There was the diesel power plant. There was the little school. For RCMP, substitute the omnipresent Chilean navy, the Armada. And up on the hill, the line-up of identical, government-supplied homes for the few fisherfolk who chose to live in this southernmost community in the whole world. "*El poblado mas al sur del mundo*," as the signpost said with such primitively scripted pride at the inner end of the dock. I would have added exclamation marks to that, but the Chileans refrained.

I took that little pebble I had brought from the beach at Grise Fiord, and I tossed it at last, as I had always intended, onto the stony beach of this tiny place.

Of course as everywhere all along the long coast of Chile, the Armada demanded to know who we were, what we were doing there, how long we were staying, where we came from, where we were going, at what speed, and when. (But they always sugared their tiresome importuning with great courtesy.) I mentioned to them this long-felt need of ours, to visit the southernmost community in the world.

"Oh, but this isn't *really* the southernmost in the world any more," they said. "You must know that we now have a *poblado* in O'Higgins Land."

Oh no, I thought, not O'Higgins Land!

The almost ludicrously Irish name of O'Higgins quite litters everywhere the long, lovely land of Chile. Bernardo O'Higgins, *El Libertador*, was Chile's George Washington, having freed the land from the rule of that black-hearted spalpeen, the king of Spain. Avenues, plazas, great edifices, banks, bridges, a multitude of things throughout Chile are named for the nation's liberator, and his name is even applied also to the Chilean-claimed segment of Antarctica, which includes the Antarctic Peninsula and the South Shetland Islands. The Chileans never pass up any opportunity to reinforce their territorial claim to "their" slice of the Antarctic pie, always vigorously dismissing the *pretenciones* of Argentina and the United Kingdom whose own claims overlap those of Chile.

How better to clinch the claim than to have a resident Chilean population in place?

"At Marsh Base," the officer explained, "we have many Chilean families. They have their own chapel, their own little school, their own medical clinic, even a supermarket is there. It is proof of the rightful claims of Chile to O'Higgins Land."

"Oh yes," I replied. "That's a great idea. Actually, we occasionally do exactly the same thing in Canada, in our Arctic lands. But one thing I must tell you: we thought of it first."

Matters Medical

Whenever Katie and I prepared to set off on our extended ocean voyages, totally cut off for long periods of time from the rest of mad humanity (which by the way was exactly how we liked it) people would say to us, "But aren't you afraid of getting sick? What if something happens? What if you get toothache or break a leg? What will you do if you get appendicitis?" In exactly the same way, whenever we went to live in one or another of those little settlements that were so exceptionally isolated in earlier times, we were asked those questions. "What if something happens to you? There is no nurse up there. What if you break a leg? What if something terrible happens to you and the planes can't get in for another two months? Are you sure you are being wise in going off into such a remote area like that?"

Actually, we were not unmindful of these things, but fear of the unknown can prevent you from doing anything. The seductive comfort and security of the soft, suburban life does not liberate; rather to the contrary, if one is not extremely careful, it can easily enslave. I could readily have added to the long list of our friends' worries. What if we are caught out on the land sometime, and we freeze a foot or a hand? What if we are camped on the sea ice, and it breaks away? What about the danger of dog attacks? Or polar bears or grizzlies? What about rabies? What if I wake up one morning at sea with a prostate problem, find I am unable to pee, and we still have two thousand miles to go? And then if, as a result of this, or something else, I happened to die at sea in my bunk, somewhere in the tropics, say, several weeks from a landfall, how for heaven's sake would Katie ever manage to lift my heavy, rotting carcass up the high companionway and out across the deep cockpit to the gunwale? Would she have to saw me into manageable pieces?

Worry about stuff like that and for the rest of your life you will stay at home.

As it was, neither of us ever anticipated or contracted any serious medical problems either at sea or in the North. The occasional massive cold perhaps, during the winter after a plane came in, the odd foolishly self-inflicted hangover.... The toughest aspect of living in an isolated settlement without access to any medical expertise was not so much having to worry about one's own health, but rather having to worry about the health of one or two hundred other people, for it sometimes fell to the teacher to deliver whatever medical care was needed, and from time to time that could be a lot of work. Even in places where a nurse had been posted, she may not have stayed around for the whole year, and sometimes the last thing she would do before getting on the plane to go out would be to pass the dispensary keys to me. Gee, thanks!

They warned us about this dispensing of medicine during our teachers' conferences in the fifties. We were all expected to learn first aid, know how to set bones, give injections, deliver babies, stitch wounds, cope with an outbreak of measles.... Even so, I never quite realized then how much work it could sometimes entail. Or worry. The older folk were forever in need of some analgesic for their creaky bones, somebody's baby was always in crisis, squalling away on and on by the hour, all night long, and accidents seemed never to be far away. I used to get weary of it all and without the radio to help diagnose our problems, I don't know what I would have done. But the poor people were so dependent on the exceedingly limited help I could give them, and so grateful, even when, in desperation and baffled ignorance, I just passed out a packet of aspirins and hoped for the best.

Even the school kids had their problems, especially in those earlier settlements in the bush. They were surprisingly thin, some of them, from their inadequate diets. You hardly noticed it until they went swimming. Many came from very deprived homes, and the poor general health of some of them was indicated in the long candles of pale mucous decorating their nostrils as they came in from the cold, sagging down to lip level, disappearing suddenly as they sniffed noisily in, sagging down again... and the frequent nosebleeds during the school day. They would grab a Kleenex when the blood suddenly flowed, twist it into a little rope and poke one end as a plug into the nostril, maybe one in each nostril, so that on some days I seemed to have groups of little walruses working at their desks. But they were so sweet and endearing, grabbing my hand in theirs as I walked to school with them, (sometimes, since I had just the two hands, numbers of them would share one hand between them, a thumb for one, two fingers for another...) or, at my desk in the classroom, leaning bodily against me as I heard them individually, or in pairs, practising their reading.

Perhaps that's how Katie and I managed to contract one little problem in our first settlement. I went home after school for a cup of tea. Katie was standing by the window where the low afternoon sunshine came streaming in, and as I was standing beside her, looking at the golden light in her soft, silky hair, some tiny thing on one of those bright strands moved. I told Katie to stay still for a moment while I reached up. Ugh oh! A louse! My fingers went sifting carefully through her hair. More! Not many, but more. I picked one out and showed it to her. "Look what I've found!"

Poor Katie, immobilized in squirming panic, screamed "Oh, yuck!"

"They probably came from me. You'd better check my hair."

Sure enough, I had not only a lot more, but nits as well, the little egg cases that adhere so stubbornly to the individual strands. Horrors! How strange we had never noticed them sooner. We both felt... infected, soiled, crawling with disgusting livestock. We felt *lousy!*

So back to the medical supplies. Of course there was a large gallon jar of the smelly shampoo that would deal with those little bastards, so deal with them we did, there and then. Wash the hair. Wash it twice. Rinse and dry. Have a bath. Change clothes. Change the bed. Sweep the floor. Wash the floor. Inspect the cat. Open the window. Open the doors. Go for a walk.

The lice didn't like it, and they went away.

Next, the kids. But there were no showers in the school and nothing remotely like one in any of the homes. The teacher of the junior room had marched all her little ones to the beach the previous June, got them all stripped off to bare skin, into the water, and deloused in one fell swoop. But that was the summer. Now all we could do was to get the kids to check each other to see what was there (but they already knew that), rig up some tubs and hot water, as Katie and I had done, and have a hair-washing afternoon on Friday. That's one way of finishing off the school week. Louisa won the contest for the best tied towel turban.

During the summer in that same settlement, an old prospector came by in his canoe and wandered slowly up to the school with a slightly pained look on his face. He had been doing a long survey away off down the river to the east, chipping at rocks and looking for God-knows-what mineral. He wasted no time on formal pleasantries. "Where does the Spencer woman live?" he wanted to know.

"Spencer? There's nobody here called Spencer."

"Must be. I was told she'd be here in the summer."

"Who told you that?"

"The nurse. Just before she left here in June."

"Well, that beats me. What was the woman's full name?"

"Dunno. The nurse just told me I'd have to see a Lady Spencer. Maybe she's English or something."

"Oh, I get it," I said. "Actually I think you've already found her. But it isn't a woman you're looking for, it's me."

"You? *You're* Lady Spencer?"

"Well, almost, but not quite. I think what you're looking for is the *lay dispenser*. And for the moment, unfortunately for both of us, that's me."

We chuckled about that for a bit and eventually he told me what his problem was. Haemorrhoids! But of course. I might have diagnosed that myself just from his demeanour. So I searched around in the medical supplies, finally unearthing an old jar of suppositories, and off he went happily again back down to his canoe, bound for the bush.

He called back to me from the shore. "Thank God it wasn't a woman. I was certain she would insist on inspecting them," he cried. "Women are like that."

In another one of those communities in the bush, I was relaxing one Saturday afternoon at the Hudson's Bay post, shooting the breeze with the boys, the "factor" and his assistant, in the little apartment at the back of the store, when there was a knock on the door. Dolphus, 11 years old, from my class, stood there. "I lookin' for teacher. Leg cut."

Dolphus had already gone to the school, on his way leaving a bloody trail behind him, found I wasn't there and limped all the way back to the Company post. He wasn't crying, but he did look a little shocked.

"Come in, Dolphus. Let's have a look."

It was freeze-up time then, and though the lake was still quite open, a lot of fresh snow had fallen and was lying everywhere on the ground, soft and uncompacted. Dolphus had been tramping around near the shore when his right foot had come down through the soft snow alongside a sharp piece of steel that was hidden underneath. The jagged edge of the steel had ripped a long gash right up the side of the boy's leg from just above the ankle almost to the knee. It was the biggest wound I had ever seen, an ugly thing inches deep. It had to be stitched back together, urgently.

This wasn't a medevac; the planes had all gone south for freeze-up and the visiting nurse had likewise retreated down-river till the lake froze. I began to regret not paying closer attention to our instructor at the teachers' conference. How do you tie those stitches again?

Anyway, I first got out a needle and syringe of local anaesthetic from the dental supplies because being slightly squeamish about other people's pain, I wanted to lessen the sting of the stitching for Dolphus. So all down both sides of the wound I jabbed some Novocaine, after cleaning things up a bit with alcohol swabs. Whether that helped or not I couldn't tell. I then launched into the stitching, but instead of making each stitch separate and independent from the next, tying each one off and cutting it, I continued lacing all the way up, into the skin on one side and out the wound, into the skin on the other side and out the wound, just as a sailmaker might do with a torn jib. About 26 stitches. Was that how it should have been done? I learned later that it wasn't, but no matter, the wound was closed.

I then gave Dolphus a shot of penicillin in the rear end, ("down in the corner of the upper outer quarter," the nurse had told me over and over to make sure I had it right, for there were many people from time to time who needed those shots) and took him home.

The lake was still open, so I supposed the river draining from it would also be open, and I still hoped to get the boy to the nursing station 80 miles downstream. I rounded up a couple of men who were willing to attempt the long, cold trip downstream with their canoe. I gave them the gasoline, and a bag of supplies from my rations, and off they went, with Dolphus bundled into sleeping bags at the bow.

But the river was running ice, worse and worse as they got farther downstream, so they gave up and the next day they returned to the settlement, cold and battered. Dolphus was stuck with me, and my radio, for the duration of freeze-up. I didn't like the responsibility but the long wound gradually healed without infection and eventually the boy was back in action again, running with the rest as if nothing had ever happened. It's amazing how resilient kids can be.

The local anaesthetic, Novocaine, of course, was intended for the use of professional dentists, not half-assed lay dispensers stitching wounds. Even in a dental capacity, I learned much later, I should have left the stuff in the cupboard. But various people had toothache from time to time, and it could only have been sheer desperation that drove them to me. They wanted the offending tooth dragged out rather than having to go on enduring their pain.

Well, I didn't like the idea. But there was a variety of tooth tongs, or pliers, of various shapes in the medical supplies, mean, sturdy, tough-looking things with inward-pointing stainless steel jaws, like a trap, for grabbing at the base of the crown, against the gum. So I had the tools and if these guys were really determined to go through with this, I supposed the least I could do was to give it a try.

My friend Joe was the first of these candidates, and I must have done a satisfactory job or there would have been no more applicants thereafter. He came along with one of the older men to see me, and they each wanted a tooth yanked. I started on Joe first. I asked if he wanted the needle before I began. He thought about that, looked a little sceptical as well he should have, and then opted for the Novocaine, his second act of bravery in one day. He got it, and although it must have been simple good luck, it apparently worked, at least a little.

Once I had a good grab of the molar I began gently easing it up, rocking it back and forth, back and forth to loosen the root away from its moorings. I hated the whole business and I felt at least as much anguish as Joe felt pain, but finally, the long, bloody thing came out, intact.

While all that had been going on, the older man had been sitting in a chair nearby, watching everything intently, and nervously wriggling at his own tooth with his thumb and index finger. His tooth was a dark brown colour, from chewing tobacco maybe, and must already have been dead and loose because just before I was finished with Joe's molar, to our mutual amazement, out came the old man's in his own hand! I thought it was only kids who could do that.

Whenever there was some big medical crisis in those little places, an interesting thing happened which was quite unlike what might be expected in our own White culture. Some old fellow might be deathly ill, for example, or someone badly injured, and as you went into the little log house to see the patient you expected a hushed, unctuous atmosphere of sorrow and restrained silence, one or two close relatives hovering nearby, talking in whispers, no one else around. But that wasn't how it would be at all. The cabin would be jam packed with people, all standing around, talking, coming in, going out, everyone showing their concern by just being there. Sometimes it seemed that the closer someone was to death, the bigger the crowd.

It was a bit like that when Therese was having her baby. The midwives were there in the back room and everyone else was milling about in the main room. I wasn't needed so I gladly retreated from the busy scene. The baby was born later that night, a little boy, and all the visitors went home. But they were all back there next day, standing about looking concerned, coming in, going out, talking, smoking, when I arrived there for the second time. Two of the women had come to see me earlier about Therese. The delivery had been fine, but the placenta had not come forth. It was still in there, and had to be removed... somehow. I rather balked at the prospect. Extracting teeth was one thing, but ....

I called the doctor on the radio and explained how things stood. He pointed out that the weather wasn't very good where he was and that it might be difficult to organize a charter, but dealing with the extraction was no problem at all, and he launched into a long explanation of what had to be done. I wrote down as much as I could understand through the static, and then prepared, a bit reluctantly, to carry out his instructions. Trouble was, I was sometimes a bit too queasy for this lay dispensing. I was just leaving for Therese's house 15 minutes later when the doctor came back on the radio and said not to worry, a plane was available and since he had never seen our little settlement before, and would enjoy a visit, he would come in right away, chase everyone out of Therese's cabin, and attend to the matter himself. Whew!

But all that delicacy and reticence on my part was really just my own Western culture showing through. The people seemed far better able to cope with life's little realities, far more matter of fact, more down to earth, and more essentially natural in their attitude than were most White people. "Why isn't Brenda in school today?" I asked one day, as I marked the register.

"She got her first period," announced 12-year-old Frederick, happy to be the first with the splendid news. Apparently everyone else in the class already knew. No surprise. No embarrassment or snickers either.

"That's nice," I said. "Good for Brenda."

Everyone looked pleased and returned to their seat work.

Time once was, centuries ago, when girls were banished to the bush, left to their own resources in a shelter of boughs for a few days and nights by way of celebrating these rites of passage, but now it was good enough that they merely stayed at home. Or so it seemed, until some time later when Rose likewise reached that turning point in her life, and she was assigned a tent all to herself, separate, a short distance back from her parents' tent, for a night or two.

But she then got a considerable cold and was out of school for two weeks. A plane had arrived only three days previously and colds were going around. Our isolation was such that those cursed little viruses never affected our settlement until they were introduced to us by visitors. Planes were almost a guarantee of a cold epidemic. Or measles, chicken pox or mumps. We had them all.

It was just the same at sea. Katie and I always knew that while we were on those long ocean passages, many weeks away from land, however weary, cold, exhausted or run-down we might

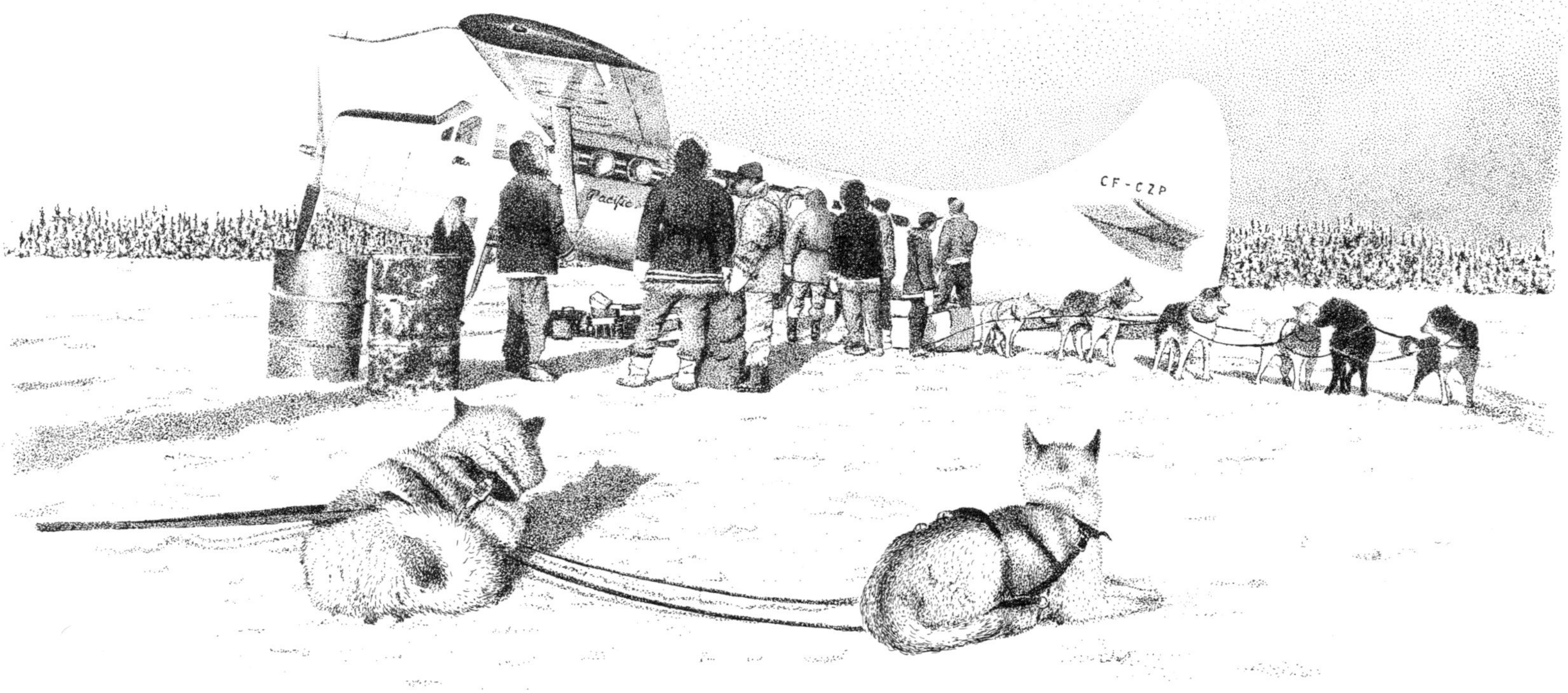

Medevac charter.

have become in protracted bad weather, at least we would never come down with any cold, flu or other infectious diseases out there on the ocean.

But in the North, the planes would bring them, and if people actually got off the plane to stay, then maybe they would bring some unwelcome venereal disease too, one of those gifts from what the priest called "the syphilised world." It took a lot of penicillin to cope once those bacteria got well established, a lot of needles "down in the corner of the upper outer quarter," and the people were forever making a big joke about it. They loved kidding each other with jokes that were ribald and rich in innuendo (no pun intended), kidding me too, asking such things as, "Teacher, how do you give a needle to *yourself?*"

At least it made it easier if people were light hearted and free of inhibitions and body-guilt. There, anything could be discussed with ease. There were no "swearing" words in the native language, nor any subject (as far as I could discern) too "impolite" to discuss. I believe there were none in the other languages of the North either, and indeed why should there be? The very idea that words could be bad was preposterous. That was a White man's concept. Equally strange was the White man's persuasion that the body is in itself a shameful thing, particularly including various assorted details that are themselves held somehow to be "bad." "Agents of the devil!" People occasionally could be partly bad, it was true, when they wandered in a wrong direction, but how could words be bad? Or things?

I was always fascinated by the juxtaposition of our respective cultures, and especially by the notion (very highly unfashionable it is true, but constantly recurring to my mind) that possibly there were some things of this native culture that may have been of value to our own, if only our collective cultural arrogance was a little less.

Just as beauty is in the eye of the beholder, so I suppose it follows that those who are dirty-minded must be those who perceive something to be dirty; that it is only through what Khalil Gibran calls "the eyes of the unclean" that the lovely human figure is seen to be unclean. It hardly matters whether the unclean are stirred by feelings of offense, rejection and disgust, or feelings of high prurient interest; they do at least have this one thing in common, that the human form in all its elegant, natural beauty is to them something shameful, secret, guilt-ridden and smutty.

To the people of that little place it was nothing of the kind. It was just a natural thing, something pleasing and normal, not deserving the high old guilt of our Puritan Western world. I suppose this happy attitude, so natural and healthy as it seemed to me, is doomed to extinction as the tidal wave of Western culture washes inexorably over those Northlands. I often imagined, with the naivete that came perhaps from long isolation, that I could play a part in helping preserve those older traditional values, but the reality was that one sandbag could not contain a flood, and that any one native person would in any case have been a far better sandbag of that kind than I was.

In one of those earlier settlements in the bush there had been no nursing station as such but just a small cabin where a nurse stayed for periods of a couple of months or so before returning to her own community. She came to visit our settlement as much as she could, but she had a boyfriend in her own community and when she left there to visit ours she also left her popular paramour to the temptations of a variety of local rivals; otherwise she might have stayed on much longer. Unfortunately, whenever she was away, I inherited the key to that cabin.

Most days in that place there were two or three people at least who were in need of some sort of medical attention after school. This was always a problem because I had so many other things to get on with and usually I was never finished working until late into the evening. The lay dispensing wouldn't have been so bad if I had had the skills to diagnose with reasonable confidence, but of course I didn't. And not having those skills meant that every case took a lot more of my time than it would have a nurse's.

The worst cases of all were the babies. I was so often baffled by their many fevers and aches and diarrhoeas and rashes and endless little troubles. I became rather terrified of babies. Every time I saw a young woman waiting for me after school, I had a sinking feeling that her baby was ill and I would have to go along to her house with a thermometer and worry myself sick with yet another insoluble baby-mystery, yet another call on the radio.

Poor Lucy! She had three delightful daughters, all of school age, and yet another girl was born to her the previous year. She was such a devoted, caring mother, very responsible and intelligent, and she loved that latest little baby so much. During the early winter it became sick, and I didn't really know what the problem was. We tried various treatments over a period of several days, but Lucy would come back each day and say that the baby was just as bad, worse even, until, finally, not before time, I decided that the little girl would have to be evacuated out. That decision might have been okay if it had not been for other factors. One of the two planes available had gone off to the Mackenzie Delta on a protracted charter. The second was having some mechanical problems, and when they were solved, the weather then was the problem. It was already turning bad even before I called to the doctor for the medevac. The plane couldn't take off, and for two days we were buffeted by an Arctic storm while Lucy stayed close to her little girl, worrying incessantly and trying to no avail all the treatments I had given her. Finally the plane arrived, and Lucy and her little one went out at last to the hospital. But it was too late. The baby died within a few hours of arriving in the doctor's care. If only I had called earlier for that plane. Poor Lucy went into a decline of grief for a time, and for long afterwards I had the recurring thought haunting me, it was my fault... it was my fault... it was my fault....

Accidents have always been common in the North. Frozen hands and feet, accidental shootings (the victims all too usually children), maulings by dogs, drownings, whole families badly burned or wiped out in house fires, plane crashes, vehicles taking their drivers with them down through the ice; there has always seemed a long litany of trauma and sorrow, and the need for adequate health care and emergency services meant that nurses and nursing stations gradually became established almost everywhere in the North and the role of the lay dispenser was over at last, and not before time. Good riddance. We often still helped the nurse in coping with problems appearing amongst the children at school, and occasionally even with other medical situations as well.

In my first years in the North I was not used to those Northern springs when daylight lasted all "night" long. There were many different kinds of migrating birds that passed through the settlement on their way north, or that came to stay for the season and raise a family, and they were all around outside my cabin at that season, cawing, whistling, warbling, clicking, cooing, singing their loud happy songs of spring, singing on and on in full-throated, sensual ecstasy, and keeping me awake in the small hours of morning.

But on one of those early mornings of springtime, it was not the birds that kept waking me up. It was another sound, every bit as raucous, insistent and sleep-penetrating, but it was not nearly as happy. Indeed it sounded terrible, and I tried over and over to shut it from my mind, to ignore it and sleep through it, for I was tired. It came from not far away, along the road a little from my cabin. I knew that there was a brew pot farther on down that road in one of the cabins (I was not sure which) and that there had been a bit of a party building up to a full head of steam in the evening. The school janitor lived down that way in one of those cabins, and in fact I think the brew itself may have been of his making. He had the wherewithal. But he was a nice old guy and in any case I would never have wished to intrude or inquire too deeply into such things. Better to stay right out of sight, especially when people got as out of control as they sometimes could.

That person, bellowing on and on like a bull not far from my cabin, was a case in point. He shouted and screamed for a while and then stopped for a minute, and I thought he'd gone away. But then he started up again, just as close, crying and shouting and groaning in some drunken falsetto agony, on and on, while other voices, more subdued, could be heard mixed in with his ravings. So he was not alone.

I just wished he (and they) would go away, back to the party, or back home, anywhere away from my cabin, and let me sleep. But finally I could stand it no longer and I got out of bed and got dressed.

For three weeks the previous year, during my first spring in that settlement, the long road, winding parallel to the river, past my cabin, past the nursing station and past the school, had turned itself into an impassable quagmire, first of deep slush, then of extensive flooding streams and pools, and finally of bottomless, gumboot-trapping mud. Each separate step through that mud required that you had to turn back on the one foot, the other in the air wearing a half-off sock, while you retrieved its missing gumboot from the vacuum of deep mud at the previous step. Even the kids had a hard job crossing that road at times (though it must be said that they navigated through it more easily and more willingly in the afternoon, going from the school than they did in the morning, going to it).

Our bosses in Fort Smith had given us a road-repair budget in the summer. (We of course had not known either that our muddy trails were really "roads" or that our "roads" needed "repairing" until we were given the money to do it.) It was left to me, as the Welfare Teacher, to figure out how the money should be spent, so I decided first to construct (or, rather, arrange to have constructed) a long drainage ditch all down one side of this so-called "road," and, naively, I hoped to have enough funds left over after that to get some river gravel on the surface. But I ran out of money, and the gravel had to wait. So for that spring at least we had a ditch, and the road surface dried off much more quickly after the big thaw.

At the little party along the road beyond my cabin, one of the women who had come up from her own cabin down by the river, Eliza by name, had imbibed a teensy bit more than she should have, and had come weaving her way back home along the road around two A.M. Eliza didn't know that we had dug a ditch, back a bit in the scrubby growth at the side of the road, and as she meandered, she fell headlong in, breaking a leg in the process. And there she lay, disabled at the edge of the ditch, bellowing yet when I arrived to look into the matter. Three other people from the party down the way stood there surveying the situation, undecided what to do about it. I couldn't understand their conversation but one seemed to be telling Eliza to stop crying, the second seemed to be telling the first to stop telling Eliza to stop crying, and the third began to walk unsteadily back to the party.

I always liked poor Eliza. She was invariably genial and well disposed whenever I went visiting her. She had a grown daughter, newly married, and two very nice younger boys at school who worked hard, and were progressing well and of whom she was very proud. And now here she was, a hulk cast upon a lee shore, a derelict in my unmarked ditch. I tried talking to her but that just released a torrent of tearful recrimination that I couldn't understand. There was a medical problem here. ("She hurt bad," was the only opinion I could deduce from the onlookers.) But at least in that community I was not into medical problems. The nursing station was no farther away from Eliza than my own cabin, not much more than a stone's throw, and I wanted to sleep. So I went and knocked on the nursing station front door. That did nothing, so I went pounding on the side door. Ten minutes of this brought a hostile nurse to the door who roundly abused me, told me what the time was and slammed the door angrily in my face. Oh dear. Poor Peggy! I gathered that she already knew all about Eliza, and that mine was not the first call made on Eliza's behalf.

There should have been two nurses there, but there was only one, so Peggy had a tough job and she used to get a little bitter and crusty at times. She herself had told me a couple of weeks earlier that occasionally when some of the young guys got all brewed up they teased her by knocking urgently on the nursing station front door in the middle of the night, and asking for a condom. Salt in the wound, perhaps, for a lonely person like Peggy.

I felt sorry for her but she should have been attending to that woman at the ditch. I waited a bit, then went around to her bedroom window and knocked on it. I called out to her, "Peggy, nobody's asking for a condom. I just want you to know that old Eliza's hurt over there, and if you want me to help, come over to my place and get me. I'm going to bed."

But the nurse refused to budge, as I found out later, holding injuries incurred in an alcoholic binge to have been self-inflicted, and that the very least a drunk can do is to sober up first before expecting sympathy or treatment. Peggy came from another time and place where it was held that we are each responsible for our own actions.

The last I saw of Eliza was when I got up at six o'clock in response to more noise coming from the road. By that time, she had been transferred from the edge of the ditch into what would have to serve in that little settlement as an ambulance. There she was, bundled like a sack of potatoes into a wheelbarrow, and her son-in-law was wheeling her along the road, weaving around the muddy bits, past the nursing station and on out of sight towards the river. There she was transferred into a canoe and taken 50 miles down the river to see the doctor.

That serious, impassive young man, who had struggled along past my cabin with such impressive dignity, wheeling his heavy but broken mother-in-law along that road in a rickety wheelbarrow, would never have made the distance, I thought to myself smugly, if I had not had the foresight and good judgment to provide for a proper drainage system last season. But then on the other hand, if the ditch had never been dug in the first place....

An accident of a very different kind occurred while Katie and I were posted to Grise Fiord in the late sixties. Throughout our time there we had a vague feeling of living on the far side of the moon, a sense of utter remoteness from the humdrum everyday world of seething humanity. And yet, of course, we weren't really so far away at all, and every day we had a reminder of this. Each evening at 7:15 precisely, two jet planes passed very high overhead flying always towards the northwest. They flew together, one immediately behind the other, like dragonflies mating in flight. The Americans in those days maintained B52 bombers in constant, around-the-clock patrol over the Arctic out of their base in Thule, Greenland, and every day at exactly that time one of those bombers was being refuelled in flight directly over the south coast of Ellesmere Island, and always, before they were quite out of our sight, they separated. We could have set our watches by those two symbiotic planes.

One day, one of those B52s crashed on the sea ice as it was approaching its base in Thule, and radioactivity was scattered far and wide over the ice from the nuclear weapons carried aboard. Great concern was felt for the possibility of radioactive contamination and a huge effort was undertaken to scoop up contaminated snow and debris and to have it all shipped south to the U.S. for containment and disposal. (This would have been laudable under the circumstances except for the inconvenient little problem that it took *people* to do all that scooping, and, needless to say, the effects of that work began to show themselves two decades later amongst some of the people involved in the clean-up, including some of the Polar Eskimos of that region.) Grise Fiord had been the nearest Canadian community to the crash site. We *supposed* we were all right but who could say? At the time of the crash, the Canadian authorities took a low profile, but several months later, long after the headlines were forgotten and the furor had died down, a medical team came into Grise Fiord to test everyone for evidence of past radiation. Oh no, no, nothing to do with B52s, we were told. Oh dear no, simply a little routine exercise. Nothing to worry about. Nothing, nothing at all. Just an academic little check into whether any abnormal levels of radioactivity could perhaps exist in the natural food chain, you know... tra la la....

Well, at least they did check. We could have used a bit more of that level of concern for people's health years earlier, but then it is highly improper to judge any action, or inaction, except strictly in the context of its own time.

Yeast and Other Problems

I HAD A game that I liked to play with the kids in one of those little settlements. They were always so sweet and trusting, and they seemed to so hang on my every word that I felt sometimes a little ashamed, fraudulent, unworthy of their eagerness to believe, their abundant and ready faith. As I told them of faraway places, strange, improbable people, turbulent events and distant exotica far beyond their own country or their own continent, they would fall silent, breathless, and their dark, almond eyes would widen in wonder. They lapped up my every word as if it came from an oracle. I think they would have believed anything.

It worried me a little for if there was any one thing that those Northern folk (the adults I mean) seemed to share with the rest of North America it was a rather-too-willing credulity, the absence, or shortage, of a strong critical faculty, of a habit of forever evaluating, questioning, weighing, doubting. Faith was considered there a great virtue and, as elsewhere, the sceptic was deeply confused with the cynic as someone lost and hopeless, groping in the darkness. You had to believe. What you believed wasn't really quite the issue, and still less was why. Belief itself was. There was held to be great virtue in believing. But of course in the fullness of his own time, the sceptic too can come to believe in all that is clearly true, and it may be that the darkness belongs to those who never search. Education should lead to the eventual empowerment of students so that they can become equipped as adults to think and act not so much uniformly (which faith and persuasion will tend to do) as independently, freely and rationally, and I think we have to begin to place a far higher value in our schools on the development of sceptical thinking, the processes of active doubt (including, especially, self-doubt) objective enquiry and evaluation that have brought us of the Western world out of the intellectual dungeons of the Middle Ages and given us the myriad discoveries of science.

So I liked to put a damper sometimes on all that willing credulity, and over a period of several weeks I warned the kids that I was going to tell them one deliberate lie every day. They had to listen, keep it to themselves, and at the end of the day they would try to identify what the lie was. The first day I told them that since spiders have six legs they must therefore be insects like flies, mosquitoes, dragonflies and ants. Only young John got it. Most thought I was lying when I told them about the birth of a new volcano in a Mexican cornfield.

They liked this little game of routine deception. Not only did it begin to awaken their critical faculty, but it helped them to pay closer attention to what I was saying, not just to hear but to listen.

To an outsider like myself, the people there seemed to have a multitude of superstitious beliefs and there were dark portents or deep significances to be found in all sorts of situations and things. Adults and children alike seemed to have their heads filled with a world of unexplainable forces and ancient spirits, the dark malevolence of the Bush Man, the secret powers of the shaman, the offended spirit of a man-killed wolf, the evil portent of a red aurora.... But such things were part of the folk tradition, their culture, and, although in adults one might deplore a too-willing credulity, still I would never have dreamed of subjecting these poetic fancies to the unwelcome, unasked-for scrutiny of sceptical science. We too had our own superstitions as children, fretting over spilled salt and broken mirrors, avoiding vertical ladders and the smelling of dandelions, deriving satisfaction from black cats, wishbones and four-leafed clovers. Whenever we found a horseshoe (a common enough thing in the days of my childhood) we would carefully spit on it, make a wish, throw it behind us over our left shoulder, taking great care not to look where it had landed, and walk away. The wish would come true! Or anyway if it didn't, its failure to come true would go unnoticed, so that was all right. Even ouija boards fell within the scope of our active imaginations as we tried to summon our ancestors in a seance. We liked these little childish games of ours and would have hated having them debunked by some pedantic scientist. But still, one grows up.

I was musing on all this as I was trudging across the lake just after freeze-up. I liked to get out of the settlement from time to time, to get some Arctic air in my lungs and some distance between me and all the concerns of that little community. My residence could sometimes seem like Grand Central Station and it was nice occasionally to get away.

The previous evening there had been a soft, red aurora glowing low on the horizon away to the northwest. As I was putting on my parka and mukluks to go for my hike, some of the kids had come in to tell me that someone was going to die. Someone here? Yeah. Maybe. Who? They didn't know. When? They didn't know. How did they know someone was going to die? There was a red aurora last night. This was scary stuff! "Hope it isn't me," I said, and they smiled and went out.

The lake, for all its gigantic girth, had finally frozen right across, a full two months later than all the surrounding ponds and streams, and at last I was able to go trekking to the far horizon, putting my legs to the test without the tedium of the snowshoe, for the lake was always windblown, and what little snow there was lying on the glassy surface was packed hard by the bitter gales out of the Arctic. It was a good feeling.

I crossed to the south shore, staying well clear of the ice surrounding the always-open waters of the outlet. There the crystal-clear liquid of the lake found its freedom, rushing forward over the deep, dark, bouldery bottom exactly as it had done unceasingly since the end of the last great ice age, and the urgent relentless current maintained the surrounding ice in a constant state of plate-thin treachery.

I floundered through the deep drifts on the far bank up to the silent, boarded-up buildings of the summer season's river transport camp, and from there I gazed back at the tiny human community on the distant shore, hardly more than a few spirals of woodsmoke curling up in the minus 35° air, and a thin grey line of log shacks, with a square white block of a building at one end as the school, a church spire in the centre and the small red and white painted buildings of the Hudson's Bay Company at the other end. From there, one could fly for hours on end in almost any direction and see nothing but this breathtakingly vast, gaunt, empty land stretching on and on beyond a never-ending horizon, a land utterly unchanged since it was tramped by the starvation-haunted companions of Franklin, or the dark, skin-clad, murder-minded companions of Hearne, and for many thousands of years before them. And there in the midst of that mighty primeval mega-land lay this one tiny human community, a final settling place of the aboriginal nomads, a place seeming, from my distant perspective, frail, microscopic, hardly believable in the surrounding immensity.

And what were they doing, all those human souls, in those distant little cabins on my horizon? Were they any more successful than all the rest of blighted humanity in their pursuit of happiness? Some, no doubt, would be sleeping, or lying awake in bed, coughing, spitting out tubercular sputum or tobacco juice, or both. Some would be in the bush with their dogs, getting a load of wood for the fire. Some might be washing mouthfuls of bannock down with sweet, dark, tepid tea, while one or two women might be busy making more of it on their steel-drum stove. One or two of the older folk could be stretching marten skins, maybe, or stitching moosehide moccasins or threading snowshoes with long strips of rawhide. A few adults might be huddled in a circle on someone's floor playing cards, gambling, an obsessive addiction from which no one seemed immune. And in all likelihood some others would be gathered together in one house or another, voices raised, children squalling or scattered, drowning their sorrows or trying to relieve the tedium of their lives with insipid home brew dipped out of some large enamel pot or basin.

The spruce trees and the willows near the outlet were coated in a lovely thick frosting from the vapour constantly rising up off the open water. I spent a little time photographing the fantasy fairyland of crystals surrounding me and then, while daylight lasted, headed back home across the miles of ice with a light but searing wind out of the Barren Lands on my face. By the time I reached the school, the daylight was half gone and my right cheek half frozen.

My return across the lake of course was not unnoticed and when I arrived upstairs to thaw out, there just ahead of me were Isadore and Napoleon. Of all the people there, I counted those two as close personal friends. They often came by to visit or to ask me to their own houses, and I never got tired of their company, whereas in the case of many of the other adults, I had to strain a bit to find common ground, quite apart from the language barrier, and there were one or two, a little of whose company could go quite a long way, especially when they were drinking. Ostensibly these two had come by to "shoot the shit" as Isadore put it so delicately, though actually they had been thinking, mistakenly, that there could have been a heel of rye whisky mouldering on the top shelf of my cupboard to help them while away a slow Saturday afternoon.

Isadore was an extremely interesting man. He was unschooled and illiterate, yet no one could call him uneducated. He had educated himself and done a fine job of it. He spoke English with the same fluency as his own native tongue and despite his isolated-native-settlement background, was completely at home in any White company, urbane, well-informed and able to join in any conversation on almost any subject. Isadore belonged easily in both worlds, Northern native, Southern White, and across the abyss of incomprehension still separating those worlds, he was possibly the best able of any person in the great wide North to provide a bridge, though perhaps few at that time realized it. He combined great intelligence with a warm heart and ready wit, and I never met anyone who did not speak of him with great respect and affection. He had a large and growing family, most of them of school age, and he lived close to the school in a large new house strategically located, so that, like the janitor and the chief, he could tap in (quite without official sanction) to the school's modest power supply. (The rest of the people had to make do as always with candles and kerosene.)

Napoleon, a tall, thin, somewhat younger man, was rather less fluent in English than Isadore, and always spoke with a soft, low voice in a sly, conspiratorial manner. In a public setting or in a group, he had little to say, keeping his thoughts to himself. But alone with one or two friends he opened up, and it was then that his zany perspective on everything was revealed. To Napoleon life was an enormous joke and his own role in it was to enjoy himself to the full, and if at someone else's expense or discomfort so much the better. There was nothing mean or vindictive about Napoleon; it was just that he was an inveterate trickster who richly enjoyed the parry and thrust of human relationships, and relished any chance to pit his wits against the world. He often came up to visit and to regale me with tales of his latest little escapade, chuckling happily all the while.

There being nothing of any interest after all at the top of my cupboard, these two fell into a desultory conversation which came around to dwelling on the considerable amount of home brewing and kai-yaiing going on at that time in the settlement, a thing one will tend to deplore far more readily while obliged to remain sober. The summer work season was long over and most of the wages were long gone. But there was a bit of unemployment insurance trickling in, so some people had money in their pockets, and those who didn't occupied themselves with balancing matters by borrowing and gambling. Apart from that standard diversion, the trapping season was still some way off and, the stockpiling of winter firewood being such a boring job, something best put off until forced on a man by dire necessity, many of the people were choosing instead to provide diversion from the tedium and poverty of their lives by laying their hands on a tin of malt and a bag of sugar at the Hudson's Bay store, and a tin of dry yeast if they could persuade the manager to let them have it. Thus outfitted, anyone had the means to enliven things a little for a couple of days. And this they were certainly doing.

Whether those ingredients could in fact be had at the trading post depended on a man's reputation, so some of the people were reduced to experimenting with other stuff in their home brew: flour, dried potatoes, white beans, prunes or even the tinned tomatoes that I was required to issue to those on welfare as part of their assistance package. (Tinned tomatoes were considered important to the native diet, but the people mostly hated them.) Still, whatever the ingredients were, yeast was the key, just as a match is to a fire, so yeast was sold discreetly, if at all, jealously guarded and very sparingly shared. (I sometimes wondered if the analogy of fire had occurred to any of those eager vintners. One doesn't really need the match, if embers can be taken from another fire. But as far as I could tell, no one in the settlement had thought of that, and I wasn't about to suggest it.)

My work took me to most of the houses in the settlement from time to time and I quite often found I had walked straight into one of those parties, if the raised noise level hadn't already warned me away. I was usually not unwelcome, but I would politely decline the proffered cup of cheer and stay only long enough to not seem to be leaving with indecent haste. I was always amazed at the transformation that that rather weak, insipid stuff could bring about in many of the people if they'd been at it long enough. The most timid could become aggressive; the most active, sleepy; the most talkative could become introverted and the most reserved as amorous as cats. Some of the adults who, I could have sworn, knew no English whatever, suddenly amazed me by launching themselves into their own slurred version of English, and not for my benefit either but also, for no apparent reason, with each other.

The problem of course with all that boozing was that no one seemed to know when to stop. A nice social drink wasn't good enough. The whole damned pot had to go in one protracted binge, come what may, sore heads or sorrow. It was something I hated. Fortunately, it was rather self limiting. Only so much brew could be made at a time, even if the yeast could be wangled out of someone else, and the brewing itself took quite a few days, and if a man's thirst couldn't survive the long wait, the brew would be so much weaker.

Of course I made no secret of the fact that I enjoyed an occasional convivial evening when invited to the home of one of my friends, Isadore or Napoleon, say, or Francis or old Joe. But they were people who drank in moderation if they drank at all, and whose demeanour at all events remained civilized and cheerful. It was quite the opposite case in some of the homes and my strong dislike of excessive boozing throughout the settlement was also no secret, though no opinion of mine could possibly have made the least difference anyway. Domestic violence was on the increase. It was a common thing to hear angry, abusive shouting and the slamming of doors as people spilled out of some drinking den or other. There always seemed to be one woman or another in the settlement with a face bruised and swollen the morning after, and the effect on the kids was especially hurtful as they witnessed the collapse of dignity and reason in those they loved. There wasn't a child in the whole school who didn't hate booze, and it was hard to know what I could do at school to help them, except to remind them that they must always love their parents no matter what, and that it was better to stay in another house with friends if they could, when all that partying started up. It was a great problem.

But this was what some of the adults, especially the younger men, called "having a good time," something that was a little hard to comprehend on the face of it. It wasn't that they needed to use alcohol to gain access to the women which might at least have made it explainable. Although that may be an Englishman's ploy, ("Have some Madeira, m'dear") or an American's, ("Candy is dandy but liquor is quicker") those guys never seemed to be without a ready pool of partners.

All these sober matters, and much more, Isadore and Napoleon spoke of before, just as they were leaving, they mentioned that Old Martha was in bad shape again, mumbling, incoherent, weak, hardly able even to cough. I went down to see her next morning, but what could I do?

Several days later, just as everyone expected, Old Martha died. *The red aurora!* She was old and she had had a good life, so everyone said. Those same kids came rushing up to my apartment above the school to tell me the news. They looked shocked and troubled, but I knew they were feeling pleased to be vindicated. Had not they themselves warned me that this would happen?

But unfortunately, they were more vindicated than even they expected for, some weeks later, a small toddler was killed when it wandered in amongst some chained-up dogs down at the settlement on the river, and this sudden tragedy too was credited to the account of the red aurora.

This was yet another reminder of the inherent danger of dogs. Normally of course it was the loose dogs that posed the real danger, but obviously even the ones tied up could pose a threat to those small enough and vulnerable enough. All the North was replete with tales of people being attacked by dogs, and savaged or killed, quite often small children, and this was the one area where I very reluctantly allowed myself to be roped in to act on behalf of the police.

Personally, I would greatly have preferred that the people could have been allowed to rule themselves and police themselves, and that the old authority of the chiefs and elders would be respected and upheld by our federal government even if it didn't quite mesh with our Western notions of democracy.

Instead, the Indian Affairs people were always bypassing the traditional figures of authority, setting up elected committees of this and that and overruling the traditional consensus style of decision-making in favour of confrontation and secret ballot, alien processes that the people were clearly not comfortable with. It seemed to me that forcing strange new democratic processes on people who didn't want them, or see any need for them, contained within it a very great irony, but it was quite lost on the bureaucrats.

But if Indian Affairs seemed to act insensitively in spelling out to the people how things were going to be done, some of those ethnocentric cops were much worse. Mostly, the police were total strangers to the people, and mostly they kept it that way. They were tall, loud and intimidating, and any confrontation seemed to leave the people with a sense of injury and emptiness, a smouldering feeling of resentment and the unhappy realization that, seemingly bereft of self-worth, they were no longer masters in their own land.

Anyway, rightly or wrongly, I was persuaded, after the affair of the killed infant, to act on behalf of the cops in trying to enforce the Dog Ordinance in the settlement, there being no detachment locally. "Dear Maurice, [the letter from the corporal read] Attached you will find your official appointment to the coveted position of Dog Officer in your community. Also enclosed for your perusal, is a copy of the Dog Ordinance of the N.W.T., and an outline of actions you might take to assist you in...." *Coveted* indeed!

There were loose dogs around there all right, a few of them constantly on the prowl. Usually I just sent a note, or told somebody to tell somebody to tie up that damn dog. And it got done, and I wouldn't see it for a week or two. But two loose dogs I did shoot in final exasperation, and I absolutely hated the business. The trouble was, the people themselves wouldn't destroy their own dogs when the time came that they were no longer wanted. Neglect them, starve them, yes. Shoot them, no. But some of the men began bringing their unwanted old dogs to the school, tying them to the fence and asking me to do the dirty deed. Though it was a miserable business, I didn't mind that quite so much; at least I was not going to need to come up with a second shot which could happen with a dog on the loose. The fact was I hated killing. But I hated guns quite as much as killing, for what were guns made for if not to kill? And so, in a way, I suppose, by extension, I hated myself.

I think the most dangerous dog in town was one belonging to a woman called Filomena who had come from the settlement down the river and was staying for the winter with her grandparents in a little old log cabin close to the edge of the lake. Like so many of the other cabins, this was just a one-room shack basically, with a curtained-off area, where the old folks slept, a single bed/settee along the back wall, a counter top along the front wall beneath the front window that overlooked the lake, a ten-gallon steel-drum woodstove in the centre of the room and two or three rickety chairs. The floor was roughly planked, and the biting wind would have blown in everywhere through the cracks had it not been for the dirt and dust that filled them. The log walls were chinked with mud. Steel leg-hold traps dangled from a nail, and a little table lay covered in cigarette butts and candle grease. It was a house about as basic as you could get without just settling for a tent.

Four or five dogs lay chained outside. The old man used them occasionally to bring wood from the bush or take him out to his nets. Every time I came to that cabin, the worst one of those dogs, a bad-tempered brute tied near the door, would lunge to the end of its chain and try to eat me. This was the dog in the settlement that seemed most in need of shooting. It always seemed rabid enough to warrant doing so, except that it had always been that way so it couldn't have been rabies. Perhaps it just hated its chain and its hard lot in life, and who could blame it? It was Filomena's dog anyway, so it was quite safe from any harm I might do even though I was always kidding Filomena that I was going to do it in.

Filomena, like so many of the other people, had a head full of superstitious fancies, and before she left to return to her own settlement she even came to think that I was some kind of White witch doctor, someone who could work magic and even influence the very forces of nature.

It happened that Filomena knew how to bake bread the way White people did it. Bannock made with baking powder was the standard fare in every home. I didn't care all that much for bannock, and I hadn't the time, patience or aptitude for making proper yeast bread, so I was happy that Filomena agreed to come to my place occasionally to bake up a batch of loaves for me. She spoke hardly any English but she was good natured and cheerful and we got along fine. Every two weeks or so I would go down to her grandparents' cabin, past that mad dog, and ask if she could make another batch of bread for me.

Filomena was rather fond of wandering off around town looking for where the action was, and I think she was quite good at finding it. She must have spent many hundreds of hours that winter sitting on the floor in one house or another playing cards, winning a little money and losing a lot more. She was always looking for a loan. I often teased her about her wicked ways and the parties she got involved in but she just retorted that she never made any trouble "like them drunkers," which was true.

In the very early summer, a short time before Filomena was due to return to her own community, she again showed up to spend an afternoon baking bread for me. I asked her what she was going to do with the dog when she left to go back to her own settlement. She just shrugged, and said "I dunno," (which in fact was the standard answer to almost all questions anyway) so I was a little more serious when I suggested that maybe it should be destroyed before it hurt someone.

At the end of the day Filomena asked me if she could have a little of the yeast in my rations. I still had a fair amount and, as she well knew, more would be coming before long in my new annual ration so it was hard to say no, though I could guess why she wanted it. Actually, she had the free run of my pantry and kitchen and could very easily have helped herself without my knowing, but people hardly ever did such a thing in those times, and I greatly respected her asking. The Hudson's Bay manager would have said no, but I liked Filomena and I said yes.

"But," I added, "only if you are going to make bread."

She hurried out happily with some packets in her pocket and I wondered a little guiltily just what it was that she was up to. Were her grandparents about to have a change from the usual bannock? Or a change from tea? *Mea culpa! Mea culpa!* What have I done?

A week or so later, I had occasion to drop by at her cabin, and make another sortie past that mad dog, to get a signature from the old man on some Indian Affairs documents: that is, the usual shaky X that passed for a signature in the case of most of the adults. (I would then surround this mark with the four words, one on each side, "Joe Blow His Mark.") Filomena of course wasn't in. She was probably off playing cards somewhere.

For a few social moments I sat down at the table beside a half-full spittoon and made a few pleasant remarks to the old couple about how good-tasting the ducks were at that illegal time of year. Surreptitiously, my eyes went searching, and I was almost certain I recognized the big tell-tale enamel pail covered with a damp cloth and partly hidden behind a printed cotton curtain hanging from the counter along the front wall not far from the entrance door. Caught you, Filomena!

Later on I had a chance to speak with her alone, briefly, when she came to the movie at the school, and I couldn't help saying, "You're in trouble now Filomena. I know what you've got in that bucket under the window in your house. You're making home brew, aren't you?"

She looked confused and sheepish and said, "How come you know 'bout dat?"

But I just smiled a little, called her a bad girl and told her she was going to be sorry.

Then, I think it was several days later, something very strange happened, something really quite unusual which confirmed in Filomena's mind my apparent status as a kind of White shaman. There was no darkness any more at that time of year and it was late in the evening when I returned from a hike with some kids to a creek in the bush where we had lit a fire and roasted some marshmallows. On my way back, I called on the lads at the Hudson's Bay Company post for a chat. They were both from the Auld Country (as so many were who worked for the Company) and so we talked of faraway places. (The Hudson's Bay Company had always tended to fill its ranks by bringing out to Canada staunch, dependable folk from the islands and highlands of Scotland, a policy best expressed by the Englishman who sailed with Captain Cook, Sir Joseph Banks of the Royal Society: "So well does the serious mind of a Scotch education fit Scotsmen to the habits of industry, attention and frugality, that they rarely abandon them at any time of life, and I must say never while they are young.")

It was long past midnight when I left the trading post to walk home through the settlement to the school. It was a quiet evening and banks of fog hung in the cold air over the lake, in places hiding the great rafts of winter ice that drifted around, persisting on the surface well into July. Some of those ice pans were still two or three miles across, probably a lot bigger than that farther out.

I felt a sudden cold rush of air on my way back to the school and noticed that a southerly wind was gusting up off the lake, bringing the fog inshore and hiding some of the houses from view. I had just reached my front door when I heard shouting away behind me somewhere. It sounded urgent, and seemed to be coming from down near the shore, but I couldn't see anything for the fog.

More shouting. Had there been an accident? Also, there was a soft, low sound like a distant waterfall. Was that the wind? I turned back to see what the trouble was, and soon noticed dimly one or two figures running down in the direction of the shore. I hurried on, and then sounds of loud voices led me through the fog to the place where Filomena's grandparents lived.

Here, for a hundred yards, the shore itself had disappeared. The sudden, sharp, onshore wind had taken hold of one of those great pans of winter ice and driven it inexorably onto the shore, up over the shore, smashing, breaking, roaring, piling itself into great ridges and advancing again, right up to the three nearest cabins, trapping the people inside so that they had to scramble out in panic through small back windows. The ice was still driving itself forward inch by inch when I arrived, and the whole front of the old people's cabin was suddenly smashed inwards with the loud sounds of splintering logs and squealing nails. The front eaves hung unsupported, the door disappeared under the advancing ridge, and broken ice spilled over the collapsed front wall onto the floor of the cabin. And then it stopped.

It seems incredible that the wind could so have concentrated its power over an ice surface as to produce such fantastic forces as we had just witnessed. But its strength could carry it only so far before friction defeated it. By the time it was all over, the sudden, mysterious wind too had eased away, and after a half hour of scrambling on the ridges, surveying the three damaged cabins and exchanging stories of back-window escapes, the people sent children hurrying home through the fog for shovels, and then the long dig-out began.

Filomena had been gambling at cards with other people in a house at the back of the settlement, and had missed most of the action. But she came running when she heard what had happened. She just stood there on top of the ice ridge, staring at the mess. Her dog was dead, and two others as well. And so too were her dreams of throwing a party.

She glanced over to me and our eyes met. I wanted to edge over towards her and say quietly in her ear, "I told you you'd be sorry!" but I didn't have the heart. I just said, "Too bad, Filomena," and then started home, but I could feel her still staring at the back of me as I retreated.

I told my kids at school next day that the South Wind was usually warmer than the other winds, but that was because it was really the breath of the Devil. It was a bad wind which often carried evil spirits with it. The spirits hated human beings and liked to take any chance to make trouble for them. When they were going to attack people, those evil spirits made fog all around themselves so that they couldn't be seen by humans. And then terrible things happened. Sometimes people died. Or they went mad and did bad things to each other. Sometimes houses burned down. Sometimes all the people got sick. Last night the spirits pushed hard on the ice and that was why the houses were broken.

The kids seemed to enjoy my little yarn. But they told me I was just telling fibs.

Doing Things

The rancid reek of old seal blubber permeated every nook and cranny in some of those small Arctic schools. To me, it was a rather nice smell, one of those slightly offensive but essentially very natural odours that, after a while, you ended up actually liking, like the barnyard smells on a farm, or the stink of guano on a desert island. Mostly, this smell came from the sealskin *kamiks* (boots) and mitts that everyone wore to school, including myself. Eventually you stopped noticing it.

So why was it, I wondered, that I had started noticing it all over again well through our winter one year, after the return of the sun? Was it my nose that was becoming more acute, or was it the smell itself? But after several days I realized that my nose could never become *that* acute; there had to be something not just rancid, but more or less putrid there in the classroom making that half-rotten stench. The kids didn't know any more than I did. They looked around for the answer to this mystery but they found none, and it was left to me finally to search about after school for the answer. And at last, I found it.

Kidlapik had a desk close to mine at the corner of the classroom. But she had left the school two or three weeks previously when her family had travelled out with their dogs to one of the camps, and it was Kidlapik who had left us with this mystery.

Most of the girls at school, especially the ones in the pre-teen years, seven to 11 or so, loved to wear the *amauti*, the women's parka of white cloth trimmed with colourful braid. The *amauti* usually incorporated two long flaps extending the bottom edge downwards both fore and aft, and included also an enormously huge hood, big enough to contain the baby that is held directly against the bare skin of its mother's shoulder. Woven bands of coloured wool cross diagonally over the shoulders to a waist belt as a bottom support for the baby. The *amauti* of course implied motherhood, and the girls loved to play at being mother.

Some of the girls had their own little *amautis* made for them by their mums. These were just play or "pretending" garments, but they were also serious outdoor garments in their own right. And some loved to borrow their mothers' much larger *amauti*, complete with the baby in the hood, and to parade about the settlement in small groups, playing "mothers" to their little siblings.

Often, they wore their own *amauti*s to school, nearly always with some object in the hood behind their shoulders as a substitute baby. This might have been a modern doll (there were a few in the settlement) or a very small husky pup (borrowed for the day from one of those cute little round dog igloos that people made with snowblocks for the mother dogs with a litter of pups), or even just a short piece of two-by-four lumber wrapped in a rag, with a smiling face drawn at the top end. I sometimes let the kids keep their *amautis* on in school if they wished, and their "babies" too, so long as they cleaned up the mess that those puppies could sometimes make, because the chances were good that some opportunity could be seized here to make use of their little domestic games in some way: perhaps to introduce something new of the English language for example, or encourage them to write something in their own words, or to sing a simple new spontaneous song of motherhood.

Anyway, the time came, after the end of the dark period, when a new kind of doll began appearing at school in the little girls' hoods, something cute, beautiful, cuddly and only very slightly gruesome. The common ringed seals had been giving birth to their pups at about that time, and when a hunter got one of those females in the late stages of pregnancy, he brought home for his children the little dead foetus, perfectly formed, wiped clean and dry, big black eyes wide open, white fur all over, as soft, cute and cuddly as anything in the toy stores down South, except that these ones didn't keep quite as well as the toy ones did, or the teddy bears.

Kidlapik had left hers in her desk, and I had to throw out everything in there. I almost threw out the whole desk when I found it.

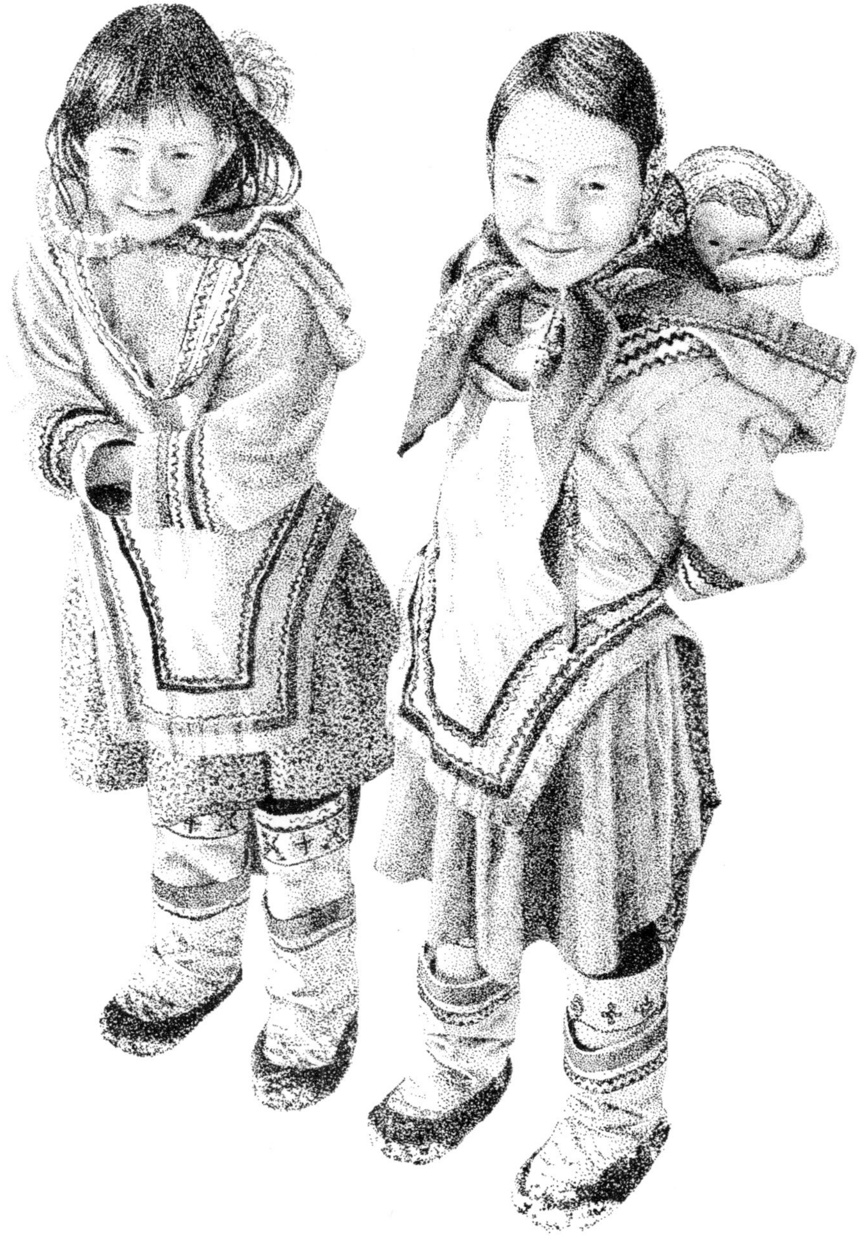

Little girls wearing the AMAUTI.

Still, I never allowed myself to worry about little things gone wrong. Potentially, there was as much educational value in an accident as in anything else. Sometimes, perhaps, more. The kids had extended their English vocabulary to include the words "search," "find," "very," "together," "help," "awful" and "rotten." The six year olds learned to use the interrogative adverb "where." Vocabularies and confidence always grew when the kids were involved in activity, when they were *doing things*, even if they were things that were unplanned, spontaneous, and from my own perspective inconvenient or troublesome.

But if at times my classroom seemed to depart wildly, even chaotically, from the traditional approach, at other times it reverted to a traditionalism that would have upset all the enlightened New Age thinkers then entering our system. It was not just Kidlapik's dead seal pup that was in bad odour in those days. Rote learning was in bad odour too, and the superintendent's long nose would have smelled that as well had he hung around frequently enough to notice it. We were not supposed any more to have the kids chanting their way in unison through the seven-times table. That was old-fashioned, wrong-headed and regressive. The children were supposed instead to be on the floor, playing with blocks or beads, or at the chalkboard, "discovering" for themselves that if you put seven caribou on each one of eight hills you will have a herd of 56. But that seemed to me a slow, tedious and uncertain way of gaining all the number facts and retaining them permanently in the mind. If I wanted my kids to respond "56" instantly and automatically whenever they were confronted by eight sevens (and to continue doing so, as they needed to, with or without a calculator, for the rest of their lives) then I believed it would have to come from practice, practice, practice.... So I still cheated, and when I was sure that there was no superintendent lurking, my class could still have been heard chanting their way through the tables. *They* didn't mind, even if the theorists at headquarters might have.

But practice could be made fun too. We took a long piece of plywood about six feet by two, and painted it. I had two of the boys drilling two separate grids of holes in it, 20 holes in each, the two grids separated by a blank space. Little, two-prong, brass paper fasteners were inserted into all 40 holes and then each fastener on one grid was connected at the back by insulated copper wire (insulation stripped at the terminals) to a fastener chosen at random from the opposite grid. So every little brass tip on the left side was connected at the back to another brass tip somewhere at the right. We called this a question board.

Then from the science kit we took an electric bell, attached it to the question board between the grids, and connected that to two long lengths of copper wire, one to each side of the question board. A six-volt battery was introduced part way along one of these two lengths so that when the left bell wire was placed on a left brass fastener, and the right bell wire placed on the correct right brass fastener, a circuit was completed, and the bell rang.

Next I glued a flashcard marked 8x7 on the left fastener and another marked 56 on the correct right one. Likewise, all the other multiplication facts I was trying to teach. The question board was then ready for action.

Anybody could challenge anybody. The challenger asked the question at the left by touching a brass tip with the wire. The other had to answer correctly by touching the correct brass tip on the right and ringing the bell. The challenger could ask ten questions.

I had a bag of marbles. Challengers got a marble if more than one answer out of ten was wrong, otherwise it was the one challenged who got the marble. Once all the marbles were gone from my bag, the children could challenge for each other's marbles. This could get vicious! On Friday afternoon, all marbles were redeemed for peanut cookies, one for one. Not everyone had marbles. Some had won a lot. However, the ethic of sharing ensured that everyone somehow got a bite. And by Friday everyone knew that eight sevens were 56 (and, fondly, I like to think that they all know it yet).

But this question board was not made just for mathematics. You could ask any question on a board like that. Science, reading, phonics, geography, Eskimo syllabics or anything else. I was not long though in changing that noisy bell for a nice quiet flashlight bulb.

Despite the massive barriers of language and culture, they were such easy kids to teach, those children of the great Northland. Their innate enthusiasm always seemed to be simmering just below the surface, and this could just as easily be fired by games, by story and song, by bursts of creative activity, as it could be held in check or suppressed by the more formal approach favoured by teachers who were afraid of a little chaos.

I depended greatly on art as a means of releasing all that happy energy, and of setting into ferment the vital yeast of language, the alien tongue of the *qadlunaat*, which alone was the one indispensable key to their education, their window on the world. We made cane baskets and woven wool scarves, carved little seals out of soap or soapstone, created stained-glass windows out of coloured tissue paper and black construction paper, made play houses, kites, sleds and plywood rowing dinghies.

In one little settlement I managed to wangle a silkscreen printing kit. The class raised the money to outfit themselves with plain T shirts, and these were then printed through the screen with a stencilled logo. Projects like that were as much a learning experience for me as for the children themselves.

In Clyde River I showed the kids how to tie-dye their T shirts, and in Resolute I showed them how to produce designs in batik, using unbleached cotton, candle wax, beeswax, tjantings and large basins of cold dye. We had batik butterflies, flowers, polar bears, stars, all sorts of things, all around the room. I was a bit nervous launching into that project because it was a rather dangerous, messy business, and the big challenge was to anticipate every possible accident — dye stain, hot wax burn, and so on — before it happened, so that it didn't happen. They had to wear aprons. Newsprint on the floor. Protective skin cream on hands. Electric hotplate, disconnected, behind a barrier. Dye basins against the wall. Only three working at a time, and no nonsense.

So I was very pleased when finally the project was over with no burns, no spills or other disasters, without anything more serious than a few small splashes of dye against the walls. The designs looked stunning, especially mounted against the fluorescent lights or stretched across the south-facing windows and backlit by the sun. I left the classroom lights on at night so that parents could admire them from the outside, backlit by the inside lights. The first impression on entering the classroom was of colours in riot.

The dyes were all poured down the sink, the chemicals, the electric iron and the tjantings all put away and the room cleaned up. I still had a fair amount of wax in the pot and I thought I would show the kids how candles were made. So I set the pot and hotplate aside for a later demonstration. The next day I had to fly out for a brief meeting and, there being no substitute available, my class was dismissed for the day. While I was gone, one of the small children from the junior class wandered into my empty classroom, saw the hotplate there, picked up the pot of hardened wax and placed it on top, plugged in the hotplate and then, curiosity satisfied, walked out. The school almost burned down!

Oh well, not to worry; things quite often went wrong. Once in Resolute Bay the kids had made portraits of each other for display on the classroom walls, but at the end of the day, the newly finished drawings had been accidentally thrown out in the garbage with a lot of other papers. So they decided instead, next day, to make black magic-lantern-style silhouettes of each other to go on the walls, but then when they knocked the spotlight over and smashed the lamp, I agreed that it might be easier just to trace the silhouettes from photographs. So photos were taken in profile of each child against a white wall, and when that was done the one who had done most of the photography opened the camera before the film was rewound, and handed me the long, curly film dangling from its cassette.

But there was a solar eclipse expected the next week, almost total, and I decided to keep the wasted film, have the kids develop it, and use it for another purpose. I enthused at length for a few days about lunar orbits, Earth orbits and so on, told them what the sun was like, how big it was, what made it so hot, and why, next Thursday, it would almost disappear and become just a thin crescent in the sky. They developed the blackened film, cut it into short lengths, and made little viewers for observing the wondrous event.

Satellite communication had arrived in the Arctic by that time and everyone in Resolute had a colour TV (except Katie and me who had black and white). For many days prior to the eclipse, the CBC repeated over and over in the Inuktitut language dire warnings of the consequences of looking at the sun during an eclipse, so that gradually, as we realized later, the people came to understand that there was a special quality to the sun at such a strange time, that the sun became actively dangerous, not just that anyone looking at it would become blind, but that even being outside in the diminished light could be a hazardous thing.

When the day of the eclipse came, the sky was nice and clear, and at the school I expected a grand opportunity to give free rein to my enthusiasm for astronomy. It was late winter and the sun was already up when school started. But only nine children came to school that morning, four from my own class, and it was then that we realized the concern people had for the sun. There was no sign of anybody outside. No matter; from the classroom windows we watched the eclipse as it gradually developed, and briefly our little frozen world was cast in the same eerie, weak, washed-out light that would pass for sunshine perhaps on Neptune. Later, as the bright orb regained its shape and customary brilliance, the school phone began ringing as people called in to ask if it would be safe now to go outside.

Generally we were given a fairly comprehensive budget in those distant little schools, but even so, it didn't cover all the things we wanted to do or have, and there was never any end to fund-raising projects. If the children discovered something they wanted — gym clothes, a swimming pool, skis, tents, a trip out, anything that couldn't be covered by our budget — then it was up to them to raise the money to get it. We always had a class account printed on a chart on the classroom wall with figures in three columns, Income, Expenses and Balance, so that they could see what progress they were making to meet their own goals. It also taught them to add, subtract and keep accounts.

For raising money, afternoon recess bake sales were best. Most kids had at least a quarter in their pockets and an edge of appetite or thirst by mid-afternoon, so for 25¢ they could get a slice of raisin cake and a glass of milk, or a cookie and juice, or some other little treat. This was popular, not only for those in the lineup out in the corridor, but even more for the kids selling behind the counter, and the others who did the actual baking or preparation. It was surprising how quickly all those quarters added up.

Sometimes we put together a settlement newspaper, and sold copies door to door. Sometimes the kids raffled off somebody's old bike or sold black-and-white portraits of each other, printed in the darkroom. One favourite money-maker was guessing-how-many-raisins-are-in-the-cake. I needed to be a little involved with this, to keep it honest, so I preferred to supervise it after school. The bakers followed Katie's recipe for making this cake. The two cups of raisins were counted before being added to the other ingredients. To make sure nobody knew the actual total number of raisins, we divided them into four or five unequal piles. I took one of the piles, counted the raisins and memorized that number. Each other pile was counted and memorized by some other person. No one knew the total.

The cake was put on display for a week and guesses were sold for ten cents. Finally all four or five raisin counts were totalled at a school assembly, and whoever came closest to that number won the cake.

Cooking was always a popular diversion, an escape from the classroom which the kids enjoyed but which conveniently served my own purposes as well. In a crowded, busy, multi-grade classroom, it was always useful to have alternate activities when one small group or another had completed their assignments. When I was too busy elsewhere to attend to them, it was good to have such an exit.

But even then, if I didn't actively supervise these kids, anything could happen. One Friday afternoon, Louisa, Phoebe and Justin, all responsible kids who had finished their seat work, were allowed into the school kitchen to make a cake to be shared later with all the others. I gave them Katie's recipe, and after the usual admonitions, left them to it.

But it didn't work out very well. The trouble was that the recipe called for two cups of sultanas, not raisins. The kids didn't know what sultanas were, but they figured out the first four letters of the word, assumed it meant salt, and threw in two cups of that.

No matter. Disasters too are educational. We wrote a story about the salt cake, and then turned it into a song. I told the kids all about the salty sea (something they had never even heard of) and described desert people who used salt as money, told them the fable of the salt-laden donkey at the river, and made salt crystals out of brine.

An occasional exit for one small group or another was a wonderful salve to the sanity of a teacher coping with several grades at once, and the school kitchen was just one of many possible routes. Katie sometimes volunteered (unpaid) to take a small group and teach them bread baking or some other such skill. With the promise of a cheque, parents too could be inveigled to take small numbers off my hands from time to time. They had their own ancient mythology to pass on, and a wonderful galaxy of skills and traditions that stood in danger of dying out. The girls had to learn how to prepare a sealskin or bathe a baby. The boys had to know how to build a snowhouse. And when the

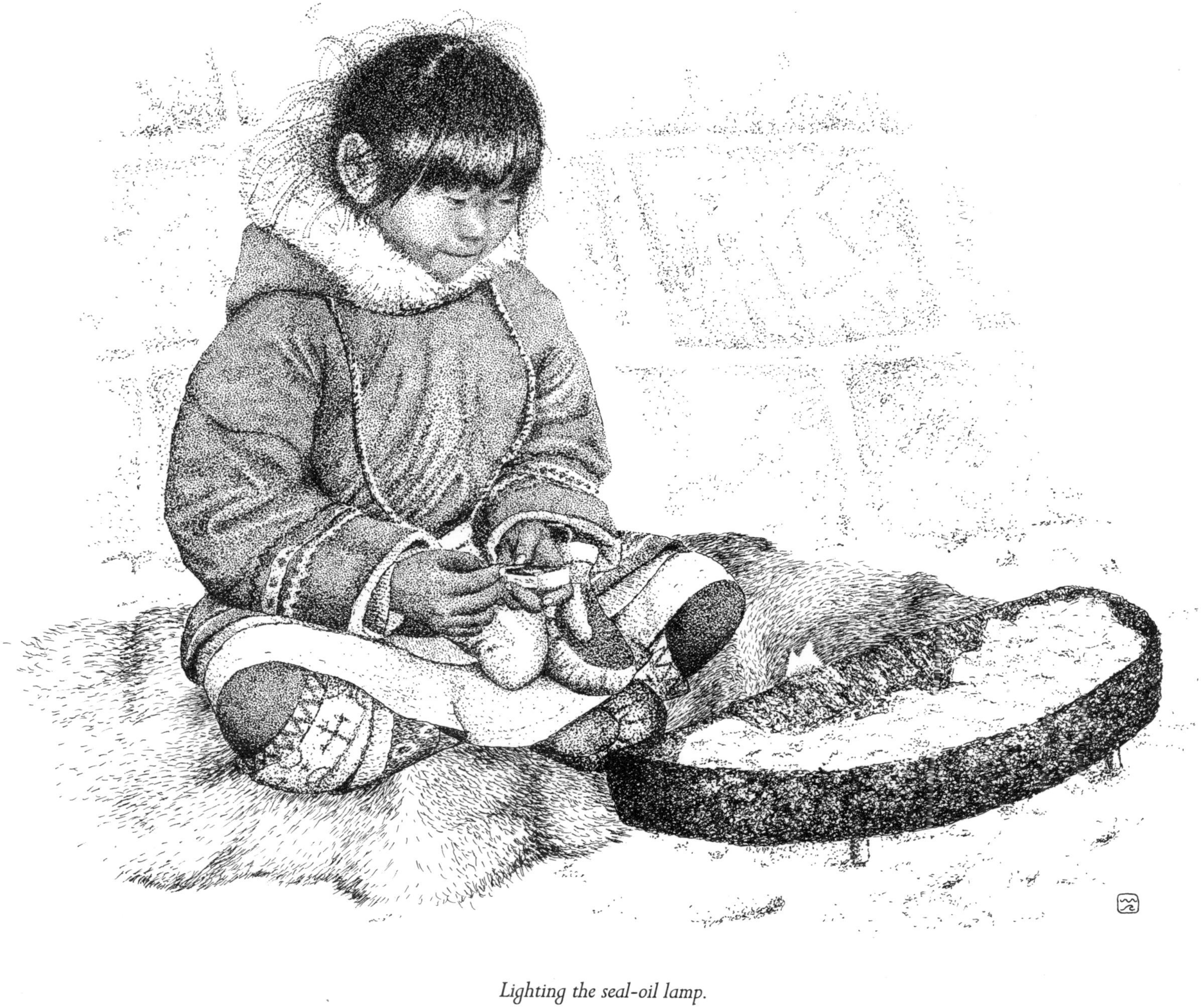

Lighting the seal-oil lamp.

igloo was finished out there in the playground, it was lined with caribou skins and used itself as a classroom for telling old stories or teaching the writing system in the native language.

Another such exit suggested itself in the last of my schools in a remote little settlement far away and lost in the lovely wilderness of the Dogrib. The notions these children had of the world were at first almost stupefyingly vague or non-existent. A few questions at the beginning of the year revealed an astonishing dearth of understanding. Canada was one of the provinces of the Northwest Territories. The Queen, who lived in Edmonton, was married to Brian Mulroney. Yellowknife was bigger than other cities like New York or Africa. Saskatchewan was the capital of Winnipeg, but no one knew what a capital was. The Mackenzie was a big river but nobody could say exactly what a river was. America belonged to the United States, a city of black people, and the wide expanse of blue to the west of the Americas on a world map was called Marrion Lake. West was where the sun came up. We didn't fall off the world because we lived on top of it. Money was made by the gummint who only let people have little bits of it at a time so they could all stay poor.

Poor kids! That last item probably came from home, but all the rest was mere conjecture. They had been taught practically nothing of human geography, nor indeed it seemed of anything much else. So I began to tell them all about their own vast country, and about the faraway wonders of an exotic, exciting world they had never even heard of, showed them slides of igloos and skyscrapers, giraffes and llamas, pyramids and palaces, mountains and deserts, of coconut-dependent atoll dwellers and camel-dependent desert nomads, and told them of our own long journeyings by sailboat over the great oceans of the world.

"Can we come with you, Maurice?" they asked, when they had seen the slides. "We wanna go there too."

Ah, but the oceans are so big it would take many months away from land. It might become very boring. You would get homesick. People get seasick too when the weather gets bad, and the waves of the ocean can sometimes become bigger even than the school, higher than the power poles, or the Band Council building. They can be far far bigger than our boat when the weather is bad. There are sharks and whales and poisonous things too. It can be scary.

"Me, I not gonna scare."

"Me too."

"We wanna go sailing Maurice, okay?"

Katie at the time had accepted a contract at the Band Council office, training two young adults to assume clerical responsibilities: answering the phone, running the little post office more or less according to regulations, doing correspondence, keeping the books and generally facing the challenge of putting in a full, seven-hour work day, five days a week, without ever actually borrowing money at any time from the cash box. Katie's contract ran until the end of August. This left me free through that final summer to search around for images and to hone my skills as a printmaker, since I had decided to try to become an artist, full-time. But it also left me with time to devote to the kids through the long days of summer if they were keen enough.

"Maybe I could teach you to sail," I replied.

A few weeks later, a plane came in from Yellowknife with a load of pine lumber and a few sheets of quarter-inch plywood, tins of resin, electric tools, paint, life-jackets, oars and other things. The airstrip was right by the school, and since meeting the plane whenever it came in was what everyone in the settlement liked to do, it was easier to re-schedule recess to coincide with the plane's arrival than to try and keep those kids confined in the classroom. I set my students to work carrying all those materials into the school.

"What's this, Maurice?" Justin demanded as he helped carry a sheet of plywood to the main entrance.

"That's going to be a boat. Five sheets of plywood, five boats."

The people had a wonderfully derisive sense of humour and this was sometimes expressed as a harsh, stilted, teasing mock-laughter, *Ee! Ee! Ee! Ee!* with a sharp glottal stop after each *Ee*. The sound of that contrived, artificial laughter always seemed to Katie and me the very soul and essence of rich derision, and we eventually adopted it ourselves whenever we felt in a mood for mockery.

The word spread that each piece of plywood was going to become a boat and I could hear the *Ee! Ee! Ee!* around the corner coming from different directions. Teachers didn't know how to make boats! And anyway, you couldn't make a boat out of just one sheet of plywood.

But we did, and for a few weeks at the end of the school year, that was the exit I arranged for small groups, a wonderful chance to sideline three or four at a time while I devoted my whole energy to the near-desperate academic needs of the rest. We ended up with three rowing skiffs, red, yellow, and blue, a sailing inflatable, and a boxy, eight-foot pram dinghy. We got tents, swimsuits, snorkel gear and fishing rods, and once the kids had learned well enough to swim, and had become used to the weird idea of sitting backwards in order to row forwards, they enjoyed their summer on the water.

Their English exploded.

And then of course, every Christmastime, there were school concerts... or maybe there weren't. All kids, of course, (and their parents) love school concerts, and nearly all teachers hate them. I have this little nightmare periodically recurring to me in which the night of the school concert has rolled around all too soon, and whereas all the other classes are eager, well-rehearsed and ready, mine have had hardly any practice and are totally unprepared....

But whenever we overcame our misgivings and launched into all the work, the concert was a wonderful experience for the kids and invariably enjoyed by all the adults. Songs, plays, dances, instrumental music, dressing up... the excitement of it all was sometimes unbearable. The plays we had to make up ourselves, for I never once found any published play suitable for a Northern audience. Sometimes I taught the kids intriguing little tricks of magic, dressed them up like Merlin, and set them to it, amazing their parents by doing impossible things, and the Magic Show was always the most popular item of all.

I had a little game I often played with the kids in the gym. It was a sailor's game from the last world war, and it went like this: whenever I called out "Bomber!" they all rushed to one side of the gym, and if I didn't change my call before they got there, the last one to reach the wall was eliminated. If I called out "Torpedo!" they all rushed to the opposite wall, the last one eliminated. If I called the two words alternately in rapid succession they were left racing back and forth changing direction with each call. If at any time I called out "Ship sunk!" they all sat quickly on the floor, last one down eliminated. If at any time I called out "Freeze!" they had to stop in mid-action and become

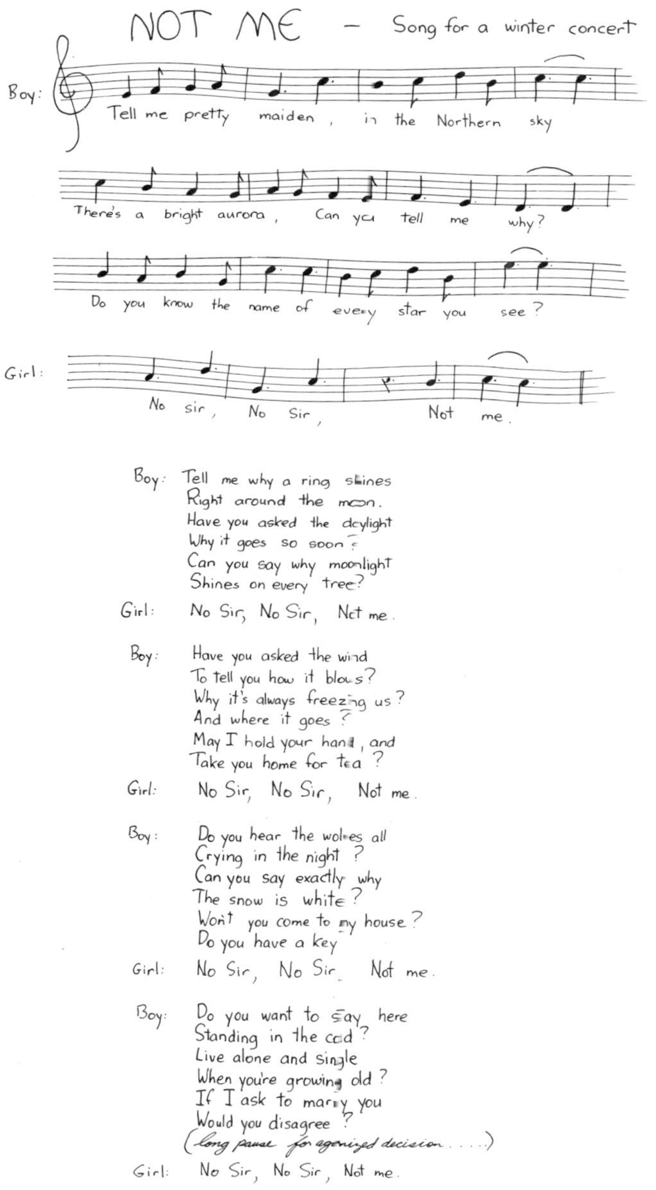

statues. Anyone moving was eliminated. Last one still in was the winner. The kids loved this game.

I used to get so tired of fads and fashions in education. Every so often, it seemed, some trendy new "ism" was dreamed up and unveiled before us at the annual teachers' conference as being the answer to all the problems that beset our schools. Everything we had done in the past was wrong, our whole approach unenlightened, and if we now adopted this new technique, new curriculum, new set of text books, new whatever, great changes would take place and all would be well. We had to be "with it." We had to embrace this new ideology, new dogma, with all the enthusiasm and energy of its promulgators and, just like these kids of mine, rush obediently across to the opposite wall. And teachers did! Nobody wants to be seen to be not "with it," to be professionally out of step.

Bomber! Torpedo!

I was always a little disappointed at the absence of debate and healthy scepticism, and the apparent willingness of most teachers to embrace every new trend as it came along, to rush so obediently in every new direction according to the dictates of fashion.

I was reminded of this as I worked through that final year as a teacher, and cast my mind back 30 years to my very first school in the North. In that last little settlement the children were so much better cared for, healthier, better housed and better clothed than were those poorer, raggeder, runnier-nosed children of 30 years earlier. And yet despite all the improvements, the changes, the many adjustments to the curriculum, the vaunted advances in education since those times, these latter-day kids with their televisions and computers and vastly better living standards and far greater exposure to their language of instruction had actually achieved far lower academic standards than had those in my first school!

Why was this? Tired teaching perhaps? Automatic promotions, and the willing acceptance of academic mediocrity? Could that have been it? If you expect nothing of children, that is exactly what you get. If you expect a little, you will get... not much, but maybe something. If you expect great things, and if with great care, love, understanding and determination you *demand* them, you will get a very great deal.

In my early teens at high school, in my little one-horse town in that faraway place and time, we studied several of the plays of Shakespeare, and though they weren't at all easy (indeed at times they were extremely hard), still we loved them all. We were *taught* to love them. We felt pleased, too, that our feeble adolescent intellects were so respected by our teachers that we could be entrusted with a study of Shakespeare, an honour that made us feel far more adult than we were. In England now, the authorities have decided that Shakespeare is too difficult for 14 year olds, and have begun setting exams instead on television soaps.

If I would aspire to achieve something but I persuade myself, or allow myself to be persuaded, that it cannot be done, then I am quite right. It cannot. But this is only because I believe it cannot. The belief itself is completely self-fulfilling. Can that be our problem?

But quite apart from a long set of lamentably lowered expectations, and an excessive delicacy about demanding good attendance, good behaviour, good work habits and serious application of our students, there is the almost opposite problem that schools can be so boring. There needs to be as much fun, creative activity and excitement in school as there is serious hard work. Children need to get right out of those desks for part of every day, doing things. The walls should shout with vivid art. The corridors should betray the smells of boiled cranberry jam, or jackfish chowder. The classroom stage should come to life with plays and pantomime. The rafters should ring with music. These are the things that bring a school to life, that bond the children to their school, and the school to the community.

I felt so disappointed with what had been achieved in that last little settlement of ours in the distant lands of the Dogrib. Half the kids at 12 years old had only a rudimentary knowledge of English and a reading level of Grade One or Two. (Oh, sure, you could ask them what grade they were in and they would say, "Six." And there it was, sure enough, in the register.) This academic shortfall, easily explainable a generation earlier, had nothing to do with family migration to winter traplines. That was a thing of the past. Half the parents didn't seem to care whether the kids got to school or not (though it must be said that some others were extremely diligent and concerned for their kids). There was so much that could have been done, but it would have taken an on-going commitment of years, and I didn't have any more years to spare. For Katie and me it was time to go, and time to start new things, to begin new careers, to sail away, north to the Arctic, south to the Horn. I hoped those children would eventually make it. They were easy enough to teach, but many of them hadn't got off to a very good start. If they could just have got to school regularly and on time (and left their chewing tobacco at home; even the eight year olds sometimes showed up with a great wad stuffed inside one cheek) and if good fortune would bring them teachers with a bit of fire and energy, they could easily yet have disproved my overpowering pessimism.

Others, after all, have done so. In my first two schools, the problems appeared so overwhelming, so insoluble, that it seemed to me then that they could be worked out only over a long period of perhaps two or three generations. Yet look back at what has happened! Those kids (some now grandparents) grew up and took their place as citizens, raised fine families of their own and played active roles in bettering their own communities. Some fell by the wayside, it is true. But most got on with their lives with varying degrees of success. Some went into business, some politics. Some became councillors or chiefs for their own people. Some are now teachers, some bush pilots. Some became advocates for aboriginal rights, one of these taking the international stage and flying back and forth to the great cities of the world. At least one seems to show every sign of having made his first million.

Perhaps in time, those latter-day kids too will flourish just as so many of the others have done. But if Fame and Fortune have each visited that earlier generation in surprisingly rich measure, still those false impostors are not at all what I would wish for these ones, nor for any of the children I have ever taught. Those two bare-faced frauds are no mark or measure of the happiness they seem so beguilingly to promise. Rather, I would wish for them other things infinitely more precious, gifts that will be theirs to inherit if they have the all-too-unusual fortune of happy homes and good schools:

for the spirit, Joy
for the body, Health
for the heart, Love
for the mind, Reason.